FOUR CLASSICS
ON THE INDIAN STAGE

The Toy Cart of Clay
*An adaptation of the Sanskrit Classic **Mrichhakatika** by **Sudraka***

The Anklet
*An adaptation from **Ilango Adigal's** Tamil Classic **Silappadikaram***

Kurukshetra Burning!
*An adaptation of **Smashana Kurukshetra** in Kannada by **Kuvempu***

The Echo
*An adaptation of **Chomana Dudi** in Kannada by **Shivarama Karanth***

Vitasta
LET KNOWLEDGE SPREAD
www.vitastapublishing.com

BANGALORE
LITTLE
THEATRE

COMMENTS ON THE PUBLICATIONS

Publication is generally the last concern of the playwright. After the excitement of performance, when the Script finally becomes the Play and meets its audience, the idea of saving the words for future readers can seem like a chore. Theatre, unique among the arts, happens in the moment. If you weren't there on the night to have your disbelief suspended, your emotions stirred and your view of the human condition destabilised or overturned, you missed it, your life is poorer and the event, unpublished, fades into legend. Shakespeare never bothered about publishing his plays. He was producing them at such a rate – three or four masterpieces a year, and performing in some as well – he must have thought posterity could wait. So it's hugely to the credit of his fellow actors Heminges and Condell that they took time after his death to assemble his plays into the First Folio. Most plays from other authors of that period are lost. It's only through the diligence of his colleagues that we have authentic versions of Hamlet, King Lear, Othello, Macbeth … What Bangalore Little Theatre has done, in the first two volumes and those that follow, is follow Heminges and Condell and put on record the texts of BLT's most ground-breaking productions – even one that has yet to be performed! These are a valued resource and as Vijay Padaki eloquently implies in his introduction, they celebrate authors past and present and their translators as well, making the local, global. Above all these plays are a theatre experience, doing what theatre does best, here particularly, replacing walls with bridges between languages and cultures. It's a delight to be asked to endorse these publications. Imagine and enjoy!

Richard Crane
Playwright-Director, co-founder of Brighton Theatre

This initiative would allow theatre practitioners from other parts of the world to access this work and look at the possibilities of staging these plays in multiple languages and in multiple cultural contexts.

Vidyanidhi Vanarase
Founder-Dirtector, International Association for Performing Arts and Research

This volume addresses the critical need for more actable and accessible versions of classic Indian plays in English. Good plays around important historical ideas are unfortunately scarce. The second admirable volume helps correct that deficiency.

Ira Hauptman
Professor of Drama, Queens College, CUNY, New York

We have eagerly awaited the publication of these volumes. They have finally arrived. They will reach performers and audiences right across national borders and far beyond.

Sai Paranjpye
Theatre personality and award winning film director

An international leader in our field, especially its serious investment in new play development, including the publication series that can benefit all of us theater makers across the world.

Bill Rauch
Artistic Director, Perelman Performing Arts Center at the World Trade Center, New York City

The new publication series produced by the Bangalore Little Theatre are an important and most welcome addition to world theater knowledge. Bravo!

Arthur Giron
Founding Member of Ensemble Studio Theatre, New York, formerly Head, Graduate Playwriting Program, Carnegie Mellon University

There is a hunger for strong dramatic texts in India, where theatre production has grown far more rapidly than playwriting. In that context, these volumes will be seen as yet another precious gift that BLT has given to the theatre community.

Anmol Vellani
Theatre Director and past Founder-Director of India Foundation for the Arts

This work is not only important for India, it also makes plays from Indian writing known across the world. It is a very important and necessary project.

Ursula Werdenberg
Dramaturg-Playwright,
Secretary General of The International Playwrights' Forum

My warmest congratulations. This is a significant milestone and a wonderful achievement that gives readers an opportunity to think about our pasts and our presents through a history of ideas.

Anuradha Kapur
Past Director, National School of Drama

Bangalore Little Theatre has reached veteran status in Indian theatre with their powerful theatrical interventions in the community, spanning 60 years...these volumes enrich our understanding of the capacity of theatre to create spaces for potent ideas, that demand our engagement.

Yvette Hardie
President: ASSITEJ (International Association for Theatre for Children and Young People)

I am delighted that you are presenting all these plays that are at one and the same time enjoyable, revealing and memorable!

Roddam Narasimha
Science Historian and Professor,
Jawaharlal Nehru Centre for Advanced Scientific Research

Your contribution to the goals of the International Playwrights' Forum, to the artistic treasures of your country, as well as for universal culture in general is indescribable indeed.

Gad Kaynar (Kissinger)
Professor, International Theatre Institute
The Yolanda and David Katz Faculty of the Arts, Tel Aviv University

ये नाम केचिदिह नः प्रथयन्त्यवज्ञां
जानन्ति ते किमपि तान्प्रति नैष यत्नः ।
उत्पत्स्यते तु मम कोऽपि समानधर्म
कालो ह्मयं निरवधिर्विपुला च पृथ्वी ॥

Those who deride or ignore my work –
let them know: my efforts are not for them.
There will come along someone who shares my spirit:
the world is vast, and time endless.

– Bhavabhuti

Bangalore Little Theatre is privileged to receive a substantial grant from ***Kusum*** *and* ***Mohandas Pai*** *towards education and institutional development programmes, which include the publication of these plays.*

Published by,
Renu Kaul Verma
Vitasta Publishing Pvt Ltd
2/15, Ansari Road, Daryaganj
New Delhi 110002
info@vitastapublishing.com

ISBN 978-93-86473-82-0

MRP ₹399
First Edition 2020

Editors: Kanagam King, Papri Sen Sri Raman
Layout: Ram Kumar
Illustrations: Ayannar C
Coordinator: Deepak Mote
Printer: Vikas Computer and Printers

CONTENTS

FOREWORD

Bangalore Little Theatre is an enormous exercise in imagination. It remains an aspiration for theatre performers and a source of inspiration for practitioners. The passion, perseverance, toil and grace is the hallmark of this intimate Institution, which has embarked on many pathbreaking initiatives, programmes and productions. If the History of Ideas programme was unique, the translation and adaptation of Indian classics in English is a huge service. In the programme Vijay Padaki has presented a pertinent model, wherein the play scripts transcend the cultural specificity and period in time to speak in a universal language that addresses our contemporary concerns. Although we read the text in English, we experience the content in the original. A truly remarkable feat.

The *Kurukshetra* play, based on a Kuvempu classic in Kannada, is as immediate as the front page headlines of any newspaper. The killing fields of the battleground with corpses strewn across the landscape, tell us the pointlessness and horrors of war. *The Echo*, adapted from a novella by Shivarama Karanth, another Kannada classic, brutally picturises the uninterrupted exploitation of a landless farm worker with the added burden of belonging to a low caste. The character of Choma represents the tragedy which continues repeatedly without escape, then, now and perhaps for years more in the future. *Mrichhakatika*, the age-old Sanskrit story of the toy cart is presented in a charming fresh version. A precious inclusion in the volume is the tale of *The Anklet*, based on the Tamil classic Silappadikaram, which is deeply moving.

BLT has had a strong play development programme for a long time. It is most appropriate that the plays are being published now. Several volumes of plays can be expected in print very soon. This is a huge contribution to the institution of the theatre in India. We can be sure they will be received with enthusiasm world-wide.

Feroz Abbas Khan
Theatre director and award winning film maker

A SPECIAL MESSAGE

For nearly 60 years, Bangalore Little Theatre has been instrumental in promoting theatre arts in Bengaluru and across the country. The ambitious project of publishing their most successful plays in a multi-volume anthology marks a great point in their story – another marker of the tremendous success they have attained.

The choice of plays for the first volume is indeed praiseworthy. In translating to English and adapting the plays for the modern stage, Vijay Padaki is conserving the best of Indian classics. Each play is especially relevant to contemporary situations, from environmental concerns to resurgent regional identities, to introspecting the carnage of wars and finally the complexities of court politics.

Classical and folk theatre in India has, due to our colonial inheritance, receded in popular memory. It has, in essence, become an untapped resource of tremendous literary, artistic and cultural wisdom. I am certain that such a project provides us the perfect opportunity to fill this lacuna and understand, perhaps for the first time in recent years, the sheer wealth of Indian theatre spanning different cultural and linguistic traditions in the subcontinent. In producing such plays, and putting them together in this volume, BLT has undertaken a public service, one which every Indian living in the 21st century can profit from, for a long time to come.

With this, I wish BLT the very best for this and their many future endeavours.

Shashi Tharoor
Member of Parliament for Thiruvananthapuram

PUBLISHER'S NOTE

Theatre is said to be the first form of communication among human species. The Neanderthals died out about 42,000 years ago. The Homo sapiens came into their own since then. The art of mimicry, scientists believe, is a carryover, however. It is said, the ears of the two species are structurally different. The ear, we commonly know, as just a hearing aid. Both species could see and hear. And they both could make sounds. Impersonation, mimicry... to explain to the fellow being...were used by both species. Genetists say, the two species intermingled at a point of time in history. The difference was, the inner ear evolved as a balancing mechanism for Homo sapiens. It helped modern man stand upright. The story of theatre begins here, not with the Athenians... much before ritual enactments in any temples, with role play. The first facepacks, coloured muds, makeup pastes and masks are about 10,000 years old, archeological finds tell us.

World's first paintings are said to have been done between 40,000 to 20,000 years ago, first book a statue carved with notations. The first university is said to be 12,000 years old. During all this business of socialising, communicating, trading, travelling, learning and teaching, the art of mimicking transformed into something more representational – something played out, enacted before a gathering of watchers, the entire community. It was at first more informative, a tool of communicating with a group – demonstrating perhaps the killing of a mammoth, a dance round the fire, enacting a death. Thus, grew theatre.

The Indian tradition can be traced back to about 3,000 years ago. The Pali *suttas* (from the 5th to 3rd centuries BCE) refer to the existence of troupes of actors who performed dramas on a stage. Buddhist philosopher Asvaghosa who composed *Buddhacarita* is considered to have been the first Sanskrit dramatist. *A Treatise on Theatre* (*Natyasastra*), dated between 200 BCE to 200 CE, is said to be authored by Bharata Muni. The first Greek plays were performed in the Theatre of Dionysus, at the beginning of the 5th century BC. Indian and Greek theatre traditions are thus contemporaries, grew up at about the same time. Aristotle said, the 'play' evolved before the epic. Western plays have no place descriptions, they begin in the middle of the story, in *medias res.* Scholars say , the original Rama story, handed down to us, was first oral literature and spread in play form. From Kamban's time song and dance was a part of it, *Mahaviracharita*, a 8th century play mentions meeting of Rama and Sita. *Thakkai Ramayanam* (1600 AD) is a temple performance, as is Ramakien from the Philippines.

Vitasta brings to its readers, a book of four plays, that begins with *Mrichhakatika,* said to be the oldest preserved play in the subcontinent. The book ends with a play of our times, also a classic, from the doyen of Indian theatre, Shivrama Karanth. With this first book from BLT, our attempt is to preserve in print for a global audience, stageable manuscripts of plays in the English language, starting with Bangalore Little Theatre's productions. Vitasta is proud to be a part of BLT's efforts at spreading theatre as art and information. *4 Classics on the Indian Stage* is our third book on theatre. Vitasta also has two earlier theatre books, *Two Classical Plays from India* by DP Sinha and *Manch Par Utree Kahaaniyaan* by Kumar Sanjay in Hindi. For theatre lovers Vitasta hopes to add to its repertoire.

•

PREFACE TO THE VOLUME

It is of great significance that the very first volume of plays being published by Bangalore Little Theatre comprises classics from Indian literature. Way back in 1963 Bangalore Little Theatre produced its first Indian play in English, an original adaptation of *Mrichhakatika* (The Toy Cart of Clay) by a founder-member, Professor B Chandrasekhara. Since then the group has maintained the conscious policy of producing Indian plays periodically – translations, adaptations, original scripts – by its own members and others.

In 1960 a small group of committed persons in Bangalore sought a theatre experience that could be a genuine alternative to the order of the day that was called BBC Theatre British Bedroom Comedy. They had a vision of a Community Theatre best described by the slogan invented twenty-five years later: *Think Globally, Act Locally.*

A brief history of the evolution of English language theatre in Bangalore may be of interest to the reader

Educational institutions and the colonial legacy

With the establishment of the Cantonment Township in Bangalore it was inevitable that the English language got to be adopted in many social transactions in the areas under the administration of the Cantonment. A natural accompaniment to the process was the emergence and establishment of schools with English as the medium of instruction. Not surprisingly, many of these schools were characterized by two features:

- a missionary origin
- staffing with expatriate/British teachers

The teaching and practice of drama in 'English' schools was integral to the British educational system. It was simply a reflection of the social context in Britain in which the theatre was a living and vibrant art form. Indeed, the amateur non-profit theatre had a far wider base in community participation than the commercial theatre. The popular expression was: 'Amateur dramatics is as English as toast with marmalade at tea time.'

It can be said that English language drama in India was essentially a colonial cultural legacy. The very term *colonial legacy* has, inescapably, a negative connotation. It must be accepted that there were some obvious positive features of the legacy as well:

- The British influence brought in technically sound stages. For instance, the original Assembly Hall at Bishop Cotton Boys' School had fly mechanisms and other backstage features not seen in other performance halls.
- Teachers coming from Britain were often trained and experienced in both teaching drama and producing plays.
- The teachers had exposure to good stagecraft – in set design, costumes, fabricating props with locally available materials, lighting, sound, and so on. Woodwork and other crafts taught at the school formed natural accompaniments to drama.

Most significantly, with good quality inputs in teaching and practice, dramatic activity in school was a respectable pursuit–as respectable as cricket and computers today.

We cannot overlook the fact that there were some obvious negative features of the legacy too:

- Drama studies amounted to a narrow pursuit of English and Western traditions. Students remained ignorant of Indian and Eastern traditions.
- There was a Cantonment-City divide. Students in the Cantonment schools were isolated from the City performance scene.
- There was an overall alienation from Indian culture. Two examples might illustrate this point admirably.
  - » The schools observed Michaelmas holidays at Dasara time.
  - » Until even the late seventies, some schools in the Cantonment area observed a holiday on Guy Fawkes Day.

Another example of the colonial legacy that remained in the Bangalore Cantonment right up to the late seventies was an association of old ladies and gentlemen called the Empire Loyalists Society. At their meetings in the premises of a Club (of colonial origin) the standard agenda was reminiscences of the good old days of British India and lamentations on the decay of post-independence India. At dinner time they would stand to attention as the gramophone played *God Save the Queen*.

The undercurrent indoctrination was evident: the superiority of all things English and Western over all things Indian.

It is now known that even the teaching of English literature in schools and colleges outside Britain was a creation of the colonisation process. It was not originally a curriculum subject to be taught like science, geography or mathematics. An excerpt from a play written in 1997 might be appropriate here. It was the year of India's Golden Jubilee of Independence, and the play was written as part of an exchange project between Bangalore Little Theatre and the Royal National Theatre in London. The conversation is between Jeet Mukherji, an Indian engineer in his sixties and Miss Alice Taylor, his teacher in a school in British India. He is ever grateful to her for the education he received in a British educational system. She, on the other hand, feels guilty for having corrupted young Indian minds and now lives as a recluse in England.

JEET

You can't take the blame all on yourself. You were one small part of a larger – what do you call it – a whole history.

ALICE

A small part that was completely avoidable. We owe you an apology.

JEET

Oh, come on, Miss Taylor...

ALICE

This supercilious island nation owes an unconditional apology to the whole of the subcontinent for at least one of its sins of commission.

JEET

It's all in the past. It's forgotten.

ALICE

You can forgive and forget the wars and the massacres and the looting of the land. All of these will be made up. But you can never forgive the permanent damage done to the mind. It is not buried with you when you die. It is passed on. It will stick for generations.

JEET

You gave us science and technology. You gave us a language to speak to the world, and Shakespeare, and...

ALICE

Shakespeare! That velvet-tongued opportunist! What do you say in Urdu for that? *Matlabi*, I think.

JEET

William Shakespeare, *matlabi*!

ALICE

The philanderer who oiled his way into the London aristocracy and charmed them with his verbosity to finance his pet projects, his adolescent fantasies.

JEET

The loquacious charm translated into a hundred languages around the world!

ALICE

Think about it, Jeet, would the name Shakespeare mean anything, anywhere, if it was not for the Empire?

JEET

It is great literature nevertheless.

ALICE

Because we taught you to believe that – that it is great. Did you know, Jeet, that English literature was never a subject for schooling before the Empire? Physics and mathematics and geography, yes, they were subjects that could be taught. And studied. Literature was something you did. You didn't teach it or study it. It was entirely in the interests of the Empire that English literature was brought in as a course of study.

JEET

Was it his fault that he stood out in history as a great writer?

ALICE

Is it their fault that hundreds like him, in every land, every bit the same in creative energy, never got to be known by the rest of the world?

Extract from *Gold and Silver* by Vijay Padaki, 1997.

Miss Alice Taylor is only echoing the assessment of many other Western scholars. Of the several examples of 'full many a gem' of Indian writing remaining unseen, the poetry of Tulsidas may be cited here. The Indologist and linguist Sir George Grierson called Tulsidas 'the greatest of Indian authors of modern times' and the epic *Ramcharitmanas* 'worthy of the greatest poet of any age'. Edmour J Babineau, author of an important book on *Ramcharitmanas*, says that if Tulsidas had been born in Europe or the Americas, he would be considered a greater personality than William Shakespeare. Ironically, Tulsidas was indeed a contemporary of Shakespeare.

Phases of Development in English Language Theatre

We must begin by accepting that English language theatre has remained an urban phenomenon in India, restricted to the larger cities. Bangalore certainly has been one of the cities to nurture English theatre over a long time. Four broad phases of development are recognizable in the English language theatre in Bangalore:

- *The pre-sixties era*
- *The sixties*
- *The seventies*
- *Eighties onwards*

Bangalore Little Theatre (BLT) was created in 1960. In its very first three years, English language theatre moved out of the Cantonment to reach all of Bangalore. BLT very decisively sought an alternative theatre experience in a post-colonial social context. Reaching out to those active in the Kannada theatre in the city they created a truly inclusive theatre society. BLT was influenced greatly by the Little Theatre movement of the fifties in the UK, decentralizing theatre activity from London, disseminating high quality theatre widely through training, outreach and community involvement.

Within a year of inception, BLT arrived at a character and identity for itself: to maintain pride in its strictly amateur status, but to conduct its affairs in a thoroughly professional manner. The group gave itself a constitution and, through that, a participatory style of functioning. The group was seen as belonging to a membership, and therefore to be managed by a transparently elected management committee. The founding members were the first to give way to younger members to take the group forward.

Of special significance was the group's positioning as *Community Theatre*, relating to the Indian socio-economic reality. In sum, within a short space of five years BLT was:

- an *Indian* theatre group with a global outlook
- assimilating the best of British theatre traditions in a new Indian environment
- relating to Kannada and all other regional language theatre groups – actively assisting them.

An important indicator of the *Indianness* that was being set was as early as 1963 – BLT produced an original adaptation of a Sanskrit play (*Mrichhakatika*) in English. It was performed specially for an international conference on Asian Education.

Related to the last point is one other indisputably important feature of BLT. It is the only English language theatre group in Bangalore (perhaps one of the very few anywhere in India) with strong links to the local-regional theatre, building bridges across language divides. Many of the stalwarts on the Kannada stage and screen have been either life members of BLT or have been prominently involved in some capacity or the other. Indeed, BLT has been a substantial support to Kannada theatre groups in their startup stages.

The seventies were the decade marked by several upheavals in the larger socio-political environment. There have been many scholarly analyses of the many turning points in the India of the seventies. (The emergence of 'protests' had, coincidentally, a parallel in other societies of the West as well.) It was only natural that the theatre was also drawn to a deeper recognition of these contextual realities. While this was evident in writing for the theatre in most regional languages, the English language theatre, too, was beginning to find its place in the new Indian identity. In Bangalore the seventies witnessed, among other things:

- *A renaissance in Kannada theatre*: This was reflected clearly in new writings, new performing groups and directors, new directions in stagecraft, and a bold new identity.
- *Beginnings in Play Development in English*: The context was the acute paucity of Indian plays in English. It led to the emergence of a playwriting activity within BLT that would only grow stronger over the years. It began with reworking available English language translations of plays in other Indian languages, making them more stage-worthy. It then took on fresh translations and adaptations of plays in regional languages. It then went on to original scripts that were clearly Indian in character, but in the English language.

Indeed, as recognized by many in other parts of India, the thrust given to play development in Bangalore was to also influence English language theatre in other Indian cities.

Eighties onwards, Bangalore showed a sizeable increase in the volume of theatre activity in the English language. Because of the open developmental platform presented by BLT, along with a participative climate, many interested in the theatre began with BLT and went on to start their own groups. These new initiatives were even encouraged and aided by BLT. The decade witnessed two important developments:

1. *Major advances in play development:* Bangalore was clearly emerging as a centre for original playwriting in English. For instance, in the very first year of *The Hindu* awards for contemporary play scripts, two prizes went to BLT members: the First Prize for Vijay Padaki's *Credit Titles* and a Special Prize for Ambika (Poile) Sengupta's *Mangalam.*
2. *The Deccan Herald annual theatre festival:* The first of its kind in India, emerged as a major encouragement to English language theatre in Bangalore. It was also a place for new play scripts to be presented. Mahesh Dattani's early successes were in the Deccan Herald festivals.

A publication programme

In 2008 BLT was restructured. A public Charitable Trust was created with a non-profit status. Theatre development activities which were pursued in an on-and-off manner till then were now placed in a newly created Academy of Theatre Arts, with well-planned, long-term, programme thrusts. One such long-term programme is titled *New Voices*. It integrates three streams of work that were pursued separately in the past:

- New play development
- Training new directors
- Promoting new talent for the stage.

When integrated, they find opportunities for presentation on stage.

Play development has been led by me over many years in BLT. The large number of plays written never got published so far—not the least important reason being my own disinterest in publication. In 2019 the active group managing BLT decided to take charge and have all the plays published. And here we are!

I am personally delighted that the very first volume has the classics. Three of the four plays included in the volume have been produced by BLT. The fourth, the adaptation of Shivarama Karanth's novella *Chomana Dudi*, has had two rehearsed readings and is to be produced in the near future. Most readers will be aware that writers from Karnataka have won eight awards of Bharatiya Jnanapith. Kuvempu was the first awardee in 1967. Shivarama Karanth was the third, in 1977. A comparative analysis of the contributions from the eight writers is very instructive, reflecting the richness of Kannada literature The first six are conspicuous for both the range of writing and the volume of output. Kuvempu and Karanth stand out as giants. We are particularly pleased that the first volume of plays from BLT has the works of both of them.

Each of the four plays in the volume has its own introduction including notes on the first production in Bangalore. The plays are meant for performance. However, from the innumerable comments we have received over the years, we are sure they will make enjoyable reading as well.

Vijay Padaki
Series Editor

STAGE DIRECTIONS

with the actor facing the audience

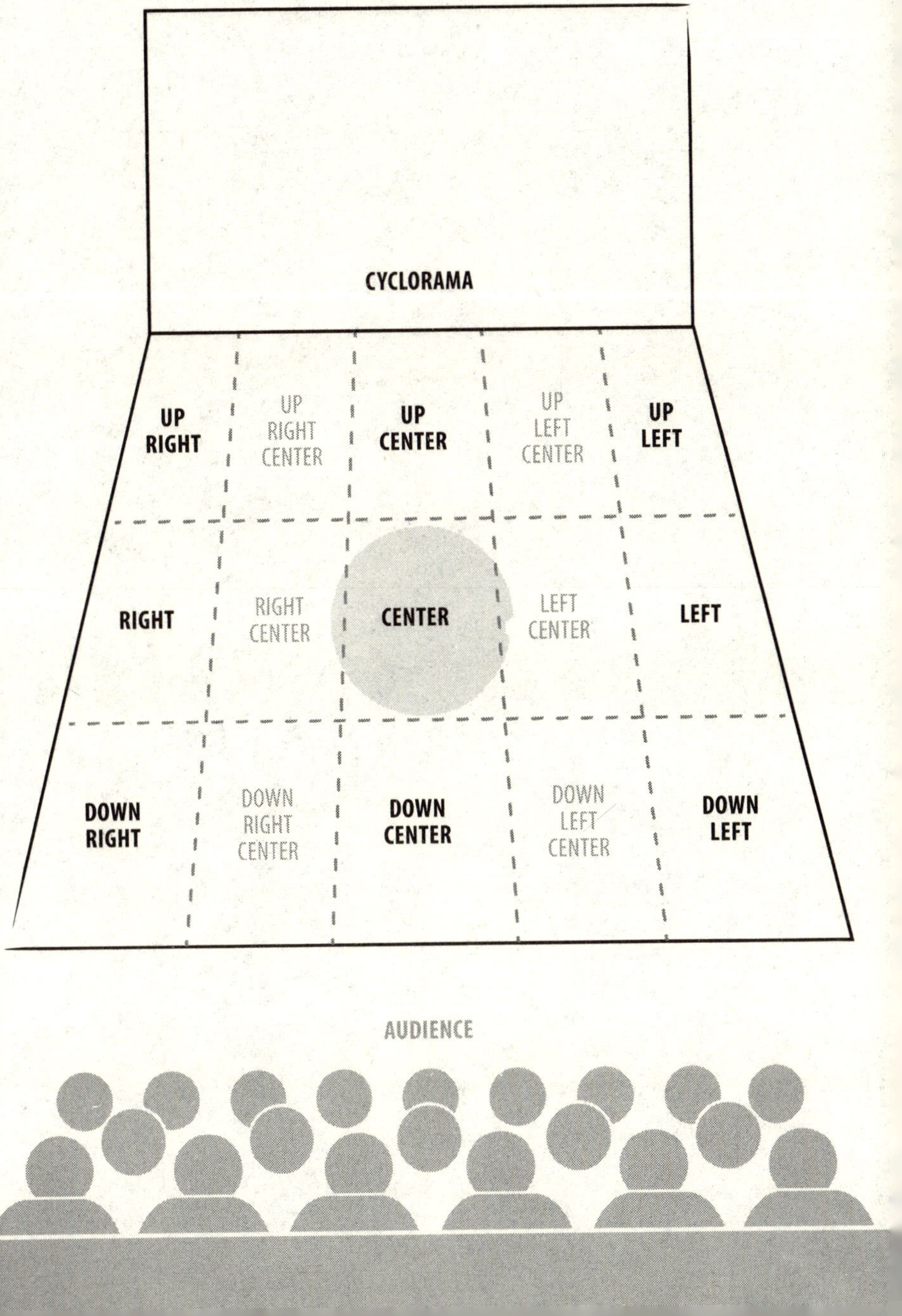

The Toy Cart of Clay

An adaptation of the Sanskrit classic
Mrichhakatika** by **Sudraka

FOR

B CHANDRASEKHARA

CHARACTERS IN THE PLAY

STAGE MANAGER (SUTRADHAR)	*Vasanthasena's Maid*
STAGE MANAGER'S WIFE (NATI)	*Steward*
MAITREYA, A BRAHMIN	*SHARWA*
CHARUDATTA	*Rohasena, Charudatta's son*
VASANTHASENA	*Clerk of the Court*
KUMANTRI	*Judge*
PRINCE SANSTHANAKA (SHAKARA)	*King's Investigator*
COACHMAN	*Vasanthasena's Mother*
RADANIKA	*Shakara's Servant*
1ST GAMBLER	*Gardener*
2ND GAMBLER	*Soldiers*
3RD GAMBLER	*Court Messenger*
REFEREE	*Litigants*
MADANIKA	*Spectators*

SCENES

ACT I

Scene 1: Charudatta's house and the street adjoining it

Scene 2: The street adjoining Charudatta's house

Scene 3: Vasanthasena's house

Scene 4: Charudatta's house

Scene 5: Vasanthasena's house

Scene 6: Charudatta's house

ACT II

Scene 1: Charudatta's house

Scene 2: The Spring Garden

Scene 3: The King's Court of Justice

INTRODUCTION

THE PLAY IS set in Ujjain, one of the great cities of India a thousand and five hundred years ago. Vasanthasena, a famous courtesan, seeks refuge from Prince Sansthanaka's snare in the house of Charudatta, once a wealthy man, now broken in fortune. In malice, Sansthanaka, also known as Shakara,* lures Vasanthasena into the spring garden where he leaves her for dead. Charudatta is accused of murder, but is saved from a death penalty by a fortunate turn of events. The play provides a vivid picture of the busy life in the great city, with its princes, courtiers, merchants, gamesters and the ordinary folk with their big and little schemes in which matters of state are interwoven with the lives of the people.

The original Sanskrit script of the play was in ten acts. It was accepted that the duration of the play in a traditional form of performance through the night would be highly variable, depending on the mood in the gathering and the extent of impromptu diversions taken. Musical interludes and dance sequences were integral to these performances, usually led by the Sutradhar and Nati. The English language version presented here has a compact, two-act structure, but retains the essential content of the original play. The performing group can decide on the need for music and dance. The narrator roles of the Sutradhar and Nati, however, must be maintained.

The evidence from historical research suggests that Sudraka was the pseudonym of King Shiladitya Dharmaditya of the Maitraka dynasty, circa 590–615 AD. (For instance, the work of Dr SV Sohoni at the Bhandarkar Oriental Institute in Pune.) Interestingly, one of the characters in the play, the activist, is named after the founder of the dynasty, Sharwa Bhattaraka.

Shiladitya's kingdom was spread over western and central India, with the capital in Vallabhi in what is currently the Saurashtra area

---

**sh + akara: for the prince's mannerism in speech, the s sounds being mouthed by him as sh*

of Gujarat. He was acknowledged by Buddhist and Jain scholars of the time as an accomplished poet and writer. As with many plays of the genre, Mrichhakatika celebrated the triumph of good conduct in trying times. The playwright-king was also critical of the politico-economic system introduced by the legendary Kautilya in the kingdom of Magadha. A brief reference to it is made in the play. The much-loved courtroom scene in the play, taking up the entire last act, is often regarded as the prototype of the dramatic device. The political satire in the act is also clearly recognisable, as relevant today as it was in the reign of the play's wicked king.

There have been many scholarly analyses of the play, mostly by Western writers. Almost all of them have been from a literary perspective, rather than a performance perspective. Sadly, no thanks to a prolonged colonial influence, Indian theatre folks have tended to be awed by the Western analyses, suspending their own native intelligence derived from centuries of folk theatre. It is now being recognised that the play can indeed be viewed as a farce, but with a strong political commentary, and a dash of romance thrown in for good entertainment. That was a thousand years before Moliere!

FIRST PRODUCED

The Moon Shall Rise by B Chandrasekhara
Bangalore Little Theatre, August 1962.

Stage Manager.......B CHANDRASEKHARA
Wife.......NINOO BHAGWAGAR
Maitreya.......A GANGULI
Charudatta.......S VIJAYSHANKAR
Vasanthasena.......DHUN LAL
Kumantri.......EDDIE LAWYER
Shakara.......VIJAY PADAKI
Coachman.......BK NARAYANA RAO
Radanika.......JENIFER VAZ
1st Gambler.......S RAMASWAMY
2nd Gambler.......AK SESHKUMAR
3rd Gambler.......CR SIMHA
Referee.......A RAMA RAO
Madanika.......FRENY LAWYER
Maid.......SA PRATIBHA
Steward.......T GANAPATHI
Sharwa.......R FRANKLIN
Rohasena.......P RAGHUNATH
Clerk at Court.......S VISWANATH
Judge.......VV SUBBA RAO
Investigator.......K VASUDEVAN
The Mother.......LAKSHMI FENN
Shakara's servant.......S RAMACHANDRACHAR
Gardener.......KK GEORGE
Soldier.......MS RAMA DOSS
Court Messenger.......T GANAPATHI
Stage Director.......SG RAMACHANDRA
Stage Manager.......BOBBY MEIKALJOHN
Stage Assistants.......S RAMA RAO. SEETHARAM
SRINIVASA VARMA. SESHKUMAR
Lighting.......SHIVASWAMY
Make up.......SHIVA RAM. JULIA STUFF
Costumes......VIMALA RANGACHAR. MANGALA RAMACHANDRA
Tailor.......SHAMA RAO
House Manager.......MP ANANTA DEVARAJ URS
Front of house.......SRINIVASA GOPAL. DL VISHALANATH
Designed and directed by.......SCOTT TOD
Assisted by.......MARGARET TOD

First revision produced by The Play Cart Ahmedabad, 1983.

The homes of Charudatta and Vasanthasena may be set in the same stage area, with suitable changes in the props, and entries/ exits from alternate directions. The homes may either have doors for the purpose or have open access through imagined doorways.

Scene changes are executed by the Sutradhar and Nati.

ACT I

SCENE 1

The play opens to reveal the Stage Manager Down Centre bowing to the audience, hands pressed together in namaskar. Presently he lifts his head and speaks to the audience.

STAGE MANAGER

Noble gentlemen and gracious ladies! May He that dwells in glorious light and speaks in thunder, shower his choicest blessings on us and teach us to walk in paths of restraint, compassion and charity. (*Tosses flowers into the auditorium*) I am your humble servant, the Sutradhar, the Stage Manager. The story that we wish to present today is an ancient Sanskrit play of the great poet Sudraka. It has been made famous over countless generations, and is well known in many lands as *Mrichhakatika*, which means *The Little Cart of Clay*. It has entertained people in the past, and we hope it will entertain you. On an occasion such as this, it is the invariable custom, made sacred by immemorial practice, for the Stage Manager to introduce the play. It is a duty I accept with unconcealed pleasure. It gives me the satisfaction of observing hoary tradition. It makes me proud that the actors have done me the honour of entrusting this noble task to me. The actors, the backstage company and I hope the pains we have taken to realise the idiom, the manners and the motives of the people of the past will be rewarded with your generous approbation. Now the actors and the stagehands are all ready. (*Looking off in various directions*) Now, where the devil have they gone? The green room is deserted... And the wings are empty and silent...Nobody here either...(*He scans the auditorium*) And I am hungry and tired. Well, as long as people are still coming in and settling down, I can dash home, snatch anything left over, and run back to get the show going. (*Takes a few steps Left and points off*) This is my house...But what is this? What is happening? Women weaving garlands...Making sandal paste? What delicious odours of sweetmeats frying! I wonder...I wonder...(*Calls off*) Wife...Wife!

WIFE *(Entering)*

Here I am, dear. But why are you not at the theatre?

STAGE MANAGER

I have been at the theatre. I have been working the whole day there. And I am hungry. I am famished. Is there anything to eat?

WIFE

Yes, of course there is. There is everything under the sun.

STAGE MANAGER

What do you mean everything under the sun?

WIFE

All kinds of delicious dishes, and ghee, and sweet curds, and the fruit salad that you like best, and of course...

STAGE MANAGER

What? All this in my house?

WIFE

Hubby dear, don't get so angry. Man's temper is full when his stomach is empty.

All these dishes are always there...under the sun...in the market.

STAGE MANAGER

Wicked woman! You will swallow the flames of hell for this.

WIFE *(Placating him)*

Now, now, now, don't get so angry. I didn't mean to hurt you...I should have known better.

STAGE MANAGER

All right, all right. What is the new scheme in your head? What is all this going on inside?

WIFE
I have undertaken a fast.

STAGE MANAGER
A fast! Great heavens, why?

WIFE
So that the great heavens may grant me a handsome husband.

STAGE MANAGER *(A thundering voice)*
In this birth or the next?

WIFE *(Sweetly)*
Of course in the next, my dear.

STAGE MANAGER *(To audience)*
You see, my friends? That is all a wife could cook up. She feasts on a fast, she squanders your money away in penance, and she longs for a handsome husband...in the next birth.

WIFE
There, my dear, you are upset...Didn't I tell you in front of the sacred fire at our wedding? I want you to be my husband always, in birth after birth. That is why I have undertaken this fast.

STAGE MANAGER
Hmmm. That is better...but tell me, who is to officiate at this fast?

WIFE
A worthy Brahmin.

STAGE MANAGER
And where will you get a worthy Brahmin?!

WIFE
Is there not a single one in this great city?

STAGE MANAGER
What! In Ujjain? Don't be stupid. You can't find the man you want even if you turn the city inside out and upside down.

WIFE

How very sad!

STAGE MANAGER *(Looking off)*

There goes Maitreya, Charudatta's friend.

WIFE

Aren't we lucky! He is a worthy Brahmin.

STAGE MANAGER

Ha! That clown? Well...at least he is the friend of a worthy man. (*Stepping off stage and calling*) I say, Maitreya, come and dine with us.

MAITREYA *(Offstage)*

No, I will not.

WIFE *(At the wing)*

Will it please you, sir, to visit us and grace our home with your holy presence?

MAITREYA *(Still Offstage)*

I am sorry, lady, I cannot. Something has made me very unhappy today. Ask somebody else.

STAGE MANAGER

We are famous for our dinners. There are gifts...and some money too.

MAITREYA

I've told you. I'm not coming. And nobody can force me.

STAGE MANAGER *(Re-entering)*

So...that's that. Well, you go in and observe your fast now, and I will go out to the park and gaze at the moon starving. No! No! I have to be back at the theatre and get the play started. I have to rush...

WIFE

But my Brahmin!

STAGE MANAGER

We will find a substitute. You have to feed a hungry man to please the gods – I will bring you one. Leave that to me. Keep everything else ready for the evening. *(Exit wife. To audience)* Perhaps I'll find a hungry man in the theatre. There is always somebody popping peanuts into his mouth through our most tender love scenes.

Well, my friends, the play must start now. We begin with a scene at the home of Charudatta. What can one say about Charudatta? For now, let us say he is a gentle and upright man. *(Exit)*

(Charudatta's house. He is seated in the courtyard. Maitreya's voice is heard off stage, repeating the earlier protest. He enters into the street area. On his shoulder is an expensive shawl, neatly folded.)

MAITREYA

I will not come, I tell you. Well, they are gone. *(Sighs)* I was a fool to tell them I would not come. I can have a proper meal only when I am invited – and that is not often these days. Just my luck – two invitations on the same day, and this second one so soon after a feast at the first!

In the past, when my friend Charudatta was prosperous, how I would eat those delicious puffs fried in ghee! *(Shakes his head and sighs)* I would eat and eat, and I would lie down in that very courtyard, drowsing like a big bull. Now...he is so impoverished. I must wait for chance invitations to fill my belly. *(Enters the courtyard)* How are you, my friend? *(Shuts and bolts the door)*

CHARUDATTA

Have you had good hunting today? Come, tell me how your day went.

MAITREYA

You know the habit of cows and oxen? They fill their bellies only when they are brought to food and drink. And every time they eat and drink it is only in bellyfuls. That is how I live. However, here's something for you, a bit of business. You remember that one-time friend of yours? Old Man Dust I call him. He has sent this jasmine scented shawl to you as a gift. He is sorry he cannot come himself... Why that face? Have I said anything wrong?

CHARUDATTA

It is well to come out of darkness into light. Misery after happiness is worse than death.

MAITREYA

Don't pity yourself because you are poor. You did not gamble. You did not speculate. You gave in charity.

CHARUDATTA

It is not loss of wealth that makes me sad. What pains me is that I no longer have any guests or visitors. I am poor, but to be avoided...

MAITREYA

Don't you worry. One of these days they will all flock back to you.

CHARUDATTA *(Rising)*

Well, the household evening worship is over. You must go now and offer evening worship at our shrine.

MAITREYA

I won't go.

CHARUDATTA

Why not?

MAITREYA

Because I can't. It is not proper. I may anger the gods if I worship them in my present state.

CHARUDATTA

Your present...

MAITREYA

A bursting stomach.

CHARUDATTA

Don't talk like that. To worship is the daily duty of all mortals. The gods are pleased by our sincerity in prayer. Now, go.

MAITREYA

I won't. Tell someone else. Everything looks topsy-turvey to me like things in a mirror, the left looking like right and the right looking quite wrong. Look, it is getting dark. The streets will soon be full of all sorts of bad characters – streetwalkers, pimps, thieves, playboy courtiers. I dare not go alone into their midst. I will feel like a frog meeting a serpent that is chasing a mouse.

CHARUDATTA

It is dark, but not so late. Go, now, do not waste more time. *(Charudatta enters the house area through a doorway. Maitreya sits on the courtyard seat.)*

SHAKARA *(Offstage)*

Stop, woman! Stop! *(Vasanthasena enters the street, followed by Kumantri, Shakara and Shakara's coachman.)*

KUMANTRI

Stay, lady. Do not run and tire your tender feet.

SHAKARA

Stop, girl! Scuttling away like a mouse! I am not going to kill you, you know. My heart burns for you – with love – like...like choice mutton over a fire.

COACHMAN

There is nothing to fear, madam. *(Vasanthasena turns to go)*

SHAKARA

Ha! Where do you think you can go? You just cannot escape. I am as sure of scent as a pedigree mongrel. I am the king's brother-in-law. I shall use all my power and spirit you off, just as the vulture carries off a rabbit.

COACHMAN

Did you hear, madam? My master, Prince Shakara, is the King's brother-in-law.

SHAKARA

She knows that, damn it!

COACHMAN

Indeed, sir, she does. Amuse him, madam. He has gifts for you.

SHAKARA

I do? Oh, yes, I have gifts for you.

VASANTHASENA

Women! Women!

SHAKARA

No, No, Men! Men!

KUMANTRI

Do you think she is calling us names? She is only calling her maids.

SHAKARA

Ah! She is calling her women? All right. Let her call them. I am not one bit afraid. Even if a hundred women come along, heh heh, I can kill them all. *(Vasanthasena looks about in panic)* Hey, Vasanthasena, call your women, all of them, a thousand, if you like. I am in hot pursuit, and no one can save you. *(Grasps her)* Now, look, I have you by the hair. My sword is sharp. Shall I slice your head off, or will you go with me?

VASANTHASENA *(Appealing)*

Sir, I am a woman.

SHAKARA

That is why I have not killed you yet.

VASANTHA

Sir, you are kind. But your words frighten me.

SHAKARA

They do? I am so sorry. But that is only what you see above. Down below I am very different. I am an angel...I am a god...I am a man. Be mine!

VASANTHA *(Angry)*

I have told you – day after day, week after week – it is impossible. Please leave me alone.

SHAKARA

I shall make you a wife – the king's brother-in-law's wife.

VASANTHA

You waste your breath. Don't tire yourself needlessly.

SHAKARA *(Clapping and laughing)*

Kumantri, the wench loves me. She says to me, 'Don't tire yourself, preserve your energy'. *(To her)* If you don't want to be a wife, I will permit you to live with me, if you think that is better.

VASANTHA

Oh! You are so stupid.

KUMANTRI

Your conduct is puzzling, madam, contrary to the custom of your kind. It is your duty to entertain the man who seeks your services.

VASANTHA

Money cannot buy love. Only character can, and only one man has it.

SHAKARA

Hah! I have been following her all evening, through every lane and street, but she won't listen to me. All because of that bankrupt Charudatta. Isn't that his house there? Come on, let us catch her before she goes in. It is no good being soft with her anymore. *(Kumantri has a plan to help save Vasanthasena.)*

KUMANTRI *(Loudly)*

You are being very clever, aren't you? So, that is Charudatta's house over there. I don't suppose she can see it in this darkness.

SHAKARA

Come, let us carry her off.

KUMANTRI

Wait. Let me talk to her and try to persuade her. She might change her mind. *(To Vasanthasena, taking her aside, into the darker area of the stage)* You are known in this city by your birth in a trade, but you seem to be a good woman. You must have a gentle heart, since you love Charudatta. Now you know where his house is – there, slip in there quietly and all will be well.

SHAKARA

Hey, Kumantri! Where are you? I can't see you.

KUMANTRI *(Returning to Shakara)*

Here...I cannot find her. *(Vasanthasena edges towards the entrance to Charudatta's house.)*

SHAKARA

She must be there, but has made herself invisible, like a piece of charcoal in a heap of black gram. But oh ho ho, I'll find her. She cannot escape.

KUMANTRI

It is so dark, you cannot see her at all. But you are so clever. There must be some special sign by which you will find her.

SHAKARA

Ha ha ha, find her I will! Hmmm, what did you mean by 'special sign'?

KUMANTRI

Oh, I thought your sharp senses would detect the sound of her anklets, or the scent of the jasmine in her hair.

(Picking up the cue, Vasanthasena takes off her bangles and anklets, ties them up in her sari, and throws away the flowers in her hair.)

SHAKARA

Of course! I can hear the smell clearly! But there is darkness in my nostrils, so I cannot see the jingle of the jewels.

VASANTHA

Thank god, here is the door. *(Tries to push the door open, but it does not yield)* It is bolted! *(She pushes herself into a corner of the frame)*

SHAKARA

I will track her down now. She is as good as cooked. Watch me.

KUMANTRI

Very well, I'll watch. *(Inside the house we see Charudatta joining Maitreya.)*

CHARUDATTA

Haven't you gone?

MAITREYA

My friend, I told you I was not going.

CHARUDATTA

So now you ignore me too. It is but natural. When poverty overtakes a man, relatives forget him, friends abandon him, and pain from all directions is heaped upon him.

MAITREYA

Don't appeal to the soft side of my nature, please, with such trite philosophy. However, if you must have me go, you might consider sending Radanika with me – just for company, you understand. I can't carry the offerings, the lamp, the stick and everything. *(Picks up a lamp)*

CHARUDATTA *(Smiles, calls out)*

Radanika, bring the flowers and other offerings. *(To Maitreya)*
It would be safer if you went alone.

MAITREYA

Have no fear. I will take good care of her. *(Radanika comes into the courtyard, carrying a basket of flowers and fruit, and a small vessel of water.)*

Come along, Miss. I shall hold the door for you. *(He picks up a stick and puts it under his arm. Radanika follows him. He opens the door. Vasanthasena comes in quickly and hides in a corner. The lamp goes out. Maitreya gasps.)*

Save us, lord!

CHARUDATTA

What is it Maitreya?

MAITREYA

Nothing, nothing at all. I opened the door and the draught blew the light out. What do you think? Am I afraid of ghosts? Radanika, you stay here by the door. I will go in and light the lamp again. *(He passes Charudatta, halts, returns and takes Charudatta in with him.)*

Better two than one. *(Radanika steps out into the street to wait. We see Shakara's group)*

SHAKARA

Yes, Kumantri. Tonight we celebrate! Vasanthasena will make a fine stew in my cooking pot.

KUMANTRI *(To himself)*

The celebration of an empty pot on a blazing fire. *(Shakara gropes in the dark)*

SHAKARA *(Grasping Kumantri)*

Kumantri! I have her.

KUMANTRI

Oh, but it is I!

SHAKARA

Oh, but it is you...Well, you stand here, as a guide post. *(Groping again he grasps the coachman)* Ah! I have her now!

COACHMAN

But sir, it is I.

SHAKARA

But, sir, it is he...well, you stay here. *(Moves between them, feels them, and assures himself of their positions.)* Kumantri here. Coachman here. Kumantri – Coachman. Coachman – Kumantri. Stay just where you are. *(Shakara gropes again and...catches Radanika)*

Kumantri, it is she! I have caught her. She was running away in the darkness. I have caught her by her forelock, jingling anklets and all!

RADANIKA

Sir, will you let go of me? *(Shakara hands her to Kumantri)*

KUMANTRI

It is not her voice. It is some other woman.

SHAKARA

You know what? She is even cleverer than you thought. She has disguised her voice, like a cat lapping up curds in the kitchen. Sly! More than a snake! But not more than me. I have caught her!

KUMANTRI

Disguise her voice? How could she? Yet perhaps...she has learned music and dancing and acting, and so she might have altered her voice. *(Maitreya returns to the courtyard with a lighted lamp and the stick under his arm. He talks as he walks across to the street door.)*

MAITREYA

Look at this lamp, fluttering like the heart of a cow lost in a jungle. *(He is at the doorway and sees Radanika between Shakara and Kumantri.)*

Radanika! What is the meaning of this? Gallivanting with strangers!

RADANIKA

Sir, they are being very insulting.

MAITREYA

Insulting you?

RADANIKA

Insulting you, and hurting me.

MAITREYA

What? Are they using force?

RADANIKA

Tugging me by the hair.

MAITRIYA

Oh, that's all? I am not insulted by that.

RADANIKA

But they intend to take me away, sir.

MAITREYA

What! Are you sure?

RADANIKA

Certain.

MAITRIYA *(Raising his stick)*

Under his own roof even a lap dog can turn into a lion. Look, I am a Brahmin. See this stick, crooked like a Brahmin's luck? I shall beat your brains out with it. *(Kumantri intervenes, approaching Maitreya with a namaskar.)*

KUMANTRI

Sir, You are a holy man. Pardon us this little indiscretion, an inadvertent error in judgement.

MAITREYA

You are not to blame. *(Maitreya goes up to Shakara and examines him with the lamp.)* This is the culprit. You are from the royal family, I see. You are the King's brother-in-law, aren't you? Do you think this is proper for you? All Ujjain holds Charudatta in high esteem. And here you are, creating a scene outside his house and dishonouring his household staff.

KUMANTRI

Sir, I beg you to pardon us. We did not mean any discourtesy. We were looking for someone the prince loves.

MAITREYA

Who? She?

KUMANTRI

Good heavens, no! Not she. It was another young lady. She slipped away in the dark. We thought this young lady was that one and... and...we have been guilty. *(Radanika goes into the courtyard, taking the lamp from Maitreya. She puts it back in its place and goes in.)*

MAITREYA

I am sorry I barked at you without reason. *(Turns to go)*

KUMANTRI

It was understandable. Only, I beg you, do not tell Charudatta what has happened.

MAITREYA

No, I have no intention to pain him. *(Turns to go again)*

SHAKARA

Halt! *(Maitreya stops)* Kumantri! Why do you abase yourself before this boy and beg his pardon?

KUMANTRI

Because I am afraid.

SHAKARA

Afraid? Hah!

KUMANTRI

Afraid of god's displeasure.

SHAKARA

Goddy Goddy's displeasure?

KUMANTRI

For belittling Charudatta's noble character.

SHAKARA

His noble character? That starving beggar!

KUMANTRI

You must not talk like that. In happier times, when he was well off, he was indeed noble in word and deed. He did not insult anyone. He helped every man that went to him. Come, let us withdraw to our part of town.

SHAKARA

Not without Vasanthasena.

KUMANTRI

But Vasanthasena has vanished.

SHAKARA

How did she vanish?

KUMANTRI

You want an answer?

SHAKARA

Yes, I want an answer.

KUMANTRI

She has vanished, like the smile on the village idiot's face.

SHAKARA

Ahh...I see.

KUMANTRI

It is now the time to frown. Let's go.

SHAKARA

No, not until I have her with me.

KUMANTRI

Wise men have said that you can hold an elephant with stout rope, and you can hold a horse with a halter, but you may hold a woman only by the strings of her heart.

SHAKARA

Go on if you want to. I will not come.

KUMANTRI

Very well, I will go. *(He leaves)*

SHAKARA

Go to hell! *(Turning to the house)* I know she has gone into this house. I'll wait here for her. *(Shakara sits on a stone seat near the door and talks to Maitreya)*

Here! *(Maitreya approaches)* You may sit if you feel like it – but over there. *(Points to the ground)* You are from a humble station.

MAITREYA

He has made me humble. *(Sits on his haunches)*

SHAKARA

Who has?

MAITREYA

Fate.

SHAKARA

All right, then. Let us see you rise.

MAITREYA

I will rise. I will.

SHAKARA *(After a pause, impatiently)*
When? When?

MAITREYA
When fortune smiles upon me.

SHAKARA
Weep until then, weep.

MAITREYA
I am weeping for it.

SHAKARA
For what?

MAITREYA
The death of good fortune. And the pall of helplessness.

SHAKARA
A laughing matter. *(He laughs)* I order you to laugh, then. Laugh, laugh.

MAITREYA *(Rises)*
I will, I will.

SHAKARA
When?

MAITREYA
When prosperity returns to Charudatta.

SHAKARA *(Rising)*
Enough! Take this message to your precious Charudatta. The courtesan called Vasanthasena, wearing scented anklets and tinkling jasmines in her tresses, has run away from me, Shakara, the King's brother-in-law. If he surrenders her to me, it will work out well for him. If he does not, I will crush him like a squashed cabbage leaf and make minced meat out of his mashed potato head. Tell that to your bankrupt master. *(He strides away, followed by the coachman. Maitreya shakes his head sadly and enters the courtyard, closing the door behind him.)*

MAITREYA

Radanika, the insult was not meant for you, nor for me. It was aimed at the good Charudatta. But do not tell him. It will pain him. *(He looks about and does not see anybody)*

The heroics on the streets of Ujjain have embarrassed even the gods. *(He exits. Charudatta re-enters the courtyard with a lamp. He sees the figure of Vasanthasena, but takes her to be Radanika.)*

CHARUDATTA

Ah, Radanika, it was good of you to have accompanied Maitreya. By himself he would never have returned so soon, dropping in at every shrine on the street. Go to bed, my dear, it is late.

The night air is chill. Take this shawl and cover the child with it. *(She takes the shawl from him)* See that he is warmly tucked in. Why do you not go? Why are you silent?

(Hearing Charudatta, Maitreya and Radanika re-enter the courtyard.)

Come, Radanika, it is quite late. By the way, where is Maitreya?

MAITREYA

I am here, and this is Radanika.

CHARUDATTA

Then who is this stranger I gave my shawl to?

VASANTHA

We are not strangers.

MAITREYA

I know that voice. It is Vasanthasena.

CHARUDATTA

Vasanthasena!

MAITREYA

Yes. Shakara was telling me about her just now. It seems that for all his froth and fury he could not lay his hands on her. She escaped into this house. If you do not give her up, he will destroy you...or so he says.

CHARUDATTA

Give her up to him? That rake? Oh, pardon me, Vasanthasena, I have been discourteous. The light is so little, I did not see clearly.

VASANTHA

There is no need to blame yourself. You were not to know.

CHARUDATTA

But tell us how it happened. How did you come to be so far from your house? At an hour that is no longer safe in Ujjain?

VASANTHA

It was late evening, but not so late that I could not worship briefly at the shrine of the goddess of love. But there was such a big crowd there that I was delayed. My maids were separated from me. As I was returning, I saw Shakara following me. I ducked into one street after another. Finally, thank god, I was able to come in here.

CHARUDATTA

I am glad you were able to escape. Now...

VASANTHA

If you will send someone with me, I shall return home immediately. And oh...could you do me the favour of keeping these jewels with you? I will send for them tomorrow.

CHARUDATTA

This house is not a safe place.

VASANTHA

But I trust you.

CHARUDATTA

Maitreya, will you take those jewels please?

MAITREYA *(Holding out his hands)*

Will I? Of course!

VASANTHA *(Giving Maitreya the jewels, speaks to Charudatta)*

Thank you.

MAITREYA

Oh, lady, we should be thanking you. We don't know how to thank you enough.

CHARUDATTA

Poor fellow! He is under a spell. Maitreya, they are left here only for the night, for safe-keeping.

MAITREYA

Oh! They are not meant for you and me?

CHARUDATTA

They will be returned tomorrow.

MAITREYA

Is that so? Hmm...How do I know they are genuine? Or not stolen goods?

VASANTHA

Sir, if you will send this man with me, I shall be going.

MAITREYA

No, no, no! No, miss...I am only a bachelor. It is dark in the streets, and you are beautiful. If I go out there with you something may happen. Something will happen. Something always happens to hapless Brahmins. I will be pounced upon and torn to ribbons by all kinds of...

CHARUDATTA

Stop jesting, man. Go with her.

MAITREYA

Must I? You know what? Better you than I. You are older. Don't worry about the jewels, miss. I shall guard them well tonight and leave them in charge of the steward in the morning.

VASANTHA *(Smiling)*

At this rate, I shall have to spend the night here.

MAITREYA *(Horrified)*

That won't do, that won't do at all! Here. *(Gives the jewels to Charudatta)* Come along, then.

He opens the door and strides out, followed by Vasanthasena. Charudatta stands at the door gazing after them for a moment.

SCENE 2

The street. The first gambler appears with a loosely bundled change of clothes under his arm. He speaks to the audience.

FIRST

My friends, you are fortunate in your bliss, and blissful in your state of complacence. You do not know how dreadful it is to gamble. I should know. I am a gambler, have been one so far at least. You can lose everything – first your money, then your house, wife, children, the hair on your head, everything. A gambler is a very special kind of fool, with neither honour nor self respect. And you are always on the run, with mad dogs chasing you.

Voices off stage. The third gambler and referee are shouting.

» Thief!

» I'll kill you!

» Wait till I get my hands on you!

» Stop! Thief! Come back here, you!

» You run that way! I'll chase him from here...

FIRST

You see? *(Begins to tiptoe out)* Dogs, did I say? My old friends, such affectionate hyenas...*(Stops)* But why should I be scared of this lot? I shall soon be in the camp of Aryaka's rebel army. What a triumphant return it will be when Aryaka marches through these streets to the seat of government and is crowned king again. Oh how we long for his speedy return! And with him the cheer on the face of Ujjain. *(He seats himself in a corner. The second gambler rushes in, breathless, in some panic, freezes at entrance. The third gambler and referee rush in.)*

THIRD *(Entering)*

Where the devil did he go? The cheat!

REFEREE *(Entering from opposite side)*
Did you find him?

THIRD
Didn't you?

REFEREE
No!

THIRD
He should be here somewhere.

REFEREE
He has vanished.

THIRD
Just let me get my hands on him. I'll knock all his teeth out.

REFEREE
Well, no use hanging about here. Let's call it off. What do you say?

THIRD
What do you say we...

REFEREE
Good idea! Here?

THIRD
It is only about midnight. Come, let's play a couple of throws. *(Sits near first gambler)*

REFEREE *(Sitting)*
What do you bet if I beat you in the first game?

THIRD
You are a good referee, but it's different when you're playing.

REFEREE
Go on! What do you bet?

THIRD
I give you four to one. *(Shakes the dice)*

REFEREE
It'll be a clean sweep, you know.

THIRD

For me, of course. I'll beat you all the way. *(The second gambler cannot help himself. He comes down to the two players and joins the game.)*

SECOND

I can beat both of you together.

THIRD *(Springing up)*

Ha! We have you! Rascal! My ten pieces of gold...out with it!

SECOND

You will have them, of course. You will have to let go of me for that.

THIRD

Cash down first.

SECOND

Why must you be so crude? Am I running away?

REFEREE

It's the game, good fellow. Pay him what you lost.

SECOND

Just a moment, let me think.

THIRD

Pay now, think later.

SECOND

What do you take me for? My dear sir, I consider it most improper not to pay up on a debt of honour. I am not a common cheat. I am only thinking of the mode and the manner of payment that would be most fitting.

THIRD

I don't care how you pay, as long as you pay, and pay up now. Pay it in instalments if you like – one piece of gold every two seconds.*(The second gambler takes the referee aside)*

SECOND

Hmm. I shall give you half the sum if you will have the other half written off.

REFEREE

Uhuh...I should say that sounds reasonable.

SECOND

All right?

REFEREE

All right.

SECOND

Thank you. *(He then takes the third gambler to the other side)* I say, could you advance me half the sum like a gentleman? The other half will be paid in instalments.

THIRD *(In some doubt, but taking out the money)*

I should be thankful if I got back at least half my money.

SECOND

Thank you. *(Standing midway between the two, to referee)*

You agree to forward trading of half the amount in proxy?

REFEREE

I...do.

SECOND

Thank you. *(To third)* You agree to remitting half as a secured debenture.

THIRD

I do.

SECOND

Appreciated. *(To audience)* You have heard, gentlemen? Thank you for being witnesses to the transaction. *(To the other two)* Thank you gentlemen for your confidence in the banking system of Ujjain. Goodbye. *(Starts to go)*

THIRD *(Catching him)*

Ah! Up to your old tricks again! I'll kill you if you don't pay up right now.

SECOND

I have nothing. How can I pay?

THIRD

Sell your father, for all I care.

SECOND

He is paying up his old debts in the other world.

THIRD

Sell yourself and pay. *(Shakes his fist)*

SECOND

Oh...I say! But...

REFEREE *(Also shaking his fist)*

A debt of honour, you know.

THIRD *(Hitting him)*

Cough it up, you old jackal! *(Hitting again)* Out! Out, I say! *(Shaking his fist)*

SECOND

All right! All right! Don't kill me, please. Have it your way. Take me to a public place and put me up for sale.

THIRD

Idiot! At this hour? Which market is open now? But let's go. I'll keep you tied up in my house till the morning, and then we'll see.

SECOND

Don't be so hard. I'll come to your place myself in the morning. I am starving now, and I want to get myself something to eat.

THIRD

You will earn your meal tomorrow from your new master and enjoy it much better.

SECOND *(Appealing to referee)*

Stop him, I beg you. Can't you do something?

REFEREE *(To third)*

The city inn, you know. It's never shut. Big merchants, filthy rich foreigners and their local toadies – transactions at all hours. You can put him up for auction there.

THIRD

That's a damned good idea. Come on! *(The referee and the third gambler drag the second gambler to face the audience.)*

REFEREE *(To second)*

Now, tell them. *(Second is silent. Third hits him on the back.)* Go on, tell them.

SECOND

You tell them, you are the referee. *(Sees referee shake his fist)* No, no, no, let me do it. *(Addresses the audience)* Noble sirs, I owe ten pieces of gold to this man to whom I lost at dice. Will some kind gentleman pay him the money and buy me? (*Listens)* What did you say? What sort of work can I do? Any kind of work you ask me to do – wash your clothes, scrub your floor, dig your garden... What does he mean, turning away. *(Turns to another section of audience)* You, sir, you look a prince of merchants...I'm sure he heard me before leaving his seat...Oh, sir...They are all turning and waddling away...Oh, if only Charudatta were here, I would not be abandoned like this.

THIRD

My money now.

SECOND

But how do I raise the money?

THIRD

The money!

SECOND *(Looking heavenwards)*

The money! The money! *(To audience)* Isn't there a single decent man there to help me out? *(The first gambler now decides to step in. He moves to the group.)*

FIRST

The poor fellow is being persecuted needlessly. Perhaps I can help settle the dispute. *(Going to them)* Salutations for the evening, gentlemen.

THIRD

A thousand to you. Come on, my money!

FIRST

What is the trouble?

THIRD

This fellow owes me ten pieces of gold.

FIRST

Is that all? Ten miserable pieces of gold?

THIRD

(Examining him, then snatching his bundle from him to exhibit them) See for yourselves, gentlemen. He carries a beggar's wardrobe, and speaks like a member of the royalty – of ten miserable pieces of gold.

FIRST

Come on. I dare you to play with me.

THIRD

Tchha! What good will that do?

FIRST

If you lose, he is quits with you.

THIRD

I know your tricks. I'm not playing any game with the likes of you.

FIRST

All right, play with him.

THIRD

He has no money. He is broke.

FIRST

Lend him ten pieces more and play.

THIRD

Lend him...Why am I even listening to you?

FIRST

Because you are smart. You know a good deal when you see one.

THIRD
So I lend, and we play. What then?

FIRST
If he wins, you will be paid back in full.

THIRD
What if he does not win?

FIRST
You will have won the loan back.

THIRD
You think you are smart, huh? I'll tell you what I think. I think you are a common dirty rogue, and I know how a rogue like you plays.

FIRST
Exactly. That is how I play. Pray, who are you to question my style? *(Stands nose to nose with him)*

SECOND *(Egging on the first gambler)*
Go on, man! Show him! *(There is a scuffle. The third gambler hits second, who falls, dragging referee down with him. The first hits the third. All four are on the floor in a heap. The third extricates himself.)*

THIRD
You blood sucking beast!

FIRST *(Rising and retreating)*
Now, now, now...careful, careful. If you do me any harm now, I will go to the Court of Law first thing in the morning and have you hauled up there and whipped for assault and battery.

THIRD *(Advancing)*
Go on, try it. Let's see how you get there first.

FIRST
You want to see? You really want to see?

THIRD
Yes, show me, and I'll keep my eyes wide open to see how you do it.

(The third gambler opens his eyes wide and cocks his head forward. The first throws sand into the eyes of the third and runs away, while the second escapes in the opposite direction.)

REFEREE *(Consoling third gambler)*

There, there, old fellow. It is too bad, but at least you are not hurt badly.

THIRD *(Recovering)*

Where did they go?

REFEREE

They've given us the slip. One ran that way and the other this way. Here is the blood from the rat who owed you money. Come on, let us follow the trail.

SCENE 3

The Stage Manager is busy setting up Vasanthasena's house. He is muttering to himself. Presently he speaks to the audience.

STAGE MANAGER

Women! If only the duties of a stage manager had included an oath of celibacy! First, I must go hungry so that the play starts on time. Then my senses are subjected to the torture of a feast in the making – a feast to begin a fast! Then I return to the theatre even more famished. And now she says she has changed her mind. She will undertake a pilgrimage of eleven ashrams south of the Vindhyas she says.

(The wife has appeared by now. She positions herself silently behind him in the manner of a coy apsara in a rock carving. She is dressed grandly.)

Just one change of clothes, hand spun and plain, not a thread of gold, not a stud or stone on her, not a speck of colour but the vermilion on her brow – that was her firm resolve half an hour ago. I wonder what else she is surrendering to the gods now to please me in my next birth. Oh, the cruel fate, the occupational hazard I have to live with, to husband a stage manager's wife. Well, if that is god's wish, so be it.

WIFE

The wife shall be where the stage manager must be – so do the gods wish.

STAGE MANAGER

What? You here! And what's with all this festive finery?

WIFE

Have I ever missed a new play of yours before? I had to come, and it seemed such an august audience attending.

STAGE MANAGER

What happened to all your missions of renunciation?

WIFE

I renounced them.

STAGE MANAGER

Why am I wasting time arguing with you? Go and sit in the wings. You can watch the play from there. No, wait! Help me set the scene...this way...put this upstage right... further right...that's better...now this piece... *(He and his wife set the scene hurriedly)*

Ah, good. Vasanthasena's home. Hush, here she comes. Quiet! *(They slip out. Vasanthasena is with her maid, Madanika.)*

VASANTHA

And then? And then?

MADANIKA

I beg your pardon?

VASANTHA

Did you not speak?

MADANIKA

Not I. It was you murmuring something. You were talking like that in your sleep too. You retired so late, and here you are pacing about the house before the break of dawn. You act strangely, and you look so different. Is anything the matter? I only ask out of affection.

VASANTHA *(Sitting)*

How do I look and act?

MADANIKA

As if there was some anxiety, buried under secrecy, but struggling to come up for fresh air.

VASANTHA

It is what happened last evening.

MADANIKA

That man! Is it about that man?

VASANTHA

Surely he has a name.

MADANIKA

He lives in the merchant's district, does he not?

VASANTHA

I asked about his name, not where he lived.

MADANIKA

If the name can please, it is Charudatta...but he is bankrupt!

VASANTHA

That is why I still love him. No blame attaches to a woman who loves a poor man.

MADANIKA

But you don't see each other. Why don't you invite him here and entertain him?

VASANTHA

Because he thinks he is too poor, that he cannot visit me without gifts.

MADANIKA

Hmm. I think I know why you left your jewels with him last night.

VASANTHA

I believe you do.

MADANIKA

Suppose he loses them, or they are stolen?

(Offstage, Voices of the third gambler and referee. The women are startled.)

» Stop! Thief!

» There he goes...after him!

» Catch him...he has my money!

» Don't let him get away!

VASANTHA

Heavens! What could that be about?

MADANIKA

It seems to be right outside our doorstep.

VASANTHA

The front door! *(As Madanika goes towards the door the second gambler rushes in, stands a moment looking at the two women, runs past Madanika and falls at Vasanthasena's feet. Vasanthasena rises.)*

SECOND

I surrender to you, lady. Save me, save me!

MADANIKA

Who are you, sir? What is the meaning of this ugly intrusion? Is this part of your profession?

VASANTHA

You look like a stranger. Are you in some trouble?

SECOND *(Rising)*

I am not a native of this city, lady. I belong to Magadha. I was employed in the palace there, as the King's masseur. It was a good job, but Magadha is a peculiar place. The King's chief economist wants to make everybody buy more things. Borrow more to buy more. That way they are to become more prosperous. Spending more by borrowing more, so that they can have more – so that they can prosper more, or something like that. Buying more than earning is the new order lady – even buying before earning. People appear possessed. They want more and more. They want anything, everything, by any means.

VASANTHA

Is that what you ran away from? It was wise of you.

SECOND

More than that, my lady. There were thefts in the palace. I was unlucky. There were stories cooked up about my character. They began to suspect me seriously. They would not believe me. I could not prove I was innocent. I had to run away. I'd heard that Ujjain was a great city, full of opportunities. So I came here.

MADANIKA

You will soon see that you have to run away from this great city as well.

VASANTHA

Did you find no opportunity here?

SECOND

At first I was lucky. I entered the service of a good man. He was the best of men. He always helped others but never spoke of it. *(Vasanthasena and Madanika exchange glances.)*

VASANTHA

And then?

SECOND

His charity was such that he gave freely and...

VASANTHA

And lost everything?

SECOND

Lost everything.

MADANIKA

What is his name, sir?

SECOND

He lives in the merchant's district, and is called Charudatta.

VASANTHA

Madanika, a seat for this good man. *(Madanika brings him a stool)*

You seem to have had an interesting time. Please be seated – and make yourself at home. You served Charudatta. Madanika, fan him, will you? *(Madanika fans him)* And then? And then?

SECOND

I was happy in his service, though in later months he could not pay me my wages. I did not ask for it. Then I fell into bad company. I started gambling. *(Offstage - Voices again)* They are after my blood, lady. They will kill me!

VASANTHA *(Taking off her bracelet)*

Madanika, take this to them and say that this man has given it to them in full settlement. *(Madanika goes out)* How much do you owe them?

SECOND

Ten pieces of gold, and they are ready to hang me for it.

VASANTHA

Gambling is exciting, isn't it?

SECOND

While it lasts. When the tide goes out, the money goes out even more swiftly, and you are left sinking in the bog. *(Madanika returns)*

MADANIKA *(Entering)*

I gave it to them, madam.

VASANTHA

Were they satisfied?

MADANIKA

They said, 'We take it in full settlement of the debt. What is past is past. He can come back and play again.' *(Vasanthasena smiles at him.)*

SECOND

Goodbye to gambling, I say. I shall never, ever, never gamble again.

MADANIKA

Well, that's that. You may go home now.

SECOND

But my debt to you, lady? Let me serve you until that is discharged.

VASANTHA

Better go and serve your old master.

SECOND

I am too ashamed to return to him now. And after what you have done for me, my guilt is doubled. Let me work here, please.

VASANTHA

Your master and I are old friends. Think of what I have done as giving you wages that he would have given. I will tell him about it in good time. There is no danger now. Go back to him.

SECOND

Not to him, lady. He, a saint, and I, a common sinner! I know what I must do. I shall retire from city life and take the ascetic path.

VASANTHA

Don't do anything in haste.

MADANIKA

Don't do anything rash.

SECOND

I am decided. Thank you, lady, for helping me see the light. I may now walk with my head erect. As long as I live this worldly life I will need wealth – to buy, to give and to lose. If I choose to remain poor, I can neither give nor afford to lose. Yes, I am going to give up everything and free my soul. I am going to become a monk and a mendicant. I am decided.

SCENE 4

Charudatta's courtyard. The following night. There are two simple beddings spread on the floor. Enter Charudatta, followed by Maitreya. Maitreya shuts and bolts the door.

CHARUDATTA

What a wonderful night of music it was! What a beautiful rendering of the midnight raga! Such sweetness in a man's voice is so exceptional. I kept imagining it was a woman singing. *(Washes his feet and returns to his bed)*

MAITREYA *(Sitting on his bed)*

My friend, your head is full of music and, I suspect, more full of a certain woman. My head is full of sleep. It is hours past midnight now. Why, even the dogs in the street are silent. *(Lies down)*

CHARUDATTA *(Laughing)*

You are right, you are so right. Why are you going to bed without washing your feet?

MAITREYA

What does it matter? I need neither bed nor blanket. I just lie down and roll about like a worn-out donkey. So why should I wash my feet? *(The steward enters with a bag of jewels and goes to Maitreya)*

STEWARD

Here you are, sir, the bag of jewels. It was all I could do to take care of it during the day. It is your turn now. *(He goes out)*

MAITREYA

Oh! Dreadful! I did not get a wink of sleep last night, which was just my luck. And now, this. I will not sleep tonight either. What if a thief drops in tonight to steal them?

CHARUDATTA *(Lying down)*

A thief in here? He will have to be out of his mind to choose this house to rob.

MAITREYA

I shall put them in the rice bin in the pantry. They are safer there.

CHARUDATTA

Keep them with you until the owner sends for them.

MAITREYA *(Lying down)*

Oh, well! I think I'll sleep in peace only when they are taken away. They say it is a cowardly act to enter a house and steal things when people are asleep.

CHARUDATTA

Of course it is.

MAITREYA

But I think there are others who are lower and more guilty. Your politician, for instance. What does he do but rob others to feather his own nest? I think you punish the thief because you can't punish the politician.

And what about the opportunist jackals at the heels of politicians? The thief is certainly better than those oily men, tailing people of wealth and power like dogs, licking their sandals and sucking up to them. Give me the thief anytime.

The thief is so independent and adventurous. Don't you think so? *(Charudatta only grunts)* The thief is an artiste. How skilfully he makes the hole in the wall! How athletic, as he climbs in from the window! What patience! What self-control!

What? Are you asleep already? Sleep on, man. You have no cares like me. I am the one in danger if a thief breaks in. He is like the serpent, you know...silent and sly and dangerous. *(He is increasingly drowsy)* I cannot help admiring him. I wish I could be a thief. Now that I think of it, I have never seen one at work...a thief...leaping over walls like a cat...the thief...a fine thief...wonderful thief...

(The thief has entered now. He stops when he hears the muttering of Maitreya. Soon Maitreya is asleep. The thief goes to the door, opens it, goes up to Charudatta, feels under the pillows, and then goes to Maitreya.)

CHARUDATTA *(Half asleep)*

My hands are cold...very cold...the door. *(The thief freezes)* Maitreya, the door. Ugh! *(Charudatta turns over, away from the thief, who then goes to the door, closes it, and stands there.)*

MAITREYA

Jewels safe...hug them...thief...can't get them. *(Chuckles)* Get them...get them... *(The thief waits a moment, then walks over to Maitreya)*

You take them...safer...take them. *(The thief gently picks up the bag of jewels)* Go on, take them...got them? What?

THIEF

Yes, I have.

MAITREYA

Good...thank you...sleep now...peace. *(Maitreya turns over and goes to sleep. The thief crosses swiftly back to the door and goes out, leaving the door open. The lights fade out and go up again. Radanika enters the courtyard from the house.)*

RADANIKA

Wake up Maitreya, it is morning. Trust men to wake up by themselves! *(She sees the open door and gasps. She runs to Maitreya, shakes him and speaks in a hoarse whisper)* Get up, get up! There are thieves here!

MAITREYA

Thieves! *(Chuckles)* Someone to steal my heart...

RADANIKA *(Shaking him)*

Wake up! There are thieves!

MAITREYA *(Sitting up)*

You? What do you mean, thieves?

MADANIKA

Look there, look at the door.

MAITREYA *(Jumping to his feet, shouting)*

Wake up, Charudatta! Wake up! The house is burgled!

CHARUDATTA

Don't talk rubbish first thing in the morning. *(Draws the sheet over his face)*

MAITREYA *(Going up to Charudatta's bed)*

Thieves! Robbery! Assault! Murder! *(Charudatta sits up)*

CHARUDATTA

What is the matter?

MAITREYA *(Pointing at the door)*

Look there! *(Pointing in other directions)* And there! And there! There must have been a hundred of them – over the wall, in by the window, out through the door. The house has been looted!

CHARUDATTA

What could they get here? Poor fellows! A few brass vessels and odds and ends...people will only have more contempt for me now!

MAITREYA

They saw the house was big. They thought they could get heaps and heaps of gold and silver and jewels...Oh! By the way... *(He crosses to where he had been sleeping and looks about with a puzzled frown)* Now, where is the bag? Ah! I remember. Thank god, I handed them over in time. *(He returns to Charudatta)* Look, man, you used to call me foolish, clumsy, this, that and what not. Now you see how clever I am? If I had not given the jewels to you, the thieves would have walked away with them.

CHARUDATTA *(Laughing)*

That is a good joke, even first thing in the morning.

MAITREYA

I am not joking!

CHARUDATTA

When did you give them to me?

MAITREYA

Just before we went to sleep.

CHARUDATTA

But I don't have them.

MAITREYA

I even remember saying your hands were cold.

CHARUDATTA

Did you put the bag in the kitchen after all? See if it is there, Radanika. *(Radanika goes in. He moves to where Maitreya lay and looks about.)* Is it not anywhere here?

MAITREYA

I tell you, I gave it to you.

CHARUDATTA

Is that quite certain?

MAITREYA

As certain as a Brahmin's appetite.

CHARUDATTA

Then I am afraid the jewels are indeed gone.

MAITREYA *(A mirthless laugh)*

Let us be happy. The thieves have got something for their pains.

CHARUDATTA

I'd be happy if they were mine, but they belong to somebody else.

MAITREYA

The fool in you remains! Only you can be sad when somebody else's jewels have been stolen.

CHARUDATTA

Who will believe it if we say that we have been robbed? Till now I had lost only my wealth. Now my honour is gone too.

MAITREYA

Don't you worry, man! Jewels? What jewels? Who was it that gave you the jewels? Who says you took them? Where are the witnesses? Let them try to make a case of it. I will outshout them all and silence them.

CHARUDATTA

I would much rather beg and slave to repay the loss. I cannot tell a lie.

MAITREYA

Who is telling lies? It is merely the due process of law. And these days you can't live if you keep heaping obligations upon yourself. *(Radanika re-enters from the house.)*

RADANIKA

The jewels are not there, sir.

MAITREYA

The rice bin!

RADANIKA

I looked there too. *(Charudatta sits down with his head in his hands.)*

Have they hurt you, sir?

CHARUDATTA

No, no...I am all right. That the jewels should be stolen now!

MAITREYA

You are right. Gossip is always deadlier than crime in the streets. They are sure to say all sorts of things about you – about us. She and that greedy old cow of a mother of hers. They will haul you up before the King's judge. Your honour is hardly at risk, it is mud.

CHARUDATTA

The old saying is proved upon me – wealth flows through a man's life like water in a sieve. What remains is the misfortune – wave after wave. All the good things in life fly out of the windows – the laughter, the joy, the troops of friends who feasted in my hall. And now is my sun set in a grey horizon.

RADANIKA *(Producing a necklace)*

Will she take this necklace of rubies in settlement, sir?

CHARUDATTA

This necklace? But it was my wife's parting gift to you!

RADANIKA

It was bought, sir, was it not? You can buy it back later, or one better than this. *(Charudatta shakes his head)* It is true she gave it to me before she left us forever. But I remember her words: 'Radanika, you have been good to me. Take this necklace. It is from my mother as a wedding gift. Keep it with you, take care of it. It will be of use to you some day.' And so, you see... *(Addressing Maitreya with a knowing smile)* When am I ever going to wear this myself? I can't put it to any better use, can I?

CHARUDATTA

It is now that I am indeed bankrupt, when I have to redeem my honour with my wife's jewels.

MAITREYA

Wait! I cannot approve your giving this great necklace in place of the lost jewels. They could not have been as precious as these rubies. Why, now I think of it, how do we know they were not paste? Did we weigh them? Did we test them?

CHARUDATTA *(Quickly)*

Radanika is right. I owe a duty to the memory of my wife. I also owe it to my own honour – you said so yourself. But you know I have a far more important duty than either of these two. It is to my little son. He must not grow up in a jungle of hostility, with whispers all around, and clacking tongues and snide remarks and pointing fingers. I have his soul to guard against blight. So you understand. Take the necklace from her, Maitreya. Go and give it to Vasanthasena.

MAITREYA

But let's not be rash. These rubies...

CHARUDATTA

Take it, man, and go.

MAITREYA

Oh well! Have it your own way. As always. *(Looking at Radanika)* I suppose I have to go by myself.

SCENE 5

Vasanthasena's house, the next morning. She is holding a picture in her hand and looking at it lovingly. Madanika is with her.

MADANIKA

That is a picture of Charudatta, I am sure. *(Vasanthasena does not reply)* It is a beautiful picture.

VASANTHA

It is beautiful. *(Looking up at Madanika)* How do you know?

MADANIKA

You were looking at it so lovingly.

(A maid enters from the back of the set)

MAID

Madam, my mistress, your mother, has directed me to tell you that the carriage has come.

VASANTHA

Has Charudatta sent it?

MAID

No, it is Prince Shakara's. He has sent a gift too, a bag of gold pieces.

VASANTHA

Get out of my sight! If I hear such rubbish again, you will be dismissed!

MAID

Beg pardon, madam, I only obeyed the orders of your mother, my mistress.

VASANTHA

It is the order of your mistress, my mother, that makes me angry.

MAID

But what shall I say to her, madam?

VASANTHA

Tell her that if she wants me not to kill myself, she should leave me alone. She must not ever speak of that monster to me again.

MAID

Very well, madam. *(She goes into the house)*

VASANTHA

Madanika, put this picture in my room and bring me my fan. I am going out to the terrace.

(Madanika takes the picture and goes into the house. Vasanthasena goes out to the terrace area. Sharwa comes in. We recognise him as the thief in the earlier scene. He looks about for Madanika cautiously.)

SHARWA

Madanika...Madanika...

MADANIKA *(Returning with a fan)*

Sharwa!

SHARWA

I have something important to tell you.

MADANIKA

Shh! My mistress is there on the terrace. Come here. *(She takes him across to another end)* What is the matter?

SHARWA

If you pay Vasanthasena the bond money, will she set you free?

MADANIKA

It is a large sum. But you know she is not keeping me against my will. I love to serve her. Although I stay here as a bondsmaid, she will let me go if she thinks I want to. She will not demand any payment.

SHARWA

You know how much I love you, Madanika. I would do anything to pay for your bond. But I am now in...how do I explain it... There have been some developments. Certain grave matters have demanded of me my small talents. I have to give all my time there. It has made me wretched that I have not earned enough for you. I love you so much; I can't bear to be without you. And so – I did something bold and dangerous last night.

MADANIKA

What did you do?

SHARWA *(Taking out the bag of jewels)*

I...I...took a certain risk to acquire these jewels for your release.

MADANIKA

Did you do anything dishonourable? You stole them!

SHARWA

Don't say that! I am not a common thief! I did not snatch the jewels from an old woman or child, I did not threaten to take anybody's life. No one has been harmed. I only took them from a rich man who did not even feel that he was losing them. He was giving them away. And I took them for your sake! Give them to your mistress now, and let us go. And please ask her not to disclose this to anybody for some time.

MADANIKA

What do you mean? Why should she not disclose it? Here, let me look at them. *(She looks at the jewels)*

I think I know these...Where did you get them? Tell me now, where did you get them?

SHARWA

What does it matter? Just take them and give them to your mistress.

MADANIKA

If you trust me so little, how can you expect me to marry you?

SHARWA

Aachh! Women!

MADANIKA

You won't tell me?

SHARWA

No, no, my love, I have nothing to hide from you.

MADANIKA

So, tell me!

SHARWA

All right. I stole them. I have just learned that it was Charudatta's house. *(Madanika starts)* What is the matter?

MADANIKA

You wretched man, what a dreadful crime!

SHARWA

But I did it for you! You should admire me for my courage, pity me for my plight, not jump to reprimand me.

MADANIKA

Did you kill him?

SHARWA

No, of course not!

MADANIKA

In truth?

SHARWA

I swear it.

MADANIKA

Did you hurt him?

SHARWA

Not at all.

MADANIKA

Thank god!

SHARWA

This is great! A man of respectable birth like me, friend and right hand of the exiled prince Aryaka, I endanger my life for you, and you ask if that man is all right. You have nothing to ask about me.

Wait a minute...you said you recognised the jewels. I see! So that's the way it goes – you know those jewels, do you? You are worried about Charudatta, are you? You have been leading me on all the time. I, fighting in the wars, and you here fooling around with him. I will really kill him now. And then I will come back and kill you too. *(He starts to go)*

MADANIKA

You are being stupid! You don't know what you have gone and done.

SHARWA

Hah! I know jolly well what I am going to do.

MADANIKA

These are Vasanthasena's jewels.

SHARWA

What?

MADANIKA

These are Vasanthasena's jewels.

SHARWA

Tell that to your grandmother.

MADANIKA

Ask her. There she is.

SHARWA

I don't believe it.

MADANIKA

She had given them to Charudatta for safe custody.

SHARWA

Is this true?

MADANIKA

Go on, ask her.

SHARWA

What shall I do now?

MADANIKA

You tell me. You knew jolly well what you were going to do.

SHARWA

Come on. You don't have to be so hard on me now. You said I was being stupid. So, show me the way out.

MADANIKA

You are a man, a brave hero. There is nothing for me to teach you.

SHARWA

Men only learn by practice. Women are born clever. They have instinct. Tell me what to do.

MADANIKA

There is only one thing to do.

SHARWA

And that is...?

MADANIKA

Return the jewels to Charudatta.

SHARWA

What! And be handed over to the police?

MADANIKA

He is a gentleman, not the kind to prosecute anyone for a mistake.

SHARWA

But I can't face him now. No, that won't do. Think again.

MADANIKA

All right, there's the second best course. Go to my mistress, tell her that Charudatta has sent you with the jewels, and give them to her.

SHARWA

What is the good of giving them to her when I stole them from him?

MADANIKA

Oh, the shortsightedness of stupid men in love! You see, the jewels will return to the owner. Charudatta will be released from obligation. And you won't be called a thief.

(She gives him the bag of jewels)

SHARWA

Of course! That's what I was thinking of too! *(She glares)* You are so right.

(Vasanthasena enters. Sharwa hides the bag behind his back and looks at Vasanthasena, in a dilemma. Madanika stands with her head bent. Vasanthasena looks from one to the other.)

VASANTHA

Isn't this your young man, Madanika? *(To Sharwa)* Won't you stay? She has told me about you. I have also sometimes seen you here. Just now you don't seem tired of talking to each other.

SHARWA

Did you hear us talking?

VASANTHA

No, I only saw you both. I heard nothing! I am very pleased. You may stay. You need not leave in a hurry. *(The sound of a tomtom in the street is followed by an announcement not too clearly heard, fading away.)*

Madanika, find out what the announcement is. *(Madanika leaves)* Please remain seated. I will go back to the terrace.

SHARWA

Madam, I've come...you see...

VASANTHA

I know about it. *(Starts to leave)* There is no need to be so...

SHARWA

I've come from Charudatta's house. He...

VASANTHA

I was saying...I am waiting to hear you.

SHARWA

He...that is Charudatta...has sent a message.

VASANTHA

Pray continue.

SHARWA

He wishes you to know that his house is not safe, and that your jewels should not remain there at such risk. He has therefore returned them to you. Here, please take them. And please permit me to go. *(Starts to leave)*

VASANTHA

Stay, sir. I have a message for Charudatta too. But first tell me, you and Madanika have planned to marry, have you not?

SHARWA

Yes, madam. You see...

VASANTHA

Then you will take her with you, and my good wishes too.

SHARWA

Oh, Lady! I...but...Her bond money!

VASANTHA

Perhaps Charudatta forgot to tell you of an old understanding between us – that I should freely give Madanika to the man who brought back these jewels to me. *(Madanika returns)*

The two of you are welcome here whenever you wish to come. And do remember me in your prayers. What does the town crier say, Madanika?

MADANIKA

Madam, it is a special proclamation issued under the King's seal. A rebel army led by the good Aryaka has been defeated and scattered. Aryaka himself has been captured and imprisoned, they say. The public is being warned that any underground support in the city will be crushed. Those surrendering immediately will be dealt with sympathetically, and all others providing help in any form to the rebels will be executed in public.

VASANTHA

Aryaka's defeat is unfortunate. Nothing can check Shakara now. The goodness of men and the honour of women will have little value. It will be terrible for me. It will be worse for Charudatta.

SHARWA *(Transformed)*

That is a sentiment that binds us together as common victims of Shakara's persecution. The country is groaning under the tyranny of the bandit king and Shakara's private crimes. Our resistance to the tyrant was gaining strength day by day, and we had hopes of early success. Madam, I must now tell you that the noble Aryaka entrusted me just recently with an important intelligence mission in the city. It now seems we were guilty of miscalculation. I must hold myself responsible for Aryaka's capture. But he will escape, I promise you. I must set about organising it. *(Madanika begins to weep quietly)* We had not expected the king to strike so soon. In the last hour I have become a wiser man, and have learned how misfortune strikes at the moment of greatest hope and joy. Life plays brutal tricks on a man, tossing dice before him, mocking his every foothold. Lady, let Madanika remain with you until I come back. If I don't, she can consider herself free. *(He goes out quickly)*

VASANTHA

Do not weep, girl. Trust in providence. That young man has his heart in the right place.

MADANIKA

If he is captured, or killed...?

VASANTHA

If such had been his fortune, he would have been captured last night. *(The maid has entered)*

MAID

Madam there is a visitor for you. He says he is...

VASANTHA

Would he be kind and wait a while?

MAID

Madam, he says he has been sent by Charudatta and...

MAITREYA *(Entering)*

And it is rather important business that should not be kept waiting. *(The women are unprepared for this)*

Good morning!

VASANTHA

Good morning, sir. To what do we owe the honour of this visit?

MAITREYA

The jewels you left in trust with Charudatta.

VASANTHA *(In mock horror)*

Have they been stolen?

MAITREYA

Eh? No, no, nothing so fortunate. He lost them at dice. *(Vasanthasena and Madanika exchange smiles)* And the gambler who won them has disappeared. We cannot find him, god knows we have tried. Why are you smiling?

VASANTHA

You see my peculiar fortune, sir? I admired him when he was rich. So I trusted him in his poverty. Now I learn he has degenerated into a gambler! He knows his excuse for not coming to see me is flimsy, does he not? That is why he has sent you.

MAITREYA

That is why he has sent this necklace of rubies. He begs you to take it. *(He holds the necklace forward and takes it back immediately)* I suppose you refuse.

VASANTHA *(Laughing, Madanika joining)*

I shall certainly accept it. *(She holds out her hand. Maitreya gives her the necklace reluctantly)* Tell your master that I shall call on him presently.

MAITREYA

That won't be necessary, miss. If you think your jewels are worth more than this necklace, you can tell me what the difference might be, and I shall convey it to him.

VASANTHA

He owes me nothing in respect of those jewels. There is, however, another debt I wish to settle, and I must see him personally for that. Tell him I will come soon.

MAITREYA

When? Now?

VASANTHA

As soon as I can.

MAITREYA
Now look, miss, you will only be wasting your time. He has gone out, on important business, and won't be back till very late in the evening. Let me take your message to him...

VASANTHA
I will be there in the evening.

MAITREYA
What? Oh, very well, if that is your wish. Goodbye *(Going)*

VASANTHA
Until evening, then.

MAITREYA
Eh! Oh, evening – yes, yes, evening ... *(He goes out)*

SCENE 6

Courtyard of Charudatta's house. Maitreya enters the house.

MAITREYA
I was right. I'm always right. Not one instance to prove me wrong. Women are grabbers – all of them without exception. And courtesans are the worst of the lot. She could not even be ordinarily civil. Did she ask how I was? Did she enquire about Charudatta? That much for their divine relationship! She saw the necklace in my hand, she grabbed it – didn't even offer me a seat. Let me go to hell if I look at her again. A trader who does not short-change, a goldsmith who does not pilfer, and a courtesan who does not plunder – these are impossibilities in this world.

It is almost evening, and she has threatened a visitation. Merciful heavens, do you not protect the lost and the weary anymore? Won't you answer? *(A clap of thunder)*

A thunderstorm – thank God! That will keep her home. She couldn't have left already. *(Thunder)* Ha ha, she certainly cannot come now. And when Charudatta returns, I will tell him.

(There is knocking on the street door. Maitreya opens it cautiously. There is relief on Maitreya's face and a smile on his lips as he opens the door fully. Charudatta comes in. Maitreya closes the door and bolts it.)

MAITREYA

You will live to be a hundred. I spoke your name just a moment ago.

CHARUDATTA

Well, what about your mission?

MAITREYA

Ah, the mission, the mission. Dreadful! Horrible! Disgusting!

CHARUDATTA

Did you get to meet her?

MAITREYA

Through proper channels

CHARUDATTA

Through...

MAITREYA

Her mother. Seated royally in the last of the nine chambers that make up their house. She had to approve the meeting.

CHARUDATTA

It must have been a great honour, meeting Vasanthasena's mother.

MAITREYA

A gigantic honour. She occupied the entire chamber. When you are inside the chamber you cannot see all of her at once, not without your head taking the path of the sun from the East to the West. If you step outside the chamber you can see all of the lower part of her legs through the doorway.

CHARUDATTA

She is large made, is she not?

MAITREYA

Enormous is an inadequate phrase. How did she get into the chamber, I wondered. There could only be one way.

They must have seated her there first, and then built the chamber around her.

CHARUDATTA

And Vasanthasena? Did she not accept the necklace?

MAITREYA

Not accept it! We are not so fortunate, man! She seized it. She folded her hands and said 'please, please', and grabbed the necklace.

CHARUDATTA

Then why are you unhappy?

MAITREYA

Isn't that reason enough to be unhappy? No lady would do it. What profit did her jewels bring? A thief stole them. And in their place you lose a necklace of transcendental value.

CHARUDATTA

I have not lost anything. I have redeemed the great trust that she put in me. *(Distant thunder)* The storm seems to have blown away.

MAITREYA

That is unfortunate. I have a third reason for my unhappiness.

CHARUDATTA

What might that be?

MAITREYA

She and that bag of tricks of a bondsmaid of hers looked at me, looked at each other, and looked at me again, and laughed. I am sure they meant mischief. Beware of such women! Don't let her come near you again.

CHARUDATTA

Now that I am poor, I can be no attraction for a courtesan of her standing. But you have not told me the second reason for your unhappiness.

MAITREYA

The gods in their infinite mercy are taking back that reason. Your woman friend said she would come here this evening. But now with the storm gathering she may not. I wish it had started to rain though. *(There is knocking on the door)*

CHARUDATTA

See who it is.

MAITREYA

It might be just the wind.

CHARUDATTA

It might be a stranded traveller.

MAITREYA *(Going to the door)*

I am sure it is an ill wind. *(Opens the door slightly, looks out and then tells Charudatta)* It is your banker.

CHARUDATTA

My banker?

MAITREYA

It is she. *(He opens the door fully. Vasanthasena enters, followed by Madanika.)*

CHARUDATTA

Maitreya told me that you intended to come here this evening. May I know to what I may attribute the pleasure of this visit?

MADANIKA

My mistress wishes to know the price of the necklace of rubies that you sent.

MAITREYA *(To Charudatta in a whisper)*

I now see the reason for this visit. She wants to bargain and collect something more.

MADANIKA *(To Charudatta)*

The necklace you sent, sir...my mistress has lost it at dice. The person who won it from her has disappeared, and cannot be found.

MAITREYA

Now that was exactly what we decided to tell them this morning.

MADANIKA

Until that necklace is found, my mistress wishes you to accept these jewels. *(Maitreya takes the bag she holds out, opens it, takes out the jewels and looks at them in wonder.)*

Are you admiring the workmanship, sir?

MAITREYA

Eh? Oh yes, rather. *(To Charudatta)*

These are the stolen jewels. Shall I ask how they got them? *(Charudatta nods. Maitreya goes to the maid. They exchange whispers. He returns to Charudatta and whispers to him.)*

CHARUDATTA

The gods are merciful. The maid has brought me good news. She cannot go unrewarded. *(He attempts to take a ring off his finger that is not there.)*

Take this. *(He looks at the empty finger and hangs down his head. There is a crash of thunder.)*

MAITREYA *(To Vasanthasena)*

The storm is building up now, miss. You had better hurry home. Thank you for the visit.

VASANTHA

I have something important to say to my gambler. Would you mind? Sir, it is plain that you have gambled rashly and lost all.

MAITREYA

It's late, miss! It is dark and rainy. I am surprised that you should be out on such a night.

MADANIKA

You poor bachelor! I am not surprised at your ignorance.

VASANTHA

I don't know what I should be surprised at – your rash gambling or your unthinking charity. I do not believe the one and cannot help admiring the other. You sent me this necklace, which I gather is very precious to you. I must say it was not right that you should part with it.

CHARUDATTA

I cannot disagree. But who would believe that your jewels were stolen from this house? It was fear of slander that made me send the necklace to you.

VASANTHA

And I have brought it back here.

MAITREYA

Then give it to him, miss! And get going – before it starts pouring.

VASANTHA

I was indeed happy that you sent the necklace to me. But it is fear of unworthiness I think that makes me decline it for the present. I pray you make me worthy of it.

MAITREYA *(At door)*

Come, come, miss. Hurry. I shall escort you home myself. *(Thunder and lightning)*

There! It's too late! It has come down. *(To Madanika)*

Well, young woman, you can't say I didn't warn you – but I'm afraid your mistress will have to spend the night here this time.

(*Sound of rainfall and thunderstorm as the scene closes.)*

ACT II

SCENE 1

The stage manager is seen down-centre. He addresses the audience.

STAGE MANAGER

Step lightly, dear friends. The request is not merely to respect the wishes of those in the audience who took their seats in time. We are gathering in the early hours of the morning, and many in the great city of Ujjain are yet resting after a night of thunderous rain.

Rain. Bounteous rain. Auspicious evening rain. Unfortunate the mortal that cannot see beyond the grey harshness of a downpour. For those chosen to see, the gods themselves reveal their form in the splendour of a rainstorm. They offer glad tidings to the needy, justice to the wronged, gentle comfort to the weary in heart. And for the innocent in slumber, there is little on earth to match the tranquil peace of a morning after the rain.

We return to the courtyard of Charudatta's house. *(He withdraws as the scene opens. The courtyard of Charudatta's house. It is morning. Radanika is playing with Rohasena. She is putting finishing touches to a toy cart of clay.)*

RADANIKA

What a beautiful morning!

ROHASENA

I was frightened. The thundering was so loud last night.

RADANIKA

The storm cleared well before dawn. Here, let me show you a game with this little cart I've made for you.

ROHASENA

I don't want that cart.

RADANIKA
Don't you want to play with this cart?

ROHASENA
It is clay. I want a golden cart. (*Vasanthasena enters from the house.)*

RADANIKA
Of course! A smart one like you must have a golden cart. But let's play with this one just now.

ROHASENA
When will I have the golden cart?

RADANIKA
Oh, as soon as your father can go to the market. He will buy one for you.

ROHASENA
When will that be? (*Radanika makes gestures of despair. Vasanthasena approaches the child.)*

VASANTHA
What is your name, child? *(The boy does not answer.)*

RADANIKA
His name is Rohasena.

VASANTHA
What a lovely name! He is the very image of his father.

RADANIKA
Isn't he?

VASANTHA
Are you annoyed about something, Rohasena?

RADANIKA
Yesterday, the neighbour's child brought a toy cart and the two of them were playing with it here. When the child went home, Rohasena began to cry for a toy cart. So I made him one of clay. The other one was plated in gold.

VASANTHA
Is that all? You will certainly have a nice, big toy cart of gold, my child.

ROHASENA *(To Radanika)*
Who is she?

VASANTHA
A friend of your father.

RADANIKA
And your mother.

ROHASENA
They say my mother went away a long time ago.

RADANIKA
You have this lady near you now.

VASANTHA *(With a string of pearls)*
Let me put this round your neck. *(Rohasena turns away)* Will you not wear it for me?

ROHASENA
I don't want it.

VASANTHA
Not even if I get you a golden toy cart?

ROHASENA
You will? *(Vasantha nods)* All right. But you can take back the necklace after you get me the golden cart. *(The steward enters)*

STEWARD
Madam, my master has gone to the Spring Garden. He has left word that he will be pleased to have you join him there. Shall I order the carriage?

VASANTHA
Oh no! I am not ready. But it will take me just a minute. Radanika! Do take Rohasena to the goldsmith's. Let him buy the toy he likes. Tell them to send their bill to me. *(Hurrying out, to steward)* Order the carriage in half an hour.

STEWARD
Very well, madam.

ROHASENA *(To steward)*

I'll tell you a secret? I'm going to get a golden cart.

STEWARD

Just what you should have, little master.

ROHASENA

You can come and play with it too.

STEWARD

Oh, that would be so nice.

ROHASENA

And when I grow up I'm going to have a carriage just like father's.

STEWARD

And as fine a pair of horses. *(Radanika, Rohasena and Steward exit. Lights dim briefly. Vasanthasena re-enters with Madanika.)*

VASANTHA

I am ready now. I don't think I took as long as I thought I would.

MADANIKA

Not more than ten minutes. Ordinarily you would take that long to paint your toe, just one toe.

VASANTHA

It is more than an ordinary day. Well, see if the carriage has come.

MADANIKA *(Going to the door and looking out)*

There is a carriage parked there, madam.

VASANTHA

Find out if it's the one for me.

MADANIKA *(Calling off)*

You there, my man, is that Charudatta's carriage?

COACHMAN *(Off)*

Eh? Are you Vasanthasena's woman? Tell her I'm waiting to take her to my master.

MADANIKA

The carriage is waiting for you, madam.

VASANTHA

Wait here for me. I'm off. Wait, is my hair set right? All right? Thank you. Can I go now? Just adjust the fall of my sari. Oh, hold my hand! I have never been so nervous before...so happy! *(She goes out. The maid watches a few moments, closes the door and returns into the house. The lights dim and come up again. There is loud knocking on the street door. The steward comes out, goes to the door and opens it, nods in recognition.)*

STEWARD

One moment. *(He goes to the passage leading into the house and calls)*

Miss! Miss! *(Radanika comes out)* Do you know if Vasanthasena is ready yet?

RADANIKA

But I thought she left some time ago.

STEWARD

How can that be? The carriage is at the door just now.

RADANIKA

Is it? Let me ask if she is ready. *(She goes to the passage and calls)*

Madanika, is the mistress ready?

MADANIKA *(Off)*

She went to the garden a while ago. Didn't you know?

STEWARD

But the carriage has come round only now.

(Madanika comes into the courtyard)

RADANIKA

Are you sure she went out?

MADANIKA

I saw her getting into the carriage and being driven away.

STEWARD

This is terrible! I suspect a trick. Oh god, I can see Shakara's hand in it. *(The two gasp)*

I fear the worst. I'd better run to the Spring Garden and tell my master about it.

(As he goes to the door, Sharwa and Aryaka push past him into the courtyard. They are covered from head to foot and are not recognised. The sound of a distant tom tom is heard.)

STEWARD

Look where you are going! Who the devil are you?

SHARWA

I wish to speak to your master.

MADANIKA

Sharwa!

STEWARD

Do you know this man, miss? *(Sharwa reveals his face while Aryaka remains with his back to the group.)*

SHARWA

Yes, she does. I am a friend of Vasanthasena, and an enemy of Shakara. *(Tom tom again)* This is...*(Aryaka nods disapproval)* a friend. Listen to me. There is not much time, but listen carefully. Aryaka has escaped from prison, and he's still in the city. We were recognised as sympathisers and chased. They are sealing all the roads going out and a house-to-house search has begun in the city. Anybody found to have given him refuge is to be executed immediately. We must find a way, before it's too late, to somehow get him out of the city. We need your help.

STEWARD

But, sir, you realise of course that this is all very...

SHARWA

This young woman will vouch for me. You must grasp the urgency of the matter, as I am sure your master would. If you cannot help us escape, you must at least hide us here.

STEWARD

But, sir, this is too serious a matter for me to act independently.

My master is in the Spring Garden. I shall go there immediately and inform him of the matter. You may remain here while I am gone, for my master would surely give refuge to anyone in distress.

MADANIKA

I have a better plan. Charudatta's carriage is waiting outside. Why don't you disguise yourselves as women? Radanika will give you the dresses. *(Radanika nods)* Take the carriage out. Dressed as women you can easily pass the sentries and patrols. You can send the carriage back when you are done with it.

SHARWA

That is mighty clever of you. Trust a woman for a cunning plan! Disguised as women, we will only be emulating the brave Arjuna. Come! *(Sharwa goes into the house with Aryaka, followed by Radanika and Madanika.)*

STEWARD

Gentlemen, gentlemen, I shall be obliged if, out of consideration for me, you would meet my master and obtain his approval... before you...

Oh what a morning! Heaven knows what the rest of the day is going to be!

SCENE 2

A park. The private estate of Shakara. The scene is not quite ready. The stage manager is at it, aided in starts by his wife. She sits on a garden seat.

STAGE MANAGER

And that's the way the winds blew, my friends. It was a fateful day. Charudatta had hardly left his house in the morning, and his courtyard was filled with intrigue and mystery. First, the strange disappearance of dear Vasanthasena in a carriage of unknown markings. Then...

WIFE

But that must have been Prince Shakara's carriage. It was so...

STAGE MANAGER *(Cutting in firmly)*

My dear, the seat there could do with a little shift to the left...that way now. Ah, good, now will you look after the creepers up right centre? *(He glares at her and continues with the audience)*

And then, my friends, we have a jolt of an intrusion from the thief who turned out to be a certain Sharwa, courting Madanika. He has with him a stranger, who speaks little and remains unidentified.

WIFE

That was Aryaka! He must have been set free by...

STAGE MANAGER *(With control)*

It is not for us to provide the conclusion, my dear.

WIFE

But didn't you see? It was Sharwa himself who set out to...

STAGE MANAGER *(Louder)*

Not the conclusion, not the derivation either. We may only note the possibility that it was Aryaka. The important thing to remember, dear wife and assistant...*(a long glare)* is that we have not the...

WIFE

But I saw him in the wings when he uncovered his face. It was Aryaka...

STAGE MANAGER

Not the conclusion, not the derivation, not the evidence! Oh, my sinful soul, that it should be trapped in this arena with its wings clipped! Look, my beloved, this is Prince Shakara's private garden. He does not take kindly to trespassers – especially women. Get back to your place now, and make sure you are not seen here again until the scene is over. *(He pushes her out. To audience, as Shakara enters and sits, Kumantri following.)*

To recall, my good friends, it has been a fateful morning. And more, much more, is to unfold through the day.

(The stage manager withdraws. The second gambler enters. He is now an ascetic in ochre robes. There is a twist of wet cloth over his shoulder.)

SECOND *(Chanting)*

Buddham saranam gachchami [I go to the Buddha for refuge]
Dhammam saranam gachchami [I go to the Dhamma for refuge]
Sangham saranam gachchami [I go to the Sangha for refuge]
(He repeats the chants as he wrings his cloth)

I seek refuge in the Buddha. I seek refuge in the Dharma. I seek refuge in the Sangha. I seek refuge in the Buddha. I seek refuge....

SHAKARA *(Rising)*

You spineless monk! I will make skinless mincemeat of you. *(Beating the ascetic)* I will cut you into slices like...like a boneless carrot.

KUMANTRI *(Stopping Shakara)*

Don't raise your hand against him. He is a holy man.

SECOND

Layman, know that anger is evil.

SHAKARA

See! See! He calls me a layman. Me, a prince! Me, the King's brother-in-law! *(Beats his chest, then beats the ascetic again)*

KUMANTRI *(Stopping him again)*

He meant no insult. He only meant that you are a non-ascetic believer in the Buddha.

SHAKARA

Is that so? That is all right, then. All right, monk, you may beg me to beg your pardon. But why did he come here?

SECOND

Only to bathe and wash my clothes in that lake.

SHAKARA

How dare you! Do you not know that the king, my sister's

husband, has given this park to me specially, as the best of all parks in the city? If people want to come in here, they must obtain my permission. But being a large-hearted great man I have given general permission to the heartless public to come here without permission. The only ones that may come here without prior permission are the mongrels of Ujjain. I am a great man, a big man. Even I do not bathe here. In fact, I do not bathe at all. And here you are, washing your dirty clothes in my lake.

KUMANTRI *(Stopping Shakara)*

Don't beat him again. He is only a young monk.

SHAKARA

How dare he become a monk at so young an age! He has to be punished for that.

KUMANTRI

But don't beat him. You will kill him. Punish him some other way.

SHAKARA

All right. I shall sentence him to hard labour. *(To the ascetic)* You bathed in the lake, did you not?

SECOND

That is true, I did.

SHAKARA

Go back there. Separate the mud from the water. Make one heap of the mud and another heap of the water, and then put the water back into the lake. *(He guffaws at his own ingenuity)*

KUMANTRI *(To the ascetic)*

That will teach you a lesson. Only, do not do it on this bank, lest my lord's feet should be stained with mud. Go round to the other bank and get on with it.

SECOND

May the Lord have mercy on you! *(He goes away)*

SHAKARA *(Sitting down)*

I cannot forget her. I am always thinking of her. I should have caught her that night, but she slipped away. *(Listens)* Listen. Isn't that a carriage? It must be mine. The sound is so familiar. It grunts like an old pig. Ah! Here comes my man at last.

(The coachman enters)

Have you come, my man?

COACHMAN

My lord, I have.

SHAKARA

Have you brought the carriage?

COACHMAN

My lord, I have.

SHAKARA

Have the horses come too?

COACHMAN

My lord, they came with the coach.

SHAKARA

Has Vasanthasena come?

COACHMAN

She is in the carriage, my lord.

SHAKARA

Then bring the carriage in!

COACHMAN

In here, my lord?

SHAKARA

No, out here, from in there.

COACHMAN

The carriage with Vasanthasena in it, my lord?

SHAKARA

Yes!

COACHMAN

No, my lord.

SHAKARA

No?

COACHMAN

Yes, my lord.

SHAKARA

Yes?

COACHMAN

There is a fence around the garden with only a wicket gate, my lord.

SHAKARA

Don't waste precious time talking like an idiot. Bring the carriage through the fence if you must.

COACHMAN

My lord, if I do so, the carriage will be damaged, the horses will be lamed, and I may break my neck.

SHAKARA

Look. I am the King's brother-in-law. If the carriage is damaged, I will have another made. If the horses are injured, I will buy another pair. But if you break your neck, all I will say is good riddance.

COACHMAN

It will be a great regret to me, when I die, that I may no longer serve your highness.

SHAKARA

You are a good fellow. Bring it in whichever way you wish.

COACHMAN

Here or there, my lord?

SHAKARA

Here, there, anywhere, somewhere, as long as the person in the carriage there is brought before me here and now.

COACHMAN

I wished to know, my lord, whether I should bring the

carriage in here where you are seated or drive it to the summer-house.

SHAKARA

Neither. We will go to the carriage ourselves and welcome her. Show me the way. *(The coachman turns and starts to go out, when Shakara shouts at him)*

You will hang for this! I am master, you are servant. Come behind me, fool. *(The coachman stands behind Kumantri who is behind Shakara)*

Now, that is better. Come, we shall advance. *(They walk in single file. Shakara halts.)*

No. This is not right. *(To Kumantri)* You are my friend, we will go arm in arm. *(They try that)*

No, that will not do either. *(To the coachman)* You lead. Announce Kumantri. He will announce me. *(They form a line, but do not move. Shakara gets all three to stand abreast. He gives up.)* Go and bring her here! *(The coachman does not move)* Have I to tell you everything twice? *(The coachman goes out quickly)*

I must not tire myself. She does not want me to exert and tire myself. She said so the other night. The wench loves me after all. *(Sits)* Here, fan me. *(He takes a fan from his belt and gives it to Kumantri)*

I am hot all over. I knew she would soon tire of that Charudatta. He has little to give. But I will put him in his place. You will see that Shakara is dangerous as...as a snake.

(Vasanthasena approaches. She is followed at a respectable distance by the coachman. She stands petrified when she sees Shakara and Kumantri. Shakara tries to rise, but Kumantri puts his hand on his shoulder and keeps him sitting.)

KUMANTRI

Do not rise. You should not go to her. It is not proper. She should come to you, since you are the prince. If you will permit me, I shall lead her to you.

SHAKARA

Yes, yes, do. I will pretend to be indifferent to her.

KUMANTRI *(Crossing over to Vasanthasena)*

My master conveys his greetings, madam. *(A change of tone)* I had some respect for you till now. I suppose you have cast Charudatta out and have prepared your bait for bigger game.

VASANTHA

I thought it was Charudatta's carriage. I have been cruelly deceived. I sincerely love Charudatta. This man...Oh, I hate him!

KUMANTRI

I think I can believe what you say. Do not fear. I shall help you. Come with me. *(He leads Vasanthasena to Shakara)*

Your highness, this beautiful young lady, who has inflamed every gallant heart in the city, has commanded me to indicate to your highness her desire to grant your highness her inestimable favour. Shall I escort her out of this garden to...

SHAKARA *(Cutting in)*

Madam, I was very rude to you on that inauspicious night before Charudatta's house. I ask you to overlook my uncivilised conduct. I am indeed the happiest of men now. *(He chuckles)* As a first favour *(He giggles),* the first of a long line of many, let me kiss your hand. *(He takes her hand. She slaps him hard, his turban falls off. He throws her hand away in anger.)*

I bowed my head to you. I, who have never bowed even to the gods, and you have the audacity to...to...to...I will show you! Kumantri!

KUMANTRI

Yes, your highness.

SHAKARA

Show her!

KUMANTRI

This is most serious, your highness. She must be made sorry and repentant for this.

SHAKARA
Repent, she will!

KUMANTRI
You must remain cool, and show her patience.

SHAKARA
I must think.

KUMANTRI
Meanwhile, she may be taken out of this garden to...

SHAKARA *(To coachman)*
Take her back where you brought her from! *(Kumantri moves quickly to lead Vasanthasena away from Shakara. The coachman stands still.)* Have I to tell you everything thrice?

COACHMAN
I brought her from Charudatta's house, my lord.

SHAKARA
I will cut out your tongue for that!

COACHMAN
My lord, let my tongue speak once before you do that. When I went to pick her up as ordered, I was told that she was at Charudatta's house. There I was asked by a servant-maid whose carriage it was. I said it was sent for Vasanthasena. She came out soon herself and climbed in. Perhaps she took it to be Charudatta's carriage my lord.

SHAKARA
She thought it was his carriage, did she? She has come here for him, has she? *(He strides up to Kumantri, grasps Vasanthasena's hair and drags her back.)*

The dishonour you caused me in the past is still aflame in me. This fresh insult fans it into smoke. You shall die. *(To Kumantri)* My friend, I request a little service of you.

KUMANTRI
If it is within reason.

SHAKARA

Of course, of course. I have not thought of anything unreasonable.

KUMANTRI

Very well, then.

SHAKARA

Kill her.

KUMANTRI

God have mercy on me! I am lewd and debauched, I confess. Let me not be guilty of innocent blood on my hands.

SHAKARA

Never fear, man. We will not tell anyone. There will be no witnesses.

KUMANTRI

No witnesses? When the sun and the sky and the wind and the clouds are all looking down on us?

SHAKARA

Is that all? Here, let me hold my cloak over her.

KUMANTRI

No, no. I do not wish to be damned forever.

SHAKARA *(To the coachman)*

Come here, man. *(The coachman approaches)*

That sapless owl is afraid of hell. You kill her.

COACHMAN

Oh no, my lord, I have played her a base trick already. I beg you to let me alone.

SHAKARA

You are my servant. I am your master.

COACHMAN

You are master of my body, but not of my vices and virtues. I dare not do what you command.

SHAKARA *(Drawing his dagger)*

Do what I ask, or I shall...

COACHMAN

Kill me, my lord. But I cannot kill a defenceless woman. I must have sinned hard in former births that I should become your servant in crime now. *(He bends his head to be killed)*

SHAKARA *(With cunning)*

You are good fellows, both of you. *(Laughs)* I was only testing you. You know, I love her so much that I shall not allow anybody to touch a single hair on her head. *(Lets her go)*

Go, man, bring the carriage. *(The coachman goes)* Woman, you will go with me.

VASANTHA

I shall kill myself before I go with you.

SHAKARA *(to Kumantri)*

How obstinate she is! Just like a woman! But I will not use force on her. Perhaps she is coy. Perhaps it is your presence that makes her coy. If you will leave us alone a while, I am sure I can convince her of my burning love for her. Let me talk to her. Wait for us by the carriage.

VASANTHA

Sir, I am afraid. Please protect a helpless woman.

KUMANTRI

Have no fear, my dear. My lord, I entrust her to your care. I expect to see her safely returned to her home soon.

SHAKARA

By all means! By all means! Give me ten minutes. *(Kumantri retires some distance and watches, hidden)*

My dear, you suspect me. He suspects me. They all suspect me. Only I know how much love there is stuffed in here. *(He beats his chest)* If I have been unkind to you, do not blame me, but blame the violence of my passion for you. My heart is tender like...like these flowers. *(He plucks a flower and offers it to her. She turns away.)*

Wear this flower for me, my dear. My heart is nailed into it. *(Kumantri nods to himself and goes away)* Be mine. You shall have all the jewels you ask for. I love you even more than my jewels, my dear.

My heart is as full of love as...as the fox's head is of cunning. You may marry me, if you wish. If you do not, well, that will be all right too. When the king dies, which I hope will be very soon, you will sit with me on the throne on my right. You will be my potted jasmine bush.

VASANTHA

Sir, for support the jasmine prefers the shade of the sweet mango tree and not the cactus.

SHAKARA

A cactus, am I? Be wise, girl. Forget him!

VASANTHA

How can I forget the man who is the substance of all my thought? I have no existence without him. I love him and him alone.

SHAKARA

I will kill you. I will cut your head off and kick it from here to hell! *(He grabs her by the throat, shakes her violently, and pushes her back and drops her behind the seat. He stares at her for some time. She does not move.)*

Hey! Get up! What do you mean, lying there like that? Don't die, please. *(Shakes her)*

Come on, wake up! *(Shakes her again)*

Oh! She must be dead! The people will get after me for this. *(Kumantri returns. Shakara runs down to him.)*

My dear fellow, you are back just in time. You must...I must request another service of you.

KUMANTRI

Where is the woman? I left her here in your care.

SHAKARA

She went.

KUMANTRI

Went? Where did she go?

SHAKARA
Behind you.

KUMANTRI
But she did not come that way.

SHAKARA
Which way did you go?

KUMANTRI
I went there, to the East Gate.

SHAKARA
Well, she went west.

KUMANTRI
What the devil are you talking about?

SHAKARA
I killed her.

KUMANTRI
Killed her!

SHAKARA
Even you do not believe what I say! Look there for yourself. *(Kumantri runs to where Vasanthasena is lying, feels her and strides down to Shakara.)*

KUMANTRI
You wretched man! Till now I thought you were a mere fool. Now I know you are evil. *(Turns to go away)*

SHAKARA
Where are you going, leaving me alone?

KUMANTRI
To report to the king.

SHAKARA
Don't! Please don't tell anyone about this. I will give you a thousand gold pieces.

KUMANTRI
Keep your miserable gold.

SHAKARA

Come, come, we will still be friends. You will have whatever else you wish.

KUMANTRI

I have better plans. I am tired of the present government, its ugliness, its incompetence, the callousness, cruelty, unrighteousness, corruption...

SHAKARA

I shall have you arrested for this. You will be flogged and tortured for treason.

KUMANTRI

I'll be gone before you raise a finger. The whole city is hostile to you and your brother-in-law king. People will gladly hide me. When Aryaka's forces appear under the city walls...

SHAKARA

That can hardly be soon. Aryaka is reported to have fled to a far-away place.

KUMANTRI

Not as far as you think.

SHAKARA

Where is he?

KUMANTRI

You would like to know, wouldn't you?

SHAKARA

You will not tell? *(He catches Kumantri)* You murderer! Kill a defenceless woman, will you? Murder! Murder! Help! Help! *(Kumantri shakes him off and runs away. Shakara is still shouting when the coachman runs in.)*

COACHMAN

My lord, what happened?

SHAKARA

My dear fellow, thank God you are here. Vasanthasena is dead.

COACHMAN

Dead, my lord?

SHAKARA

Yes, quite dead. Killed, murdered.

COACHMAN

But...how? By whom?

SHAKARA

Yes, murdered! By...I suspect Kumantri.

COACHMAN

That could not be, my lord.

SHAKARA

You don't think so?

COACHMAN

Not Kumantri, my lord.

SHAKARA

Then it must be Charudatta.

COACHMAN

Charudatta? That is impossible my lord. He could never...

SHAKARA

You do not believe what I say, do you? I suppose you think I did it. Did Vasanthasena come here because of me? Of course not. You know yourself that she had a tryst with Charudatta here.

COACHMAN

It seems to have been so, my lord.

SHAKARA

Of course it was so! He must have been here somewhere. He must have been eavesdropping. Ah! I remember now! I was pleading with her. I heard a sound. I thought it was a twig or something. He must have been hiding behind that tree. I continued to plead with her. At last she yielded. And then I came some distance to call you. Suddenly I heard a thud. I looked back, and there she was, groaning and writhing on the ground. He was gone. She was dead. So I shouted for help.

COACHMAN

But...Charudatta? He would not hurt a fly!

SHAKARA

You still don't believe me!

COACHMAN

I do not know, my lord. It is all very confusing.

SHAKARA

May be, may be. Perhaps it was someone else, perhaps for her jewels. Now, let us not waste time. Send the guards here. Keep the carriage ready at the gate. I shall see that justice is done. Send the guards quickly. *(The coachman leaves)*

And I will see that over-suspicious fools do not obstruct the passage of justice!

(Shakara goes back to Vasanthasena's body, takes some jewels off her, puts some into his own pocket, drops one or two near her and throws one or two away from her. Voices of guards are heard offstage, as Shakara returns to the seat. He strikes a melancholic pose.)

SCENE 3

The Stage Manager strides on in some hurry. The final scene is to commence without undue delay. He sets up the Court of Justice. In an outdoor production it can be under a tree. He moves about without speaking. The wife follows, sniffing.

WIFE

Such an evil man, that Shakara.

STAGE MANAGER

This is too much. You should not keep intruding, you know.

WIFE

And Charudatta is so good and noble. It's going to be terrible for him! Just when I thought they'd get away and live happily together.

STAGE MANAGER

If only the pages of history could be written according to our inferences! Perhaps they will be, some day – even in this great land of ours. He who pays the writer calls the tales.

WIFE

The circle of ministers around the king are already proclaiming that it is the return of the golden age, and that all of us are supremely happy.

STAGE MANAGER

And you and I know what people really say behind closed doors. It is not merely the price we pay for the private wars of kings that is unjust, it is the ignominy of being shown in their history books as being a mass support to causes far removed from our lives.

WIFE

What wickedness! What immoral abuse of station! And to think nobody can bring the villain to book because of his birth and title. Oh dear gods!

STAGE MANAGER

Be consoled, my dear, that evil, like folly, defeats itself, even as it remains undestroyed. There must surely be an ordering to life beyond the infirmity of man's convictions. In courts of justice such as this one, we gather in celebration of human reason and, once assembled, we choose to set reason free for a while, release it to the winds, a butterfly, and revel in the chase to recapture it. But we must trust in the justice of the gods. Come, the actors are waiting to resume. It is the King's Courtroom. And I have to play the part of the doorman, down there at the entrance.

WIFE

I suppose you're sending me back into the wings.

STAGE MANAGER

But of course. Well...all right. You can join the crowd of spectators in the courtroom. Sit on the last bench there.

(She takes a seat. Scene opens. A court of justice. A motley group of men and women, with the king's investigator, clerk of the court, servants in uniforms. A low desk and accessories for the judge, another one for the clerk, both on a dais. A few stools below the dais. Some of the people are standing, some are sitting on stools. The rest are squatting on the floor. A bazaar atmosphere. The Judge is at his seat. Sounds of murmurs. Voices offstage..)

STAGE MANAGER

Attention all, attention! Make way, make way. Prince Shakara approaches.

(The Court is hushed. All stand. Shakara enters and looks around with cool insolence. He struts up to a man by a stool, who gives way. Shakara sits down, and signals to the crowd to sit. Some do so, and the murmur in the group starts again. The doorman beats the floor three times with his staff and stands bowing. Silence again. All stand up and bow, except Shakara, who continues to be seated. The judge comes in and looks around with a benign smile. He sees Shakara, frowns, shrugs in helplessness and sits at his desk.)

JUDGE *(Looking at the papers on his desk)*

Are these the cases for tonight?

CLERK

Yes, your Worship.

JUDGE

Very well, summon the parties.

CLERK

All those seeking justice may approach.

(Several persons approach the dais)

SHAKARA *(Standing)*

I demand first hearing.

JUDGE

Your Highness, if your case is first in the schedule, you will be heard first. If it is not so, may it please you to wait your turn.

SHAKARA

No, it does not please me. I am a great man and I do not intend to surrender precedence to inferiors.

JUDGE

In the eyes of justice all are equal.

SHAKARA

I have heard that before. I will be heard first, and I will have my enemy beheaded.

JUDGE

As a judge I am bound by established procedure.

SHAKARA

Procedure! Rules! Tradition! Hah! All right, I will not ask you to violate rules or procedures of law. Just relax them, just a little detour, you know. I give you permission.

JUDGE

If I overlook rules prescribed for my duties, the king becomes a target of public criticism. The Court is suspected of bias. People lose faith in the King's Court of Justice. You see the danger? *(Shakara tries to speak, but the judge goes on)* You are a wise man. You will appreciate the sanctity of the process. I am sure you want justice done, and have every man and woman of Ujjain extend the respect due to your honourable position.

SHAKARA

Of course I want justice, and a little more respect from the women of the city. That is what I was saying to myself when she... *(He checks himself)*

JUDGE

When, your Highness? I will have to record what you said so to yourself. It may be useful to the proceedings.

SHAKARA

No, no, it does not matter. No. *(Sits)* You were saying... *(Smirks)* You first. Proceed.

JUDGE

Your Highness is wise and kind. *(To clerk)* Call the disputants in the first case. *(There is suppressed laughter in the court)*

CLERK

Silence in the Court! *(Calling)* Rudra and Gowra, present yourselves. *(Two men come forward, grinning)*

SHAKARA *(Vaguely suspicious)*

You mean I am to wait?

CLERK

That is the Judge's command.

SHAKARA *(Jumping up)*

I am not here to take commands! Look at them laughing at me. Start on my case first, or I shall report to the king. I will complain to my sister the Queen. I shall have you dismissed. I will make sure there is another man appointed who will have more respect for me than for your useless book of procedures. *(He twirls his moustache and strides out.)*

JUDGE

Let him be brought back.

CLERK

Request His Highness to return. *(A servant goes out)*

You may return to your places. *(The two litigants retire)*

JUDGE

If he does what he threatens to, it will be the final purge of our hallowed traditions. God knows there is little of it left. *(The judge bends his head in thought. Shakara strides in.)*

SHAKARA *(Entering, loud)*

First, you will not hear me first. Then you will hear me then. Now you will hear me now. Was ever such procedure heard of?

Well, never mind, I shall see that you are properly rewarded for this. *(The Judge smiles tolerantly)*

I mean properly rewarded. *(The smile turns weak)*

JUDGE

Won't you be seated?

SHAKARA

Of course I will be seated, and no thanks to you. This is my brother-in-law's Court of Justice. *(He sits)*

JUDGE

What is the action in which the noble prince is concerned?

CLERK

It concerns murder, your Worship. The King's Attorney will present the matter. *(The King's Attorney rises and goes to the dais)*

JUDGE

You may present your case.

SHAKARA

And make it tight. I want the fellow to be crushed...like a squashed cabbage leaf.

JUDGE

You must not interrupt.

SHAKARA

Why shouldn't I?

JUDGE

If you do you may confuse him and damage your case.

SHAKARA

Oh! Why didn't you tell me earlier? *(To the Attorney)* Go on, man! You are uninterrupted.

ATTORNEY

Your Worship, it was the morning of yesterday.

SHAKARA

It was yesterday in the morning.

ATTORNEY

Sir?

SHAKARA

Go on, I am not interrupting you!

ATTORNEY

I was summoned urgently by the guards of the Spring Garden. On my arrival, the noble prince, who was there himself, reported that he had stumbled upon the body of the famous courtesan, Vasanthasena, and that he had sent word to me immediately. He conducted me to the exact location, but when we reached there... *(He stops)*

SHAKARA

It was clear that she had been murdered!

JUDGE *(Patiently)*

It is clear so far that there was a reported murder. *(To Attorney)* Please continue.

ATTORNEY

There was no corpse when we reached there. The noble prince surmised that it was a further indication of some foul play. According to procedure we had to arrest a suspect quickly. It was done immediately. The prisoner is waiting outside.

SHAKARA

Bring him in. Bring him in right now! Have the man brought in and pronounce judgement! *(The Attorney does not move)*

JUDGE

I must follow procedure and examine the witnesses first. *(To the Attorney)* Was it His Highness who discovered the body?

ATTORNEY

Yes, your Worship. He told us so himself.

JUDGE *(To Shakara)*

Tell me what you know of the matter.

SHAKARA *(Rising)*

I come from a high family, as high as... *(Indicating)* a vat of arrack – that high. My father was the king's father-in-law, the king is my father's son-in-law, and I am his brother-in-law. He is my husband's sister. *(The laughter that had been gathering in the court bursts out now. Shakara glares.)* I mean my sister's husband! *(To the clerk)* Have you written all that down?

JUDGE

They are undisputed, universally known facts. That book is meant to note matters on which there is room for investigation.

SHAKARA

Don't write it then. Write this down. You know the Spring Garden? The king has allocated it to me as a gift, sponsored for my rest and recreation. But I hardly ever go there, except when I have business. *(Suppressed laughter)* Private business. *(Loud laughter. Shakara glares around again.)* It happened that I went there yesterday in the morning. I found the corpse of a dead woman. I did not kill her!

JUDGE

Was the woman known to you?

SHAKARA

No, she was not known to me, though I know a lot of women. She wore heaps of jewels, which must have tempted some wicked man. He must have stalked her *(A replay)*, cornered her by the garden seat, caught her by the neck, and killed her, twisting and wringing her neck.

JUDGE

You describe it quite vividly.

SHAKARA

I saw it! *(Corrects himself)* I mean I could see him do it...I mean *(Taps his head)* I see here, you know, my imagination.

JUDGE *(To the Attorney)*

Did you establish the death and then ascertain the nature of her death?

ATTORNEY

Not beyond what the noble prince told me.

SHAKARA

My word is proof enough.

JUDGE

If the body was missing, what evidence was there of the woman's presence?

SHAKARA

My word! The word of a man of honour!

ATTORNEY

We found some jewels in the vicinity. Two persons testified to her presence in the garden – the watchman on morning shift duty at the garden, and a young monk.

JUDGE

A young monk?

SHAKARA

A young monk!

ATTORNEY

He said he was a novice, initiated into the holy order only a few days ago. In fact, on the day he last met the deceased woman.

A VOICE

Maybe she drove him to it. *(Laughter in court)*

JUDGE

Now, now, silence! Let the arrested accused be brought in. *(To Attorney)* Please take your place. *(He does)*

(Murmur in the court. Shakara fidgets on his stool. The Judge whispers to the clerk.)

(Charudatta enters, escorted by two guards. Shakara looks away. There is agitation in the court. The judge thumps his desk. The clerk shouts for silence in the court, and the noise subsides.)

JUDGE *(Kindly)*

You have been accused of murdering a young woman by the name of Vasanthasena in the Spring Garden yesterday. What is your plea?

CHARUDATTA

I am innocent of the crime.

JUDGE

Pray be seated.

SHAKARA *(Jumping up)*

What kind of justice is this?! Honouring a woman-killer with a seat!

JUDGE

It is still to be proved that he is the culprit. *(Shakara tries to interrupt)*

Remember, interruption may harm your case. *(Shakara sits down)* Who are the next of kin of the deceased?

CLERK

There is only her mother.

JUDGE

I wish to examine her. *(A woman of large build stands up. It may even be a folk puppet occupying much stage space)*

Come here, madam. Are you Vasanthasena's mother?

WOMAN

That I am, Sir. Is it true she is dead? Who could kill such a sweet young thing? Do you believe it could...

JUDGE

Now, now, now, control yourself, good woman.

WOMAN

But he couldn't have done it, sir! Not him, not to her. A saint like him, though he is poor. I know what has happened. She has been kidnapped for her jewels. So precious they were too, bangles and bracelets and diamond earrings. The belt, it had a clasp that large, and the serpent-hood of rubies in her hair...

JUDGE

Please! Stop this chatter!

WOMAN

Am I talking too much, sir? It is my tongue, I know. It always runs away with me. It's been that way since I was sixteen. I don't know how...

JUDGE

Stop the jibber jabber and answer my questions. To the point.

WOMAN

Am I not doing so?

JUDGE

Let us say you are beginning to try my patience.

WOMAN

Oh Lord! I am sorry. I am sure I am. What I mean to say is that if only...

JUDGE

Please pay attention! You must first listen to my questions and then reply to them precisely, briefly, saying only as much as the question requires.

WOMAN

Only give her back to me, sir. I will say whatever you want me to in reply to any of your questions.

JUDGE

Now, then...when did you last see your daughter?

WOMAN

The evening before last, sir.

JUDGE

How was she employed? What was she doing at that moment?

WOMAN

Decking herself to go out. Wore her best clothes, her best perfume too. An admirer from Kashmir had sent it. And all her jewels – her sapphire bracelets, emerald bangles, studded mango earrings and the string of diamonds along her hairline that she had kept reserved for a very special occasion. She was gorgeous. She was radiant. I would even say she was...

JUDGE

Yes, yes. I know. Did she go out?

WOMAN

But of course she did, sir. Why else would she be decked up? I warned her not to though, what with a thunderstorm gathering and all that.

JUDGE

Where did she go?

WOMAN

To Charudatta's house.

SHAKARA

There you are! It proves that he killed her!

JUDGE

Does it? If His Highness is suggesting that this should be probed to greater depth, I can only agree fully. *(To woman)* How do you know that she went to Charudatta's house?

WOMAN

Because she told me! She told me when I asked her if it was... *(Pause)*

JUDGE

What did you ask her?

WOMAN

Well, it was this way, you see. She was all dolled up, and I asked her 'What's the big idea?' And she said, 'I am going to meet my lover'. I thought she meant His Highness. *(A giggle)*

JUDGE

Do you mean the prince here?

WOMAN

Yes, him all right. You see, he was sort of sweet on her, but she...

JUDGE *(To Shakara)*

So, do we take it that you were acquainted with her?

SHAKARA

Well, yes, in a manner of speaking.

JUDGE *(To Woman)*

Proceed.

WOMAN

You see, he used to send his carriage – I mean the noble prince. He sent it two nights ago, or was it three nights? Anyway, he sent it for her that night. Is it important if it was two nights ago or three nights? All, right, three nights. And strike me dead if it did not come around yesterday in the morning again! He has been so good and kind and all, following her like a dog – I mean, sending her presents and all – but she would have nothing to do with him. Neither him nor his jewels. Sent them both packing back.

SHAKARA

But I did not get back any jewels!

WOMAN

Did you not, indeed? Well, if you say so, it may be so. Why, now I remember, I have them. I thought the girl would come to her senses and take them one day and then take you too. Now, where was I?

JUDGE

Yesterday – morning – carriage – daughter. You said your daughter was going to meet her lover.

WOMAN

So she said. And I thought it was this prince. So I said 'Are you going to meet the prince?' And she said 'Don't be silly, Ma! I'm never going to meet that overfed dimwit wild pig.' *(Laughter in the court. Judge smiles. Shakara glares.)* I beg pardon, those were not her words, not exactly. She didn't say 'pig'. She used some fancy words. 'Beast of the feast', I think. I shut her up proper. She had no call to be disrespectful to one so high-born.

JUDGE
That was thoughtful of you.

WOMAN
Well, that's what I thought. She said she hated him and loved him – the one who didn't have a copper coin to his name. 'Well', I said to her, 'you are a fool, but have it your way. You'll come to your senses soon.' And she says 'I love him, ma.' I said 'Why do you love him, this pauper? It's sunset and dark nights with him, you know.' And she says to me, 'The sun and moon leave us a while only to return, ma. But it's not for wealth that I love. I love him for his character.' Huh! Love a man for his character! What a silly idea, fit only for women of a certain class who know no better. A girl like her has no business to get such stupid ideas into her head. I told her to have no truck with him. And she says, 'You liked it when he used to come in the past, ma.' That was different. He was rich then, and his wife had just – you know – she wasn't there. Now he is wretched poor, but she is stuck on him. She doesn't so much as set eyes on another man. Foolish, I call it. A girl like her...

JUDGE *(Interrupting)*
So she said...?

WOMAN
She said?

JUDGE
She said?

WOMAN
Who said?

JUDGE
What did Vasanthasena say?

WOMAN
To whom?

JUDGE
Did she say she would go to Charudatta's house?

WOMAN

Oh, yes, and went.

JUDGE

When did she return?

WOMAN

Not that night, and not yesterday morning. *(Sobs)* Nor evening either.

JUDGE

Very well, you may retire for the present. Did you not hear, woman? *(The woman retires reluctantly and sits. The judge turns to Charudatta.)*

I take it that you heard what the woman said. Shall we note that you were intimately acquainted with the young woman? *(He pauses. Charudatta remains silent, head bent.)*

SHAKARA

There you are! You see, he is afraid to speak. He is hiding his guilt.

JUDGE

We are all trying to uncover what is hidden. *(To Charudatta)* You must answer my questions. You must help the court to arrive at the truth. Shall we....? Your relationship, I believe, was intimate in the past. Then for some time it cooled. Was she in some way responsible for this cooling?

CHARUDATTA

No, she was not to blame. When my business went into unending decline, I could not expect her to show interest in me.

JUDGE

You did not visit each other during this time?

CHARUDATTA

No.

JUDGE

Nor meet each other elsewhere?

CHARUDATTA
I avoided her. I did not wish to embarrass her.

JUDGE
Would it be right to say that you continued to love her?

SHAKARA
Love! With his history? Hah! And she a crafty courtesan!

CHARUDATTA
God knows I loved her. And only He can chart the depths of that love.

JUDGE
Did she love you?

CHARUDATTA
I believe she did, but I cannot answer on her behalf.

JUDGE
I understand. To proceed, how do you explain her presence in your house two nights ago?

CHARUDATTA
She came to return some jewels.

SHAKARA
Return, my camel's hump! He robbed her and killed her for her jewels.

JUDGE *(With some annoyance)*
A man who gave all his wealth away in charity?

SHAKARA *(Slyly)*
Is the judge in the King's Court of Justice taking sides?

JUDGE *(Composing himself, to Charudatta)*
Were the jewels yours, and was she returning them because she wished to terminate the relationship?

CHARUDATTA
They were not mine. They were her own.

JUDGE
Pardon me, but how could she return to you what belonged to

her? You will explain that, I'm sure.

CHARUDATTA

It is a very long story, your Worship.

JUDGE

It should be an interesting story. Proceed.

CHARUDATTA

Some nights ago Vasanthasena came to my house, quite unexpectedly, seeking refuge. She said that the noble prince had been stalking her.

SHAKARA

And I say that is a damned lie! *(Murmur in the court. Order restored.)*

CHARUDATTA

I arranged for her to be escorted home later. But she left her jewels with me for safekeeping, till she sent for them. Unfortunately my house was burgled the next night and the jewels stolen.

SHAKARA

Safekeeping! Burglars! You can see he is inventing tales to save his skin. She gave him jewels! He took the jewels! Who are his witnesses? Perhaps his servants will give evidence for him!

JUDGE *(To Charudatta)*

Proceed.

CHARUDATTA

The theft was a great embarrassment, and I wished to make amends. I sent her a necklace of rubies to compensate. In the evening, she came again and teased me. She said that in return for the necklace, she wished to give me her jewels.

JUDGE

The stolen jewels?

CHARUDATTA

Yes.

JUDGE *(Increasingly drawn in)*

Are you sure? How did they happen to reach Vasanthasena?

CHARUDATTA

They were indeed the stolen jewels, your Worship. It turned out that the thief had been courting Vasanthasena's maid, and to obtain her release he took the jewels to the mistress.

JUDGE

I see. The deceased – did she return home that evening?

CHARUDATTA

She remained the night in my house, your Worship.

JUDGE

Did she return home in the morning?

CHARUDATTA

I do not know.

JUDGE

How do you not know? Can you explain that?

CHARUDATTA

I had to leave the house early, before the others rose. But I left word that I would wait for her in the Spring Garden.

SHAKARA

Aha! Now you have it! He went there, she went there, and he killed her.

JUDGE

Is that how it happened?

CHARUDATTA

No, your Worship. Before I went to the Spring Garden, I was obliged to assist two great friends of mine to depart from the city. That took some time. Then I started for the garden. I was arrested on my way there.

JUDGE

You did not enter the Spring Garden?

CHARUDATTA

I did not.

JUDGE

Is the watchman of the Spring Garden here? *(The watchman stands up and comes forward. The Judge turns to Charudatta.)*

You may sit. *(To the watchman)* Do you know this man?

WATCHMAN

God have mercy on me! Who does not know the saint of the city?

JUDGE *(Sternly)*

Do you know him?

WATCHMAN

Yes, sir.

JUDGE

Was he at the Spring Garden yesterday in the morning?

WATCHMAN

No, sir, not that I remember.

JUDGE

Are you certain?

WATCHMAN

Well, I cannot swear to that, sir.

JUDGE

He might have been there?

WATCHMAN

A lot of folks come and go. It is very difficult to remember them all.

JUDGE

Do you remember any of the persons who were there?

WATCHMAN *(Scratching his head)*

Well, sir, let me see. There was a young couple, newly married they looked, a group of five or six sundry folks on a picnic, two young lads eyeing the mangoes on the trees, but I shooed them off quickly, there was the young monk, then there was his Highness' coachman, and just before that, His Highness himself and Kumantri.

JUDGE
Kumantri? Who is that?

SHAKARA *(Laughing)*
A special friend of mine, a nobleman. Not as noble as myself, but – all right – a nobleman.

JUDGE *(To watchman)*
Could Charudatta enter the garden without your noticing him?

WATCHMAN
He could have, since you put it that way, sir, he could have.

JUDGE
Did you notice Vasanthasena's arrival?

WATCHMAN
How could I miss it? Rolling up as she did in His Highness' carriage.

JUDGE
What?

WATCHMAN
What?

JUDGE
What did you say?

WATCHMAN
What did I say?

JUDGE
Just now, what did you say just a moment ago?

WATCHMAN
What about?

JUDGE
About Vasanthasena.

WATCHMAN
About Vasanthasena?

JUDGE
In whose carriage did she arrive?

WATCHMAN

His.

JUDGE

Are you certain?

WATCHMAN

I saw it with my own eyes.

JUDGE *(To Shakara)*

Did she get there in your carriage?

SHAKARA

I don't know what he is talking about.

JUDGE

Did you or did you not send your carriage for her?

SHAKARA

Did I not? Yes, I did not!

JUDGE

The woman there has also testified that your carriage went to her house yesterday, and that it was for Vasanthasena.

SHAKARA

Servants often do things without the knowledge of their masters.

JUDGE

Is the coachman here?

SHAKARA

He is not my prisoner. I mean I am not his keeper!

JUDGE

Would you kindly send orders for your coachman and Kumantri to come here? *(Shakara does not move)*

It will help the ends of justice. *(Shakara remains stubbornly silent. The judge sighs and asks the Attorney.)*

Is there anyone to either support or contradict what the watchman of the garden has said?

ATTORNEY

Your Worship, there is a witness who says he saw Vasanthasena in Charudatta's carriage yesterday in the morning.

JUDGE

In Charudatta's carriage?

ATTORNEY

Yes, in Charudatta's carriage. It is a guard from the city's North Gate.

JUDGE

Where is he? *(At the Attorney's signal, a soldier comes forward. The watchman retires.)*

It is all very confusing. Well, did you see Vasanthasena yesterday in the morning?

GUARD

I did, your Worship.

JUDGE

In Charudatta's carriage?

GUARD

Yes, your Worship.

JUDGE

How did you identify her?

GUARD

Well, she was wearing a veil, your see, so I had to ask the coachman for her name. And he gave it promptly as Vasanthasena. Her maid was with her, also veiled. We had orders not to allow any unknown carriages to pass without a check, but since it was clearly Charudatta's carriage, the ladies inside were...

JUDGE

Where did it happen?

GUARD

At the city's North Gates.

JUDGE

At the city gates?

GUARD

I was on duty there. They were going into the country to visit relatives.

JUDGE

Did they return?

GUARD

Not in my shift, your Worship, not as long as I was on duty.

JUDGE

When were you relieved?

GUARD

When I was called to the King's Attorney to give evidence on the murder of Vasanthasena.

JUDGE

It is very perplexing. Were you acquainted with Vasanthasena by sight?

GUARD

Well...no, your Worship, but...

JUDGE

Both the women were veiled, you say, during the whole course of your short encounter? *(Soldier nods)*

So, they could be other than those they claimed to be?

GUARD

Oh, come now, your Worship, they were...

JUDGE

But they could be?

GUARD

Oh God, I hope not, because...

JUDGE

But they could be?

GUARD

Yes, your Worship, they could be.

JUDGE

Stand by. *(The guard retires, wiping his sweating face. The Judge addresses Charudatta.)*

I take it you have the jewels with you. They are required as evidence. *(He turns to the attorney)* Send some officer...

(His speech is lost in the commotion offstage, interspersed with Maitreya's high pitched exclamations.)

» You can't go in there!

» I can go in, I shall go in, I will go in!

» Impossible! Here...

» It's a public court of law!

» But the proceedings have...

» Hands off, I say!

(Maitreya storms in. He has his stick with him.)

MAITREYA *(To judge)*

This is unthinkable nonsense, sir. That good man can do no wrong. How can you even entertain the hint of a thought that he is guilty of this inhuman crime?

JUDGE

He has been accused by due process...

MAITREYA

And who is the fool that accuses him?

SHAKARA *(Standing proudly)*

I, Shakara. *(Laughter in court)*

MAITREYA *(To Shakara)*

I thought the accuser a mere fool. I am sorry, I was wrong. He is a fool of a rogue. *(Bursts of laughter in court. The Judge and the clerk look at Charudatta and smile.)*

SHAKARA *(Spluttering)*

See that? See that? Calling me names, this little fellow with the big mouth, insolent lout with the crow's foot of a tuft. *(To Maitreya)* You get a big cut of the loot, don't you?

MAITREYA

Do you recognise this stick, crooked like your mind? I have a good mind to put it to some good use here. (*He lifts his arm, the bag of jewels falls on the floor. Shakara pounces on it.)*

SHAKARA *(Displaying the bag)*

Look! Everybody look! Here are the jewels. He killed her for them. *(To Judge)*

You have your evidence. *(He puts the bag on the Judge's desk)*

JUDGE *(To the woman)*

Come here, madam. *(The woman comes to the dais)* Look at these and tell me if they belonged to your daughter. *(The woman gazes at the jewels and appears lost)*

SHAKARA

Don't just stare with your mouth, you old tart! Open your eyes and bark out the truth.

JUDGE

Are they your daughter's jewels? *(She does not answer.)* Why do you gaze at them so?

WOMAN

Ah, these jewels!

JUDGE

Do you recognise the jewels?

WOMAN

Isn't it a wonder, the craftsmanship! They are exquisite.

JUDGE

Yes, yes...

WOMAN

The best you will ever see.

JUDGE
Are they or are they not your daughter's?

WOMAN
They look like some of them.

JUDGE
Well, are they hers?

WOMAN
I don't know. They might be...and they might not be.

JUDGE
Shall I take it that they are Charudatta's?

WOMAN
Well, now...

CHARUDATTA
They do not belong to me. They were Vasanthasena's.

WOMAN
If you say so, it is so. But I can't say I...

JUDGE
You must tell the truth, woman.

WOMAN
To save that man's life, I would tell a lie and be damned, that I would.

JUDGE
I warn you, I may punish you for perjury. No false statements now!

WOMAN
Well, I should say I think I am speaking the truth.

JUDGE
Do you or do you not recognise the jewels?

WOMAN
I can't say I do. *(The Judge waves away the woman)*

JUDGE *(To Charudatta)*

Are these the jewels the deceased gave you?

CHARUDATTA

They are.

JUDGE

How do you account for their being in the possession of this man?

CHARUDATTA

This poor Brahmin lives in my house. I gave them to him yesterday to be returned to the lady.

JUDGE *(To Maitreya)*

Is that so?

MAITREYA

He says so, and I say so. It was so.

JUDGE

When precisely did he give them to you?

MAITREYA

First thing in the morning. Foolish, I thought. Bad beginning of a worse day.

JUDGE

You did not return them to her as instructed? *(Maitreya shakes his head)* Why didn't you?

MAITREYA

I thought he shouldn't. He didn't agree, of course, but I hoped he would come to his senses later. She gave him the jewels in exchange for a necklace of fabulous rubies. I saw no sense at all in returning the jewels.

JUDGE

Have you any witnesses to this transaction?

MAITREYA

No one, except her maid.

ATTORNEY

I have interrogated her, your Worship. She declares that

Vasanthasena handed over certain jewels to Charudatta two evenings ago, that is, the evening she went to his house. Further, both she and Charudatta's steward confirm that Charudatta was to meet Vasanthasena yesterday in the Spring Garden. They state that before his carriage arrived, another carriage called for her at Charudatta's house, and that she left in that carriage.

JUDGE

Thank you. Have you any other witnesses?

ATTORNEY

There are no more, your Worship.

JUDGE

Before I conclude, does anybody else here wish to give evidence? Has anyone anything more to say pertaining to this case? Does anybody wish to offer additional evidence?

In the circumstances, therefore, and on the basis of the evidence already before me, I shall proceed to make my recommendation to His Majesty. The Court's messenger will convey it to His Majesty and will return with the orders His Majesty may be pleased to pronounce. *(The messenger stands. The Judge pronounces his conclusion.)*

This is my recommendation. Charudatta has been accused by Prince Shakara of the murder of Vasanthasena. The evidence is, however, incomplete, confused and conflicting. All that is certain is that the deceased was in the house of the accused on the morning of her alleged murder, that her jewels were in the possession of the accused, that she was in the Spring Garden, and that he might have been there. In the absence of a corpse, her death is not fully confirmed. On the other hand, it is to be noted that her being dead is not inconceivable, since there is no information as to her whereabouts either in the city or in the country. I recommend, therefore, that the charge of the murder be suspended, and that Charudatta be kept in custody, until further evidence is available.

Go and bring back the sentence that His Majesty may be pleased to pass.

(The messenger starts to go out with the investigator. Shakara is unhappy with the verdict. He moves to a door, motions to the messenger, whispers in his ears and returns with a fan snatched off the servant's hands.)

SHAKARA

Ugh! Terribly hot day, isn't it? It was good the fellow carried this fan with him. *(Sits fanning himself)*

JUDGE *(To Charudatta)*

I am sorry, my friend, that the end of the road should have brought you to the humiliation of public gaze as well.

SHAKARA

I am sorry too. Oh, he is a good fellow all right. But what can you do? Justice is justice, you know.

CHARUDATTA

Your Worship, may I speak to my friend, Maitreya?

JUDGE

You may, provided nothing is said or done surreptitiously.

CHARUDATTA *(To Maitreya)*

Maitreya, I loved her. She would have healed a wound in my heart, but she is dead.

SHAKARA

There, he confesses! They were both in on it. Arrest the other fellow too!

MAITREYA

God will punish you yet for this! But what use will that be when this good man is gone? *(To Charudatta)* If I told you once, I told you a hundred times, to put that woman out of your mind. What did you get out of it? You will surely die. Your son will be thrown out in the streets. And me? Oh, don't for a moment worry yourself over a poor Brahmin's fate.

CHARUDATTA

How can I not worry about you?

MAITREYA

I will just shave my head, and go about with a copper bowl begging for handfuls of rice. Oh, you stubborn fool!

CHARUDATTA

My punishment and suffering matter the least now. I fear for my son. I must beg you now to take him to a hermitage, and look after him well. *(To the Judge)* Your Worship, I trust that the jewels will be returned to the mother of the dead Vasanthasena.

WOMAN *(Wailing)*

What will I do with them? She is gone! Who will return my daughter to me? My beautiful...

SHAKARA *(To the Judge)*

Stop this sentimental cackle! It makes me sick. That fellow has no right to be seated. *(Charudatta stands up. Shakara struts up to him.)*

I am sorry, my dear fellow. It is most indecent in a hallowed court of justice for a criminal to be seated. *(He pushes Charudatta aside and sits on the stool.)*

Only I, the King's brother-in-law, can sit here. *(Voices and commotion offstage. The coachman rushes in.)*

COACHMAN

Sir, my Lord, your Worship! I am that nobleman's coachman. I was kept locked up. I just escaped. I heard that Charudatta was charged with murder. I want to tell you he is innocent.

SHAKARA *(Drawing him aside firmly)*

Now, now, now, don't get excited. Everything is all right. These are good people here. Come on, let me take you home. *(To Judge)* He's not well – up here, you know *(Taps his head).*

COACHMAN

This man killed Vasanthasena.

SHAKARA

Oh, come now! Would I go and do something like that? A prince, a jewel of the kingdom? *(Takes a gold bracelet off his wrist and presses it into the coachman's hand.)*

Take this, you'll get more later. Come on now, let's go home.

COACHMAN

He kept me shut up in the cellar.

SHAKARA

That is true, I kept him there. He is suspected of theft. *(Frisking the coachman)*

Aha! You rascal, I have you now! Look at this everybody, this is the bracelet he stole!

(To Judge) I demand that this man be arrested at once and put on trial. *(The Judge signals. A court servant hauls off the protesting coachman.)*

You can't trust anybody in this wicked world. *(The court's messenger returns.)*

JUDGE

What is His Majesty's pleasure?

MESSENGER

His Majesty has decreed that the accused is guilty of base murder, and is pleased to sentence him to death by impalement on a stake in a public square.

(There is commotion in court)

» Horrible! Horrible!

» Talk of justice.

» Royal justice you know!

» Good men must suffer.

» I wish I could kill him!

» Why has god forsaken us?

JUDGE *(Beating his desk)*

Silence...Silence!

(The commotion continues, the Judge continues to beat his desk. The noise subsides gradually. The Judge's beating also slows down. Everybody is listening in wonder to the sound of massed drums in the distance.)

A LITIGANT

I'm going home. It sounds like a thunderstorm. *(The drums are louder)*

ANOTHER LITIGANT

They are drums!

JUDGE

Silence in the court! *(No one listens to him)*

THIRD LITIGANT

The army is out. It is war!

FIRST LITIGANT

There's fighting in the streets!

(There is a rush for the door, where they stop dead as if they have seen a ghost. They give way slowly. An ascetic (second gambler) enters, leading Vasanthasena. Shakara stares at them in horror... moves back slowly, then turns and dashes out.)

ASCETIC

Citizens of Ujjain, this nobleman is innocent. This is the lady whose murder was attempted. She will tell you that Shakara caught her by the neck, throttled her, and left her lying on the ground, supposing she was dead. I was nearby and found her on the ground. No one else was there. She was only unconscious. I took her quickly out of the garden, for the gates were unguarded. She revived in my hermitage. I heard that this good man was accused of the murder, and we came here directly to see that no injustice was done to him. *(The town crier's tom tom is heard offstage)*

VASANTHA

Sir, I am a sinful woman, for I have been the cause of so much pain to you.

CHARUDATTA

My dearest, you bring me new life. The Gods are merciful. All that happened was passing evil... forging the good that has now sprung forth. *(The Attorney rushes in)*

ATTORNEY

Attention everybody! Your Worship, everybody, listen! The tyrant king has been taken prisoner. Aryaka has assumed government again.

SHAKARA *(Rushing in)*

He is there! They are all there, they are all after me, everyone! *(To Judge)* Save me.

JUDGE

Do you wish to register a complaint?

SHAKARA

I will be killed, chopped into mincemeat! Save me! No, you can't save me, you are only a judge. They will kill me!

JUDGE

Who will kill you?

SHAKARA

Oh, I have run round and round, like a prize goat, chased by the butcher. There they are! *(Stares at the door)*

See! Look there! There! They will kill me! *(Two soldiers come in and stop at the door. Sharwa enters behind them. Shakara prostrates at Charudatta's feet.)*

You must save me. *(Sharwa takes control of the situation.)*

SHARWA

Your Worship, and good citizens of Ujjain, I have been sent by His Majesty, King Aryaka, with messages. First, the king is pleased to order the release of Charudatta as an innocent man.

SHAKARA *(To Charudatta)*

I thought they were chasing me.

SHARWA

For services rendered, the king is pleased to grant him a reward of ten thousand gold pieces, and the title deed to the royal estate at Dwaraka.

SHAKARA

He is a good fellow, after all. I have always said that, haven't I?

SHARWA

The king is further pleased to order that the young woman called Vasanthasena is hereafter provided with the title of, and shall be treated by all as, Lady of the City.

CHARUDATTA

This is indeed a happy day.

(General celebration. The townsfolk look upon Charudatta and Vasanthasena with awe and affection. Maitreya encourages the proceedings. They all leave the courtroom. Only two remain, Shakara on the floor and the Judge at his desk. The Judge smiles. So does Shakara. Finally the Judge brings down his hand for a final thump on the desk. Shakara darts out.)

Fadeout

Close of play

The Anklet

An adaptation from the Tamil classic
Silappadikaram** by **Ilango Adigal

FOR

K SREENIVASAN

CHARACTERS IN THE PLAY

in the order of their appearance

SUTRADHAR..*Narrator*
NATI..*Narrator's companion*
KANNAGI....................*Daughter of a wealthy merchant in Puhar*
DEVANTI..................................*Kannagi's maid and companion*
KOVALAN..*Kannagi's husband*
MATHARI..............*Wife of a cowherd on the outskirts of Madurai*
MADHAVI..........................*Dancer, courtesan, Kovalan's mistress*
KOPPERUNDEVI........................*Queen of the Pandyan kingdom*
NEDUNCHEZHIAN..................*Ruler of the Pandyan kingdom*
MINISTER....................................*Leader of the Palace Guards*

SCENES

Act I: Kannagi's home in Puhar

Act II: Mathari's home outside Madurai

Act III: The Palace of the Pandyan king

Note: The play may be performed with one intermission as shown in the script.

INTRODUCTION

DURING MY LONG association with the textile industry in India, I had the privilege of knowing Kasthuri Sreenivasan when he was Director of the South India Textile Research Association (SITRA) in Coimbatore. When he discovered that we shared a common interest in drama, he presented me a copy of his original translation of *Silappadikaram.* He encouraged me to work with it in Bangalore Little Theatre and gave me permission to do whatever I liked with it. I had thought about a reworking and adaptation of Sreenivasan's script many times since then but was able to get down to the task only in 2004.

The story of *The Anklet* is one of the best-known dramatic tales written by Ilango Adigal, brother of King Senguttuvan, sometime between the second and third centuries AD. The writing contains a sensitive depiction of the socio-political context of the time. The resurgence of a Tamil identity and pride in a South Indian culture are to be viewed against the backdrop of the dominance of North Indian dynastic reigns. The assimilation of Jain philosophy into the local culture is significant, a reflection of the great enlightenment in that period. The adult love triangle in the story is regarded by many as being ahead of its time.

There is no one best way to enact the story of Kannagi and the anklet. The epic qualities of the story, combining mythology with pre-destined tragedy, permit the play to be performed in a variety of styles. As with Greek tragedy or Shakespearean drama, the play can be performed in a 'classic' mould or a 'contemporary' mould with equal effect. This adaptation has attempted to strike a balance between fidelity to Sreenivasan's translation and the requirements of compactness in a contemporary performance. The narrator roles of the Sutradhar and Nati provide, as may be expected, the link between the past and the present, between the players and the audience, and between the imagined and real worlds.

Music and dance may be incorporated into the performance, if desired, in line with the style chosen. The script does not provide detailed directions for these. One traditional way of incorporating music and dance into a play has been to treat them as interludes. A group of musicians is seated on a low rostrum on one side of the stage. Beginning with an overture, the group comes in with short pieces at different points of the flow in the unfolding drama. If sung, these may be stanzas in a longer composition. These interludes are particularly welcome between scenes, through scene changes, with due coordination with the narrators.

Likewise, the dance interlude is brought in to break the monotony of the spoken word, but with the objective of aiding imagery and enriching the aesthetic experience, and not for itself. The dance interludes are usually with musical accompaniment, both instrumental and vocal.

The actors can, of course, be dancers and musicians themselves, but this would constitute another form altogether, requiring a different kind of preparation and discipline.

If a performing group has limited people resources, it should be possible to have only the musical interludes without the dance. Even here, it should be possible for the interludes to be completely instrumental (eg. just a group of percussionists, or even one percussionist), without singers.

The premiere of this play in Bangalore had neither musicians nor dancers. An original *mridangam* (percussion) audio track created for the production provided the links. It served the purpose and was sufficiently effective.

Notes on the music

In the opening opera '*Aichiyar Kuravai*' Ilango presents the many avatars of Vishnu. A part of this was made famous by MS Subbulakshmi in her '*Vadavarayai Mathakki Vasukiyai Naanakki...*' Not many know that it was taken from *Silappadikaram*. The song is in simple Tamil, understandable even today although written nearly two thousand years ago.

Interestingly, Ilango's song describes only eight Avatars of Vishnu, ending with Krishna, and does not recognise Buddha and Kalki. They must have been later additions to mythology that made *Ashtavatara* into *Dashavatara*.

In the same opera Ilango describes how the ancient musicians derived the seven basic musical notes of the octave by doubling and fractionalising the length of the metallic string to precise measure, under the same tension. This is the earliest documentation of the formulation of musical notes and frequencies in Tamil.

I am grateful to Professor Subbarayan Prasanna for the research leads provided.

The poet-playwright

Ilango (the younger) Adigal was the brother of the Cheran king Senguttuvan. In Ilango's writing the Chola kings are hailed as the exalted ones: their reign the most prosperous, the rulers the most virtuous and godlike. The playwright reveals that at that time the Pandyan kingdom was decaying, with corruption and anomie in society. In the play, however, the Pandyan king himself comes off as a just one, owning up his mistake and committing suicide to compensate for the lapse. Ilango opens his epic drama with three stanzas in praise of the Sun, the Moon and the Rains, using rich metaphors to compare their life-giving qualities to the attributes of the Chola kings.

Interestingly, this classic drama was written by a member of the Cheran royal family (in the West coast), setting the story around a couple from the Chola region (in the East coast), culminating the tale in the capital of the Pandyan kingdom, Madurai (in the Southern part of the Indian peninsula). Why would a Chera prince be so appreciative of the Chola Kingdom? One plausible explanation is in the two brothers being the sons of the Chola King Nalankilli, given to the Cheras in their childhood. Ilango was in all probability simply admiring his own ancestry and motherland.

When Senguttuvan carried out a successful expedition right up to the Himalayas, it was most likely with the help of the Cholas. He also promoted the West Coast sea trade and port towns similar to Puhar in the Chola region.

Contemporary archaeological research suggests that a massive tsunami-like tidal wave might have been responsible for the submergence of the great city of Puhar on the East coast.

* * *

This script is one of a pair of 'Sutradhar Plays' adapted into the English language for contemporary staging at Bangalore Little Theatre. The other is *The Toy Cart of Clay*, adapted from the 1500-year-old classic Sanskrit tale, *Mrichhakatika*. While *The Clay Cart* is a well-known Sanskrit play originating in the North of India, most Western audiences remain unaware of the richness of art and literature in the South.

Dramaturges will see interesting parallels between the two play scripts, including the function of the narrators. They provide the important links between the actors and the audience, between the past and the future, and between the spoken word and the imagined world. In this adaptation of *The Anklet*, however, the roles of Sutradhar and Nati have been deliberately extended. They have been given the responsibility of taking care of the many digressions in the tale, maintaining the focus on the essential storyline of Kannagi's destiny. *The Clay Cart*, on the other hand, appeared to need a simpler linking role for the pair of narrators.

FIRST PRODUCED

By Bangalore Little Theatre in March 2007

Sutradhar............EDGAR FERNANDES
Nati............DIVYA JAIN
Kannagi............NISCHAL PAI
Devanti............DEEPTHY SHEKHAR
Kovalan............PRITHAM KUMAR
Mathari............ALIYEH RIZVI
Madhavi............PRIYA RAO
Queen............SWATI SENGUPTA
King............SHASHANK PURUSHOTHAM
Minister............ANAND RAMPRASAD
Palace Guard............SANTOSH SAMUEL
Lighting............PRADEEP BELAWADI
Sound............SRIDHAR RAMANATHAN AND VIJAY PADAKI
Costumes............DIVYA JAIN AND GULSHAN DEVAIAH
Make up............RAMAKRISHNA KANNARPADI
Backstage team............RAHEEM DAREDIYA, S HARIHARAN
VISHNU RAO, BHASKAR, ARVIND, VIJAY
Directed by............SRIDHAR RAMANATHAN
Assisted by............VIJAY PADAKI

PROLOGUE

In the dark we hear the sound of hand cymbals used in ritual worship. The lights increase (fade in) slowly to reveal NATI, seated (Down Centre) with her back to the audience, playing the cymbals. Above her is seated the SUTRADHAR, also with his back to the audience. He holds an arati lamp in his right hand, a bell in his left hand, and concludes the puja to Ganesh, the elephant-headed god invoked for auspicious beginnings of events.

There is a glow on the cyclorama to suggest a sleeping city.

When the lights come on we see the full stage, which is mostly bare. Stage right has a low rostrum on which the musicians are seated. Stage left has a large, ornate, much used chest that is a property box. The sets and props are minimal, and are stacked offstage, but easily accessible. In an auditorium with a thrust-arena stage they may even be visible, but outside the lit acting areas. The scenes in the play are set and struck by the narrators. The Sutradhar is considerably older than Nati, but as a pair they are ageless. They have seen a lot of theatre and a lot of life.

Arati concluded, the narrators rise. The musicians strike up an overture. Sutradhar offers Nati the arati flame for benediction. She accepts it. The couple then places the lamp on a tray and walks down to offer the arati to the audience – moving along the front row if possible. While Sutradhar offers the flame, Nati gives away flowers.

The narrators return to the DC area, place the arati tray on the floor, and talk to each other as they wait for the flame to go out.

SUTRA

It is almost time. Is everybody quite ready?

NATI

Everybody offstage, everybody out there in front, and the two of us here, waiting for the lamp to give us leave.

SUTRA

I've been thinking...

NATI

I know what's on your mind.

SUTRA

I know that you know.

NATI

Look at that flame leaping up. Do you think it is alive? Do you think it knows?

SUTRA

It is after all a descendant of the sun, from which all things living derive the substance of life. It must have a life of its own.

NATI

It surely has a mind of its own.

SUTRA

Did we really light this flame?

NATI

Or did this flame light the fire in our lives?

SUTRA

Look at it! Do you see it dancing in celebration of this evening's performance?

NATI

I see anger and fury in the dance.

SUTRA

You are right. A dance of joy at the start, short lived, followed by the dance of pain...and then the fury, the death and destruction... *(Nati steps DC to address the audience. Sutradhar follows her.)*

NATI

The great city of Madurai was reduced to ashes.

SUTRA

It had to be done. The city of Madurai was purged of all its sins.

NATI

Cleansed of all its stains, you could say.

SUTRA

The corrupted disk wiped clean and made ready for reformatting, you could say.

NATI

Euphemisms all. In truth it was death and destruction for a city that had it coming.

SUTRA

There was no way the Council of Gods could save the city. They were compelled to act. It was hard justice, brutally delivered.

NATI

And Kannagi... (*She looks at him*)

SUTRA (*Louder*)

And Kannagi...

NATI *(Drawing him aside)*

I don't think we should do it. Not this evening.

SUTRA

We could lose our jobs. We are supposed to do what the script tells us to do.

NATI

Yes, yes, yes, I know all that. But the script was written, what, eighteen hundred years ago? And the writer is not there in the audience watching the performance.

SUTRA

But how can we just...

NATI

And one more thing, more important...

SUTRA

What's that?

NATI

Look out there. What do you see? Do you see people who look like they know the story of Silappadikaram and the transformation of Kannagi into... (*Sutradhar cups her mouth*)

SUTRA

Don't! (*He speaks to the audience*) You see, ladies and gentlemen, a specimen of modern education. (*Agitated*) Two years in a drama school, two months as an understudy, and the first chance she gets to play a proper big part, she wants to do it her way, her own way, her very own interpretation of the play, her profound view of a classic, her two minutes of fame in preparing an audience, and that is yourselves, ladies and gentlemen, an enlightened and sensitive gathering like yourselves, she must have her two minutes to preface a play that has stood the test of two thousand years! (*He is short of breath*)

NATI

Breath control. I can teach you how to increase your rib reserve.

SUTRA

Enough! And not in front of them!

NATI

There, there! Calm down, now. You know I'm with you, really.

SUTRA

But you can't reveal the end before the play has even begun. You must not spoil it for them.

NATI

But they know it all!

SUTRA

This audience?

NATI

Didn't you say yourself? That they were enlightened and well informed and all.

SUTRA

I did. They are a lovely audience. So...?

NATI

So...you can be sure they know the story of Silappadikaram, and the transformation of Kannagi into...you know...It is a well-known story.

SUTRA

So...?

NATI

So...there must be other ways to present our story to an audience like this one.

SUTRA

All right, educate me.

NATI

You see, when you play a tragic tale like this one...

SUTRA

Aha! I have you there!

NATI

What do you mean?

SUTRA

There are those who believe that the story of Kannagi is a tragedy. They go to drama schools, and read Aristotle and study Greek drama, and they think they know all about tragedy.

NATI

You are talking about people you know?

SUTRA

So, you can look at the story of Silappadikaram as tragedy, and play it as tragedy, as you think tragedy should be played.

NATI

The end clearly known to all, the players and audience alike, and the paths to be taken by the characters predestined, predetermined, the course of events set to their actions and the actions set to the events, all charted out in detail, with no chance of deviation at any point of time.

SUTRA

You took the words out of my mouth. Only, it sounds more elegant coming from you.

NATI

The complete transparency of the tragedy makes it possible to start at the end.

SUTRA

Or at any point.

NATI

Or at any point.

SUTRA

If it is to be a tragic tale...What if it is not? What if the play is really a story of celebration?

NATI

As Ilango Adigal wanted it? Or as we wish to have it?

SUTRA

It doesn't matter, does it? He has given us his play and gone away. We are here now to give the audience a performance.

NATI

And go away.

SUTRA

Not without leaving something behind.

NATI

A joyful thought? A message of celebration?

SUTRA

Camouflaged as tragedy.

NATI

All right. Have it your way, the end scene shown at the start, but not the end of the story. Hmm...All right, it's yours. But...

SUTRA

But...

NATI

The epilogue is mine. And that stays at the end.

SUTRA

And that will be...?

NATI

We shall see.

SUTRA

We begin?

NATI

We begin.

SUTRA

To the lamp, then.

(Sutradhar and Nati go back to the arati tray, pick it up, and stand above it. The flame goes out.

The cyclorama springs to life. There are leaping flames engulfing the city. Buildings collapse. Terror stricken people, trapped, disappear from view. Sutradhar and Nati prostrate in the direction of the cyclorama.

The flames subside. Sutradhar and Nati rise, move DC and address the audience.)

SUTRA

The great city of Madurai was punished by the gods. It was in accordance with the prayer from Kannagi.

NATI

The piercing pain in her heart, cloaked with insurmountable anger, had made her seek justice from none other than the god of fire, Agni. Only the truly pure and innocent are spared...little children, animals, the feeble, and the chaste, like Kannagi herself.

SUTRA

The city could make a fresh beginning if it wished to, when it was ready. *(He moves to the props chest to take out a town crier's drum)*

NATI

And now, to begin at the beginning...

SUTRA

To begin at the very beginning...

NATI

Kannagi, a lovely young maiden, is given in marriage to Kovalan, young, handsome, wealthy.

SUTRA

Kannagi is from a wealthy family herself, and in accordance with tradition, brings a good part of that wealth into the new household.

NATI

A lovely couple, made for each other, they said. A loving couple too.

SUTRA

Until...

NATI

Until he sets his eyes on the exotic dancer and courtesan, Madhavi, the one with the long laughing eyes and the petal-soft skin.

SUTRA *(Beating the drum)*

It has begun!

(The percussionists take over for a short section. Sutradhar and Nati set the stage for the first scene and exit. The music leads into a choreographed dance sequence. It may be performed either onstage or seen on the cyclorama. A small group of dancers has a ring of men seated around them. Among them is KOVALAN. After a short opener, the dancers withdraw, leaving MADHAVI at the centre, who continues with a solo piece that combines artistry with sensuousness beautifully. The men withdraw, leaving Kovalan and Madhavi alone. They are drawn to each other.)

ACT I

SCENE 1

Kannagi's house in the ancient city of Puhar at the mouth of the river Kaveri. There are stray signs of former wealth, but the present is one of severe austerity. Kannagi, a young woman, is seen sitting on an ornate divan-like couch by a window and watching the street. Her companion and maid, Devanti, enters the room balancing a large metal pot full of water on her head. She crosses the stage, places the pot of water in a corner.

KANNAGI
What is the gossip by the river this morning?

DEVANTI
There is always idle talk at the bath for those who wish to listen.
That is the only place where women congregate
Without the influence of men.
So you can rest assured there will be plenty of gossip there.
And today being the morning of Indra's festival,
There was more than the usual crowd
And more than the usual talk.

KANNAGI
Is that why you are so late?

DEVANTI
You know I never listen to idle talk
Or repeat gossip, madam.

KANNAGI
Don't they ask?
Do they not splash questions at you?
Does Kannagi still expect her husband to come back to her?

Is she upset about him?
Does she get help from her parents?
Or is she still proud?
Don't the women ask you questions and don't you answer them
With a knowing, superior air?

DEVANTI

You know I would tell them to mind their own business.
But let me ask you, madam, if you will permit me,
What is the matter with you today?
You seem agitated and not your usual self.

KANNAGI

Is it noticeable? Can you see?
I had a strange dream last night.

DEVANTI

What was it about?

KANNAGI

I dreamed that my husband and I were united once more
And that we went on a long journey.
We reached an ancient city, and while there
A great calamity befell my husband
And ever so many things happened,
I cannot remember them all.
Then I met him again on top of a lonely hill
In the company of angels
And flew away in a heavenly chariot.
It was so vivid while it lasted
And seemed so real that I was frightened.
It took me some time to realise
It was only a dream.

DEVANTI

What time of the night was it
When you had the dream?

KANNAGI
Almost morning.

DEVANTI
Then you may find yourself realising
The dream after all. It may be sooner than you think.

KANNAGI
But I am upset about that journey.
It was a strange city
And the calamity to my husband...

DEVANTI
Your husband, madam, was reunited with you, was he not?
That is what matters.
I have every reason to believe
It will come true soon, if not immediately.
As for the rest of your dream,
I suggest we go and bathe this evening
In the sacred waters of the temple tank
And the evil effects will be washed away.

KANNAGI
No, if I cannot win my husband
From another woman's snares by my love and constancy,
Or protect him from evil by the power of my chastity,
Divine intervention is of little use.
I shall not seek it for that purpose.

DEVANTI
Whether you choose to invoke divine assistance or not,
I think you are going to be united
With your husband very soon.

KANNAGI
Do not raise false hopes to cheer me, Devanti.
I have had many dreams in the past
And you have always interpreted them
To my advantage. And I have sat by this window

And watched the street eagerly,
Awaiting his arrival until my eyes hurt
And my poor heart ached. And my misery
Was all the greater at the end of the day.
All dreams are false.
I must not even sit by the window anymore.
(She moves away.)

DEVANTI
What I am telling you now is no dream.
Madam Kannagi, listen to me. I met a friend of mine
At the river and she told me...

KANNAGI
I don't want to hear it! I don't want to hear it!
How often have I told you not to listen to vulgar stories
And not to repeat them to me!

DEVANTI
But I would not repeat them unless I knew I should,
And you would be pleased to hear them.

KANNAGI
Ever the tease. All right, have your way.
Tell me what it was you heard.

DEVANTI
Our lord Kovalan and that woman Madhavi
Went to the seashore early this morning
And were heard singing duets.
At first he sang...

KANNAGI
Is that your report? I will have none of it.
Are you against me too
That you torture me with such cheap gossip?

DEVANTI
The story will end well, madam,
Even if it does not seem to begin well.

KANNAGI

I cannot stop you, can I?
Go on then.

DEVANTI

He sang a love song. It was about
A pining for a woman he had lost.
And Madhavi listened.
She has always been afraid
That he might leave her some day
And return to you.
She thought perhaps he was thinking of you.
A quick remedy was needed.
In order to make him jealous,
And there is no better method of keeping a man
Tied to the end of your sari,
She too sang as if she were pining for someone else.

KANNAGI

She probably was.

DEVANTI

No, madam.
Though Madhavi is a dancer by profession,
She loves him truly.
And in the depth of his heart
He knows it too. That is why
It is so much more difficult for him to leave her.
But wait, do not turn away.
Let me tell you the end of the story.

KANNAGI

I wish you would get to the point directly
And leave out the needless detail.

DEVANTI

Well, this is what happened.
He was so annoyed at her singing

That he left her abruptly. You know what men are like,
Big bad moods over small matters,
Working themselves up to a state over nothing.
And yet, they expect us to be forgiving at all times.

KANNAGI

Many times has he left her in the past
Only to return before he could reach my doorstep.

DEVANTI

But this time...it is different.
When he left her so suddenly,
Madhavi did not know what to do.
She thought he might perhaps be waiting
For her in her house and hurried there.
Not finding him there, she sent him
A letter and a garland of jasmines
Through her maid. She met him in the street.
He was distracted and in despair.
He was abusive.
Let us say simply that he called her
Faithless and untrue. He refused to read the letter
Or receive the garland.

KANNAGI

Is it all true?
Or are you saying things merely for charity?
Give me the truth directly, rather than
The sweet words covering the bitter core.

DEVANTI

It is the truth and there is no doubt about it.
There has been talk for some time of a break between them.
But I didn't want to say anything
Until there was something definite to tell you.

KANNAGI

I thought he was a lover of the arts,
Especially dancing and singing.

DEVANTI

He was. It was her dancing
That attracted him first. And afterwards
It was the very same dancing
That he objected to.
He would not have a public exhibition of her charms.
He dreaded other men being captivated
By her face and figure as he had been himself.
When they talked about her in huddles
And made up jokes about her
It made him angry and jealous.

KANNAGI

Do you think he will come to me now?
Do not answer merely to please me.
I do not wish to be humoured.
I ask you to tell me what you really think?

DEVANTI

He will come.
And when he does, do not lose him again.

KANNAGI

Tell me again that you speak in sincerity
And not in jest.

DEVANTI

He will come. Mark my words,
He will come.

KANNAGI

And if he does not?

There is a knock on the door. The women look at each other.

DEVANTI

And if he does?

She goes out. Kannagi raises her head in prayer.

KANNAGI

Oh Lord, you have answered my prayers

At long last. You have lent me your hand.
My pleading has not been in vain
And I am grateful.
(With determination, transformed)
This is the moment I have been waiting for.
(Devanti comes in)

DEVANTI
He is here. At last!

KANNAGI
Who is?

DEVANTI
He, of course!
Our master, your husband, madam.

KANNAGI
I have no master on this earth.
And as for my husband, I lost him years ago.
I am a widow for all practical purposes.

DEVANTI
That you certainly are not! Your head is not shaven
And the beautiful, uncombed black locks fall
Over your shoulders with customary grace.
You do not wear white.
The string that was tied round your neck
On your wedding day is still there
And the man who tied it is even now waiting at your door
Rubbing one foot against the other in impatience.
(Knocking heard again)

KANNAGI
Perhaps his impatience is not so much for me
As to return to his mistress.
It is the festival of Indra today, is it not?
The god of fire might have kindled a new flame.
He may want to surprise her with another piece of jewellery,

Another of my ornaments.
Tell him I have none left.
Tell him my arms and neck have remained bare.
My ears and nose have not felt
The weight of precious stones for long.
And this string round my neck
About which you talk so much
Is of no value to her
Who has managed without it all this time.
Tell him I have nothing more to offer.

DEVANTI

Do not be hard on him, madam.
He is thoroughly penitent.
There is misery written all over his face.
He has not come with the glib excuses
Of a profligate or the smooth deceiving tongue
Of a clever liar. He has had
A painful attack of guilt.
He is now completely awake from the bad dream
That has lasted these five years.
If you reject him now,
You will lose him forever.

KANNAGI

How dare he cross my threshold,
Humble but pure, bringing with him the scents
That woman has pasted on him,
Wearing the clothes tainted by contact
With that woman's bed!
His heart may still be there,
Hankering after newer ecstasies
From that woman's trade.
Perhaps she has no more need for him now.
She has found someone better, wealthier,
And the wretched man who was once my husband
Has nowhere else to go.

That is why he is here. Send him away.

DEVANTI

Madam, you know that is not possible.
Yes, Madhavi loves him with a woman's heart.
True, she has taken all his wealth from him.
But it is only to protect him from his own foolishness.
For he is quite capable of losing it all on the maddest ventures.
True, she might not have given him up.
Truer still is the fact that he is here.
If he is here it means he is tired of her.
The moment of her misfortune
Is the turning point of yours.
Seize it, madam. Do not let it go past you.

KANNAGI

Of course I will not let it go past me.
For this is the moment of my redemption.
Do you think I am going to let it go?

DEVANTI

No, madam, the line is blurred
Between redemption and revenge.
This is the moment of fulfilment,
Of victory if you like.
But certainly not revenge. It is the end
Of your long and lonely vigil
And the beginning of joyous days, calm and serene.
Being wise, you must be generous
In your moment of victory. Women are gracious
By nature. It does not become us
To be vindictive with our husbands.

KANNAGI

How many nights have passed when the moon
Shone bright and the galaxy of stars
Shed their divine light on this miserable earth.
I have sat alone in that moonlit parlour

And watched the billows at the pebbled shore.
On how many nights have I pined for a husband
While he was in the arms of another woman,
Afraid of my own thoughts,
Ashamed to meet other people.
How many days have I spent inside,
In this miserable room. How often
Have I sat by the window and watched
Other husbands returning from far-off lands
With wealth and fame to their waiting wives.
And yet you want me to forgive him!

DEVANTI

Yes, dear child, if I may call you that.
I call you madam by custom,
But I have been your nurse and companion
In your loneliness and a mother
In your silent grief.
I have stood between you
And the malicious gossip of the outside world
Just as I have blunted the full force of your sorrow
Even from yourself in making you proud
And unbending. Please listen to me now
And be guided by my words. You are a woman.
Your heart may bleed with pain over and over again,
But there is nothing you can do. You may call it fate,
But it is our duty to suffer in silence,
To curse fate, and offer prayers to the family gods.
You may shed tears of sorrow, longing and bitterness,
But you must accept any happiness
That comes your way in all humility.

KANNAGI

I shall never accept such a fate.
Not for myself, not for any woman.

No god in any heavenly seat above
Ever decreed that man and woman should be unequal
In pain or in pleasure.

DEVANTI

At least accept your husband when he comes to you.

KANNAGI

No. From now on I, too, shall fight.
If I can suffer pain as much as this
I can inflict pain too.

DEVANTI

Upon him or upon her? Or upon yourself?
The best way to inflict pain on your
Adversary is to take back your husband.

KANNAGI

What do I care for her?
She must be glad to be free once again,
To practice her ignoble scheme on others.
But what about him?

DEVANTI

To hurt him is to hurt yourself.
Are you so fond of pain
That you do not want to part with it?
Have you lost the capacity for joy?

KANNAGI

In truth, I do not know. I am confused and frightened.
What if he should leave me again? What if it should be
Nothing but a trick of hers, a cruel prank
To laugh at my suffering?

DEVANTI

Do not be unduly anxious, madam.
The story of their quarrel is quite true.
When he left you the last time
You were young and artless
And trusted him blindly.
But now, you should be able to keep him.
For your beauty is no less than hers
And you have the advantage of being his wife.

KANNAGI

Enough of your cheap advice! Do you think
I will demean myself by practicing tricks
That smack of a public dancing girl?
Do you want me to be like her?

DEVANTI

Not tricks, but arts, artistic skills.
Womenfolk must perfect the skills
To keep our husbands from straying.

KANNAGI

I shall never stoop to methods
That prop up womenfolk, but pull down womankind.

DEVANTI

You are proud, madam, but not very wise.
May I bring him in before he chooses to depart?

KANNAGI

If you bring him in here against my will,
I shall lavish on him all that is stored up
Over the years, all the anger held suppressed.

DEVANTI

Yes, do that, but afterwards,
Lavish all your stored up love, too.
Abuse him by all means, but abuse him to his face.
At this distance and with the door shut

He cannot hear your words.
And my unschooled repetition of them before him
Will not compensate for the sincerity
And the beautiful ringing tones of your voice.
Yes, abuse him. Do not let a single detail
Escape your notice. Tell him all that you think.
And even more than what you think. Make him feel
Thoroughly miserable, ashamed and abject.
But in the end, forgive him graciously.
A man with a bad conscience
May relapse into his old habits
If you let him harbour it too long.

KANNAGI

Is he really miserable? Tell me,
Does he look ill?

DEVANTI

He tells me that his misery can be obliterated
By the sight of your face, and his wounds healed
By the balm of your soothing words.

KANNAGI

I have waited for this moment so long,
Oh, ever so long. Seated alone
On that unsoiled bridal couch
I have imagined playing this scene over and over again.
I have worked on the script in the minutest detail,
Each syllable and inflexion, every pause and thrust.
I knew he would return
One day, a beggar at the doorstep.
My greatest pleasure would be in rejecting him,
To make him suffer the same loneliness,
The shame and the indignities heaped upon me.
Now the moment is here,
But my plans have deserted me. I am confused.
I do not know what to say, what to do.

I thought I was strong and unbent.
But I am weak like any other woman
Who weeps over losing her husband
To the wiles of another. Tell me what to do, Devanti.
But let it be in keeping
With my dignity and my pride in love.

DEVANTI

Your dignity is not lost in accepting
Your husband when he returns with remorse
For his past, madam. It is your sacred duty.

KANNAGI

If you say so.

DEVANTI

You will see him, then?

KANNAGI

Must I not? Let him in.

DEVANTI

He must not come in with you looking like this.
Comb your hair and straighten your sari.
You do not want him to suspect
You have been pining for him all this time.
Let your grief not be too evident. Replace the spot
On your forehead and I will get you some flowers.
(Devanti hurriedly helps Kannagi)

KANNAGI

Hurry up, Devanti. What if he should get
Impatient and leave?

DEVANTI

It will not do him any harm waiting a while.
After all you have waited five years!

KANNAGI

Oh, I am so happy!

DEVANTI

Control it, madam. Do not be too spontaneous.
Keep your anger in balance with your happiness,
Deliberate and measured
In the correct proportions to suit the moment.
Keep a firm hold on your emotions.
A little sarcasm followed by anger
Will be quite proper.
And virtuous indignation, interspersed
With a few well-chosen sobs.
And when he is really miserable,
A final melting away in a flood
Of tears and love. That is what will make him
Your slave for a long time to come.
(Devanti goes out to bring Kovalan in)

KANNAGI

As if emotions can be measured
In bushels from bags of rice!

(Sutradhar and Nati enter for an interlude. They guide Kannagi to one side of the stage and seat her. They have a page of script each or a clipboard, which they glance at as they set the scene.)

INTERLUDE: KOVALAN'S RETURN

NATI

Aah...Look at her! Such composure, such fortitude.

SUTRA

Steely resolve.

NATI

The moment she has waited for all these years, taming the storm within herself, the patience through the agony, the longing controlled with dignity...

SUTRA

Why is she doing this? Why can't she...

NATI

Why? How can we expect you to understand? A mere stage decorator, paid to do what the script tells you to do!

SUTRA

She should put her foot down! She should send him packing, send him straight back, right at the door. She shouldn't see him at all.

NATI

What do you know about womanhood? All that is beautiful and divine in the feminine?

SUTRA

It will not do! Ask the 'feminines' there in the audience. Not in this day and age!

NATI

There, there, there. Give Kannagi a chance to show what she is capable of. Give the modern slogan-shouting critics a length of rope.

SUTRA

The only thing she should... *(He stops abruptly, looks at his script closely, looks at Nati's, takes her aside and speaks angrily to her)*

You switched scripts!

NATI

Bhasa! Circa third century AD. From his science of dramaturgy. You go deeper into your own character by putting yourself into the other's role.

SUTRA

That's cheating!

NATI

It works!

SUTRA

You are getting me confused... should Kannagi see Kovalan or not?

NATI

She has a mind of her own.

SUTRA

Should she forgive him?

NATI

A mind of her own. She has a purpose.

SUTRA

So, does the playwright not have a purpose?

NATI

Let it go with the flow!

(She withdraws. Sutradhar follows. Kannagi is seen seated, upright, her back to the entrance.)

SCENE 2

Kannagi prepares to receive her husband, who enters without Devanti.

KANNAGI

What brings you here, my lord?

KOVALAN

A guilt-ridden conscience and a broken heart,
Repentance for folly, remorse for the past,
Love reawakened for a neglected but dear wife,
Dormant so long, but never extinguished,
And empty hands.

KANNAGI

I can see the empty hands.

KOVALAN

I cannot expect you to feel the anguish in my heart.
Should I tear it open to prove to you
My shame and my misery? Does it not show
In my face? Can you not hear it in my voice?

KANNAGI

Your voice and face have the benefit of training
By an actress and dancer, my lord.
And I hear you are not a bad singer yourself,
Though I have never had a chance to know.
But I am no expert in such matters.
Therefore I cannot judge.

KOVALAN

While others made their name in commerce,
Like my worthy father, or became
Ministers to the king by their wit and wisdom,
Or earned glory in the service of this land,
I was merely a man of fashion.
Flattered by the idle, scorned by the virtuous,
Blinded by the darkness of an unholy passion,
I could not see the light.
Drunk with the devilish beauty of a temptress
Faithless but possessive,
Caught in the web of cunning design,
I have been beaten into a stupor.
My conscience was chained and kept prisoner
By a tyrannical infatuation.
I was robbed of my wealth. I lost my honour too.

KANNAGI

If your mind is as confused as your figures of speech,
It is best that you go back.

KOVALAN

I have come to you a broken but wiser man.
The cobwebs of the mind are swept,
The drunken state lifted, the confusion cleared.
The morning light is sharp and piercing.
My mind is awakened to a pervasive sadness.
Do not forsake me now. This is my plea.
A plea to one who remains a wife
From one who remains a husband.

KANNAGI

I knew a husband once.
He made promises
Before the assembled nobles of the state,
Before the rising sun and the North Star,
Before a sacred fire, before the unseen power
That watches over all our deeds, before the whole world,
To take me as his lawful wedded wife
And to live thereafter in domestic bliss.
That was you, was it not?
You left me then to the shame and loneliness
Of a neglected wife. You spurned me.
Have you the face to ask me now for comforts
Of home and not be spurned yourself?
Or, perhaps, it is a mere ruse.
You are here to see if I have any other ornament
Left for you to pawn, to maintain your mistress.
If that is so, it will be your last call.
I have with me an anklet.
Take it and leave without further ceremony.
It is one of a pair, a gift from a mother
On her daughter's wedding day.
She said I was not to part with it except as a last resort
To save my life, or that of my husband.
I have no other ornament
Except the sacred wedding string
Which even you cannot remove except by your death.
So, you may pick up the anklet and leave.
Do not cross this doorstep ever again.
(Devanti comes in carrying a tray)
What is it?

DEVANTI

I have brought some flowers and fruit, and rose water
With sandalwood paste. Our lord may be tired
And may need refreshing.

KANNAGI

Take them away, foolish woman!

DEVANTI

Yes, madam. *(She leaves with the tray)*

KOVALAN

How can you be so cruel?
Your face the softness of a morning rose
But your heart so hard?

KANNAGI

Yes, my heart is hard. It will grow harder still.
I have had to protect it against grief,
Against malicious gossip,
Against the unwelcome sly glances of men and women
As I walked alone. I have not waited
With love and tenderness like other wives
For a husband to return from across the seas.
When storms broke over the ocean
And it rose in a mighty roar to dash against the shores,
I was not afraid like other wives were
For the safety of their loved ones.
I was glad that the skies were dark and the waves violent
So you would not be able to lie on the beach with your mistress.
But the hour of dreadful sorrow was when the seas turned calm
And the sky cloudless, and the gentle southern breeze
Brought the ships to harbour
For I would see then
Other wives dressed in all their finery
With scents and sandalwood paste
Going to the shore to meet their husbands.
It was then I cried
For I had no husband to welcome.

KOVALAN

My own remorse has pierced my heart
A thousand times more deeply

Than all the cruel words you can muster
And hurl at me, quite rightfully.
If it were possible to retrace my steps,
I should do it gladly, even if it cost me my life.
But the past can never be retraced or obliterated.
It is made, never to be unmade.
I merely ask forgiveness for the past, pity for the present.
Love and affection can surely return
In the future into our lives.

KANNAGI
My heart is dried of all pity and love and turned brittle.
The broken edges sharpen the grief.
There is nothing but bitterness
In the black depths of sorrow and suffering.
Do not probe my heart any deeper.
Return to her, go back to where you have come from.

KOVALAN
Is all hope lost? If that is your last word,
Then I fear it must be so.

KANNAGI
Who am I? Merely a discarded wife,
Eclipsed by one more cunning, more beautiful than I,
Trained in the art of making men her slaves.
Nature shuns me. Spring bears no charm.
The white heat of the sun or winter's biting cold
Are equal in disdain.
They ignore me in this miserable room.
Life has assured me no joy. Death will bring no grief.
Thoughts of love have no thrill and sweet words
Give no relief. Laughter has no excitement
And fond affection gives no peace.
My eyes no longer blink in silent merriment,
My bosom holds no warmth,

My heart no pity and my mind no hope.
I feel only the acute pain of parting and separation
And bleed even at the touch of friendly hands.
That is the woman I have become.
Can you love such a woman
After one such as Madhavi?

KOVALAN

Torture me all you wish,
Aim your darts into my deepest wounds.
Only relent and let me stay, for I love you deeply still.

KANNAGI

If we are to be reconciled and seek a life together
Once more as man and wife...

KOVALAN

Do I see hope?
Or is this another cord to keep me suspended?

KANNAGI

I said IF we are to be reconciled. If so,
We must purge ourselves of the past
And start afresh. Clear our minds of all poison
That has overrun our souls.
Reveal to each other the deepest wounds.
Expose the venom
To the light of each other's searching eyes
And expel it for all time to come.
Only then can we start a new life,
Protecting each other from our weaknesses,
Making allowances for our follies, guarding
Against evil that is inherent in us all.
I must understand the peaks of your folly
And you the depths of my shame.
Only then can we lead a new life,
Untainted by the crimes of our hearts.

KOVALAN

Listen, then.
I was a simple youth when I married you.
I was a dreamer,
Dreaming many dreams of two persons in love,
Love in togetherness and togetherness in love.
I dreamt of flowers surrounding our nakedness,
Lonely moonlit beaches, secret hiding places
From where we could watch departing ships
Against the rising sun.
If only you had given me time, flattered me
For my silly escapades, satisfied my foolish manly pride
Pretending you were weak, cajoling my pretended strength,
I might have grown to what you wanted me to be
In time. But in your tender wisdom you chose to be
A taskmaster, a very hard one.
You wanted me to be greater than I was.
I yearned for a woman to love and to protect,
To feel superior to and to please.
It was not to be. You were the exacting leader,
I, the reluctant follower, ready to desert
At the first opportunity.

KANNAGI

And the dancer Madhavi was the opportunity?

KOVALAN

I am ashamed to admit it.

KANNAGI

Tell me, how did you get to know her?

KOVALAN

Do you insist on rubbing in my folly?
Can we not bury it?

KANNAGI

If you survived living in folly so long,
You can surely bear recounting it for a while.

I want the truth, not a fairy tale.
Tell it boldly with your newfound manliness.

KOVALAN

When I left our home that fateful evening
There was not the faintest trace of the whirlwind
That was to carry me away.
On my way to the garden...

KANNAGI

No fairy tales!

KOVALAN

I heard the king's drummer announcing
The inaugural performance
Of a new and accomplished dancer named Madhavi
In the Hall of the Nobles
And in the presence of the king himself.
I went there intending to spend only a few minutes.
I came out well after the end, hours later.
My senses were stunned by her charms,
As were those of many others gathered.
All reason had been enslaved by her seductive art.
The king presented her a garland
Which clung to her bosom every moment of the evening.
When it was offered in auction,
I bought it for a thousand and eight pieces of gold.
A tribute to her art, I said.
It was rash but it was rapturous.

KANNAGI

Didn't you know the custom,
That when you bought the garland
You had become her lover?

KOVALAN

I was weak and I was possessed.
Life with her was going to be a service
To the noblest art of dancing, I thought.

My life was meant to be full of music and poetry, I told myself,
In a higher plane. What a fool I was!

KANNAGI
And wasn't there poetry and music?

KOVALAN
There was, for a while. She made me believe so
In order to keep me there till my wealth was exhausted
And I was spent.
She started complaining about cheating servants
And tradesmen overcharging.
She could find solace only in dance, she said.
She spent longer hours and whole days away from me.
I was left alone. I was jaded. It was just as dull...

KANNAGI
As the days with me?

KOVALAN
I am wiser now.

KANNAGI
Why did you leave her?

KOVALAN
It took me some time to grasp things. I realised slowly
The nature of a woman who was but a dancing girl,
Her body for sale to the highest bidder.
I had won her as a mistress, she was mine.
But she belonged in truth to her art,
An art that demands constant practice
In turning strong men into weak submission.
I was alone.
I was turned loose but held captive.
She was free.

KANNAGI
Do you mean unfaithfulness?
As sometimes seen between husband and wife?

KOVALAN

Does it make a difference what it is called?

KANNAGI

It might, to one such as you,
Who has knowledge of these matters.

KOVALAN

You taunt me now.

KANNAGI

Only to be of service.
Is not a person held innocent until proven guilty?
You suspect Madhavi, you say.
On what grounds, I ask.

KOVALAN

She had a new composition.
Seeing me downcast she said she would perform it for me.
It was a lover's lament. When she sang
It was a face and voice I could not tell.
In dance it was a body I did not know.
I knew only it was time to go.

KANNAGI

So, you suffered too. My poor husband!

KOVALAN

Yes, I did, if that is what you wish to call it.

KANNAGI

So you suffered.
But what you display is the suffering
From the agonies of a jealous heart,
Not the agony of a guilty conscience.
Is it with such stale offerings
That you come to me for forgiveness?

KOVALAN

Are you playing with me, Kannagi?
Are you goading me to recall my pain
That I may suffer all the more?

KANNAGI

Your tale of woe begs the question:
Why did you not return
The moment you realised your folly?

KOVALAN

Realisation was in truth the beginning of the suffering
That I hope will end today.
I saw no one I could blame,
Abuse or punish to ease my conscience.
There was no peg on which to hang my excuses,
No faith to harbour my weakness, no hope to urge me forward,
No confidence left in myself. I was alone.
I was ashamed of the past, suspicious of the present,
Frightened of what the future could hold.
I was impaled on my misdeeds. I struggled to live by the hour,
Countering pain and unholy desire.
There are no illusions now to taunt me.
But wisdom has come too late, and all our wealth
Has been spent in acquiring it.

KANNAGI *(Calling)*

Devanti! Devanti!
(Devanti enters)

DEVANTI

Did you call, madam?

KANNAGI

How long you are with those refreshments!

DEVANTI *(Brightening up, as she exits)*

I shall bring them instantly, madam.

KOVALAN

Does that mean I am forgiven?

KANNAGI

What is there to forgive, my lord?
I remain your wife. We are joined by sacred bonds

That even death cannot sever. You accepted me once
When I was young, beautiful and wealthy.
I am still young, but my beauty has been ravaged
By my grief and my wealth by your folly.
It is for you to accept me as I am now.

KOVALAN

I accept with joy!
But I long to hear you say I am forgiven.

KANNAGI

You are, if that will ease your conscience.

KOVALAN

I deserve neither pity nor tolerance.
Heaven has given me a faithful and chaste wife
Who loves me. I can now dare to seek attainments long discarded.
You will be my inspiration. I will hold my head high
As I go into the world to earn wealth and fame
As you once expected me to do.
I shall start life anew.

KANNAGI

The names of our families are known and respected
Across the seas, but we have lost our links.
We cannot afford to live in this city any more, to be
Talked about in whispers, laughed at in secret,
Humoured by friends and patronised by our blood relations.
The names of our parents must not be dragged in the dust.

KOVALAN

We can wipe away the past, you and I.
It is but an incidental memory, an unhappy burden
Weighing needlessly on the future.
We cannot afford to carry the load all our lives.
Let us leave this accursed town and start afresh elsewhere.
You once spoke of the ancient city of Madurai,
The city famous for its learning and its wealth.

KANNAGI

But it is far away, my lord.
Can you not choose a place somewhere near?

KOVALAN

No place is too far away if we choose to put
The scene of our misfortune behind us.

KANNAGI

How can I, the only daughter of a merchant prince,
Go wandering by foot into strange lands,
In search of wealth? How can I leave my home,
My friends and those who once were friends?
What should I do with cherished memories
From a happy and loving family?

KOVALAN

Do not be afraid, I shall work hard.
Our necessity now and past sufferings
Will spur me on to great deeds and successes
Though ready affluence failed to accomplish it.

KANNAGI

There is no need to work hard.
I still have the pair of anklets I told you about.
It is most valuable and will fetch a great price.
With that as capital, you can engage yourself
In a business of your choice.
With your skill and my turn of luck
We shall find prosperity again.

KOVALAN

So be it, then. If ever you are homesick and we must return
To our dear Puhar, It shall be as honoured citizens.
My folly would by then have been forgotten
And we should be welcomed straight back. *(Devanti enters)*

DEVANTI

Here are the refreshments, madam.
I hope I haven't kept you waiting too long.

KANNAGI

Devanti, we are going on a long journey.
We must start before dawn tomorrow.
Prepare yourself quickly.

DEVANTI

Yes, madam; I shall be prepared.

KOVALAN

To Madurai, then! And to our fortune!

KANNAGI *(Stepping aside)*

Oh...

KOVALAN

What is it?

KANNAGI

That awful dream...

KOVALAN

What did you say?

KANNAGI

It was nothing, my lord.
Just something I remembered.

INTERLUDE: THE JOURNEY TO MADURAI

Possibilities: *Choreography. Kovalan, Kannagi and Devanti journey to Madurai on foot. It is a long, arduous journey. On the way they meet the wise Jain nun, Kavundi, who befriends them. Sensing troubled souls, she counsels them on the subject of human conduct in line with fate and destiny. She then accompanies them to the outskirts of Madurai and leaves them in the care of Mathari, a cowherdess, who readily takes them in.*

A counselling scene with the wise nun is a possibility, but is being omitted here. Instead, a link scene by the Sutradhar and Nati is suggested below.

Percussion/music. Sutradhar and Nati enter to introduce the second act.

NATI *(Dreamily)*

Wipe away the past. We can
Together you and I now
Leave behind accursed loads,
Step lightly with our love restored.

SUTRA

Not the best rendition, but it should do.

NATI

It must do. As if anybody can do justice to the original in a translation.

SUTRA

Especially in converting poetry to prose.

NATI

Contemporary prose too! Beautiful images and eloquent metaphors have no place on the stage anymore.

SUTRA

Four line stanzas, exquisite poetry...

NATI

Puhar, Puhar, we leave you now.
Your glory must spread wide.
Our heads are bent as we take leave.
Held high they will be on return.

SUTRA

Hmmm. No need to get carried away. Da-d-da-d-da-d-da-d-da-d-da-d-da-da...It will sound like Jack and Jill soon.

NATI

Iambic pentameter. Invented by Chaucer. Usurped by Shakespeare. You remember him, of course. It was fifteen hundred years after Ilango Adigal.

SUTRA

That will do! You see, ladies and gentlemen, Ilango Adigal didn't merely tell the story in verse, he set it to tune.

NATI

It was an operatic composition, to be sung, to be really enjoyed, to be heard as music to be really understood.

SUTRA

We would love to tell you more about the original. *(Turning to Nati)* But there's just that much we can do in one evening.

NATI

Put it into the programme! Let's move on!

SUTRA

The scene describing the journey away from Puhar is one of the most beautiful compositions in ancient dramatic literature.

NATI

What a journey that must have been! From the city of Puhar at the Kaveri delta to the city of Madurai in the middle of the great South Indian peninsula.

SUTRA

A good three hundred miles.

NATI

Or more.

SUTRA

A good two weeks on the road.

NATI

Or more. On foot. Don't forget, there were no roads then. It was mostly cross-country. First, the hills...

SUTRA

And then the forests. They had neither the horse-drawn carriages nor the palanquins that a household of their standing would press into service for any sojourn out of town.

NATI

Kovalan and Kannagi chose to walk, all by themselves.

SUTRA

Their only company was the faithful Devanti.

NATI *(Abruptly)*

Done? Can we get on with the play now?

SUTRA *(Annoyed)*

Always at a gallop! Will you ever learn to slow down? To take a link scene nice and easy?

NATI

But why?

SUTRA

First, that's the way a play like this must be done. Second, because I say so.

NATI

There you go, pulling rank again.

SUTRA

Three, we have to tell them about Kavundi.

NATI

The wise Jain nun they meet in the forest! We should be playing that scene and not just talking about it.

SUTRA

You know what each addition to the cast does to us?

NATI

We beg harder in the market-place.

SUTRA

That's what the theatre has come to, begging sponsors for our bread.

NATI

With a little bit of butter, please.

SUTRA

And where will you get an actor to play the nun?

NATI

I can play the nun!

SUTRA

You!

NATI

When I was eleven I played a ninety-year-old great grandmother.

SUTRA

And you giggled so convincingly.

NATI

In my first year in this company I played an elephant calf, a lamp post and an invisible potato.

SUTRA

The company is honoured to have such talent on its rolls.

NATI

Sticking on too.

SUTRA

Not snapped up by another company, not yet. Why not, we wonder...

NATI

They may be there right now, among the audience!

SUTRA

They might well be. There will be phone calls. So...

NATI

So...I suppose we skip the scene?

SUTRA

Under the circumstances.

NATI

We do the usual thing? Provide an intelligent narrative link?

SUTRA

Better than that. We put it into the programme. The audience will read it by themselves.

NATI

We go straight on, then.

SUTRA

Straight on. Kovalan, Kannagi and Devanti are on the outskirts of the great city of Madurai, at the home of Mathari, a humble and pious cowherdess.

NATI

Is there a part of a cow?

SUTRA

Offstage!

(They leave the stage, now set for Mathari's hut)

ACT II

SCENE 1

MATHARI

Are you rested enough? Did you sleep well?
You are from the richest in your land.
The comforts we can provide are few.
If you can ignore the austerities
Of a peasant's home we will be happy
To share our little joys with you.

KANNAGI

You give away the fat of the milk and butter
To the rich in the cities, but you keep
The lean strength of the buttermilk with you.

MATHARI

I can give you all the buttermilk you need, dear lady.

KANNAGI

I am a stranger to you, and yet
You have taken me into your home
And ministered to my every need.
I have shared all my thoughts with you,
My past trials and my future hopes and fears.
You are more than a mother to me.
I have not shared these secrets even with her.
Too ashamed, I have run away,
And she knows not where I am.

MATHARI

It is not uncommon.
We can sometimes tell the most intimate secrets
To a stranger while it seems unthinkable

To repeat them to loved ones.
The stranger takes you as you are,
While the loved one judges you by the past.
But do not be afraid. Your secrets are
As well concealed in me as in the innermost
Recess of your own heart.

KANNAGI
To provide us with shelter alone
Has been extremely kind, but you have given
Comfort and solace for my mind as well.
My body, broken by the hills and forests
No longer aches. Mind and body refreshed
In a new found peace, I am now ready
To even help you in your household tasks.

MATHARI
You will do no such thing! I will not have it said
That we extracted work from a noble lady
In return for shelter. But where is your husband?

KANNAGI
He has gone into the city to sell my precious anklet,
To see what scope there is for trade in this land.
Merchants from many lands East and West
Visit our shores. We know their ways.
We can provide links with your own markets.

MATHARI
I know nothing of such matters. I only know
My dear that your troubles are over now.
You are in a country where wise philosophers
Grow on trees, the king is just, the land
Is prosperous and the people honest and true.
Hence the rains do not fail us, the harvests
Are bountiful and our granaries are always full.
Your husband will have all the facilities of honest trade.
Our king welcomes foreign merchants to this city

So that they may see for themselves
The glory of his capital and sing its praises.
Soon you will have a house of your own
And all the luxuries to which you were born,
And the added bliss of children.

KANNAGI
You have persisted in being kind and encouraging.
I have overcome the pangs of homesickness.
The miseries of past years already seem distant.

MATHARI
I must go out for a while now for some deliveries.
My daughters will be here soon. They will entertain you.
(Devanti enters laughing)
It seems Devanti is set to entertain you too.
I must be off.
(She leaves, carrying a pot on her head)

KANNAGI
What do you find so funny, Devanti?

DEVANTI
The people in this city!
Such a funny language, such queer expressions.
And they laugh at me for my proper speech.

KANNAGI
And that makes you laugh?

DEVANTI
Their clothes and their manners too. They are frightful.
They wear the oldest styles and strut about
As if they were the leaders of fashion.

KANNAGI
So, you don't like the people of Madurai?

DEVANTI
I wouldn't go so far as to say that.
But they do seem to think rather a lot of themselves.

Take our hostess for example, the wife of a cowherd.
In our city she would not be allowed to speak to you directly.
And here she is, treating you as one of her own kind.

KANNAGI

You are forgetting, Devanti, she has given us shelter
And has been very kind to us.

DEVANTI

I am sure we could have done better
For ourselves somewhere else.

KANNAGI

You are being very ungrateful, Devanti.

DEVANTI

You are too trusting, madam. I could not sleep
All of last night because you told her about the anklet,
And I kept thinking they might be after it.
You never know with these people.

KANNAGI

Listen to me, Devanti.
My worries lie elsewhere. I am anxious about my lord.
He is upright, brave and honest, but inexperienced
In the arts of negotiation. In a strange city
Where none knows him or his family by name
He may be easily cheated.

DEVANTI

He is more than a match for a roomful of these foreigners.
He will easily manage them.
He can teach them a few tricks of their own trade,
Whoever they may be.

KANNAGI

It is so late. He should have been back long ago.
While I wait I see evil signs lurking everywhere.
The oil in that lamp has gone dry, the flowers
He gave me have faded, the fruit given us

Just this morning have gone stale. All these
Are signs I find difficult to ignore.

DEVANTI
Evil signs, madam? These are merely the result
Of passing time. The lamp has gone out because
Your dear hostess failed to replenish the oil.
The flowers faded in the heat of the day.
The fruit was overripe even yesterday.
Do not look for danger where there is none.
Your husband will return safely.

KANNAGI
It is that dream. So much of it has unfolded so far,
In such detail. Oh, that I had awakened sooner, or taken
Your advice and bathed in the waters of the temple tank.

DEVANTI
You should have, madam.

KANNAGI
I was proud then. I had nothing but pride
To sustain me in my unhappiness.
But I have a husband to care for again.
I have no more pride, only anxiety for his safety.

DEVANTI
If it is written in the book of fate
That if something must happen, none can alter it.
I hear the laughter of girls.
Mathari's daughters are here to entertain you.
Go out and watch their dancing and forget your cares.
I shall join you soon, madam.

(Kannagi goes out. Music is heard in the background. Devanti kneels and prays.)

DEVANTI
Do not cause my lady any more unhappiness
Oh, god. She has suffered enough.

Give her peace of mind and much needed
Domestic bliss in this quiet retreat.
There are rumours afloat. Let him
Return in safety, unharmed by the strange ways
Of the strange people in this strange city.
(Madhavi enters. She watches Devanti at prayer.)

MADHAVI
Is this the home of the cowherd
Where Kannagi stays with her husband?

DEVANTI
You? Here!

Intermission here

INTERLUDE: MADHAVI MEETS KANNAGI

Devanti is kneeling in prayer as at the end of the last scene. Sutradhar and Nati enter on tiptoe.

NATI
Hush. She is in prayer.

SUTRA
We are at a crossroads here.

NATI
Should we get on with the story of Kannagi?

SUTRA
Or should we take a diversion? A small but interesting side excursion?

NATI *(To audience)*
The way he puts it, you can be sure he has decided already. A diversion it will be.

SUTRA
Have you wondered about Madhavi? She has been talked about, but not seen.

NATI

Madhavi? Here, on stage? My turn to raise eyebrows. It's not done, you know.

SUTRA

Why not?

NATI

Give me one good reason to bring her on.

SUTRA

I will give you three. First, Kannagi and Madhavi, the two women in Kovalan's life, may appear to be opposites, but they have really influenced his life in a complementary way. They are the Yan and Ying in Kovalan's life.

NATI

Yin and Yang.

SUTRA

Whatever. And, second, equally important, many women would secretly wish that Kannagi and Madhavi should meet. *(Nati tries to react, Sutra cuts in)* Educated women like you!

NATI

And so, Madhavi undertakes the journey herself, tracks them down, and meets Kannagi in Mathari's hut. Why would she do that?

SUTRA

Let her explain it herself. *(He starts to leave)*

NATI

The third? *(Sutradhar stops)* The third good reason.

SUTRA

We have already seen her on stage before the intermission! *(Sutradhar and Nati leave quickly. Madhavi enters. She watches Devanti at prayer.)*

SCENE 2

MADHAVI

Is this the home of the cowherd
Where Kannagi stays with her husband?

DEVANTI

You? Here!

MADHAVI

Yes, it is I. You are Devanti, I believe.
Where is your mistress?

DEVANTI

And I had foolishly imagined we were safe here!
How did you find out? Who told you we were in Madurai?
What mischievous tricks are you about to play now?
Can you not leave us alone? Explain yourself.

MADHAVI

I shall, since you ask.
When my letter was returned, my message spurned,
I thought it was a passing mood, a lovers quarrel.
It was not easy, but I decided
The next day to go to Kannagi's house myself.

DEVANTI

Such audacity! The doorstep of a chaste and virtuous woman
Crossed by the husband's lover herself.

MADHAVI

It was love that gave me courage.
I found the house abandoned, and saw the emptiness of the place
Where my lover's wife had spent five unhappy years. I saw
The poverty that had crept in and the pride that hid it all
From the world and even from her own parents.
I realised then my part in her sorrow and decided to make amends
And to return all the wealth that he had lavished on me.
A poor recompense, but...

DEVANTI

Are you really capable of regret and remorse? If so,
Prove it in deed, not in syrupy outpouring. Leave this city immediately.
Do not disturb once again a happy household.

MADHAVI

I will, when I have proved my innocence
And returned the wealth into rightful hands.

DEVANTI

How did you get here?

MADHAVI

When I found the house abandoned, I went
To your parents, hers and yours.

DEVANTI

What, there too?

MADHAVI

Yes, there too. I went to expose myself,
Acknowledge my sins, and to ask where you were,
And when you would return. They had no idea.
Worse, I was a messenger of sorrow.
They did not know you had left the city.

DEVANTI

You carry sorrow like an infected vermin.
Is it not time for your riddance?

MADHAVI

I carry a fate too. I had to follow it. I left the city
By the very same route that you took and trailed you
From one village to the next. I saw the temples where you had prayed,
The hutments where you had rested. My heart ached
For all the sufferings you had undergone.

DEVANTI

Fancy talk from a woman steeped in evil!
Charmer, seducer, destroyer of homes,
Priestess of immorality, listen to me.
Our lord Kovalan has no more wealth to offer you.
His love, or what remains of it, is pledged
To his wife. Your offer of help even if true
Will never be accepted, your innocence never believed.
You will be spurned, insulted and reviled
By him and by us all. You will gain nothing by staying here.
You sow the seeds of sorrow wherever you go.
Your looks are evil, your words poisonous, your intentions
Persistently foul. Go away and do not return.
I shall pray every day to all the gods for your salvation.
But go. If you remain here, your sins will multiply.
You will then face the tortures and miseries of hell for all eternity.
(Kannagi comes in)

KANNAGI

What is the noise here?

(She sees Madhavi. A long pause, held with great control. Finally, Madhavi chooses to address Kannagi.)

MADHAVI

Dear bonded sister, I hope you will let me
Call you my sister, for we have both loved
The same man and suffered for it.
I, unfortunate woman, am the cause of your misfortune
Without realising it. I have come to make amends for what is past.
I come not as a rival for your affections,
For I will not presume to compete with one as beautiful as you,
But as a humble slave, to do your bidding, to atone for past sins.

DEVANTI

Go away before my lady's rage is unleashed.
Go and do not return ever.

KANNAGI

Let her stay. Let her try out any seductive art
Newly acquired on my husband if she so desires.
If he is to fall for them again,
Then I do not deserve a husband.
(A pause)
Miserable woman, have you not a shred of virtue for cover?
No modesty or shame, no dignity or self-respect,
Nor even the pride of your profession, that you must take the road
In search of another woman's husband?

MADHAVI

Dear sister, dear lady, you are a respectable wife.
Society guards your honour, protects your rights,
Upholds your claims and condemns the husband if he leaves you.
Custom bars you from following the man you love,
Demands that you wait and suffer.
I have no such rights, nor the duty to detain myself for the man I love.
My name is at the mercy of every rogue. My house is marked
As a place of ill-fame, a den of vice.
The men who claim to protect the virtue of women
Readily besmirch my name.
Though I practice the noblest of the arts,
No one dares or cares to protect my chastity.

KANNAGI

What protection did I have when my husband deserted me
Squandering all his wealth on you?

MADHAVI

Your wealth was not protected, but your honour was.
(A pause)
Listen to me awhile and then condemn me if you will.
You married him by the wish of your parents, to the chant of hymns
Presided over and blessed by Brahmins.

Duty bound you to him for life as he was to you.
No duty compelled me.
No virtue, honour or chastity held me back.
My freedom was the reward for bearing scorn.
The goddess of love must have sent your husband to me.
She tossed an enchanting net around us both,
Trapping us like helpless birds. We lived as such,
Sharing the ecstasy of a love so sweet that all else was ignored.
No bonds but those of love held us together
Until our daughter arrived.

KANNAGI
You have a daughter...

MADHAVI
Yes, the image of your husband.

KANNAGI
Devanti, you didn't tell me our lord has a daughter.

DEVANTI
I didn't think you would like to know, madam.

KANNAGI *(Turns to Madhavi)*
Then, lucky woman, be satisfied.
Do not aspire for more and cause
Needless unhappiness all around.
You have had his wealth, then his child
And you have had his love, not without passion,
For more than a few casual nights. What more can you want?

MADHAVI
I have not come here for my wants.

DEVANTI
Do not listen to her madam. Did you not hear what our lord said?
Her words are cleverly play-acted, perfected with practice.
Her eyes and gestures are trained to express any mood needed.
Her face is a mask that can be changed at will.
All these are aids to her cunning designs.

Send her away before you too fall a victim to her snares.
(Kannagi motions to Devanti to wait outside. She exits. A pause.)

MADHAVI

Not for my wants. Yes, I have desired him in the past.
In truth the desire persists, but now his love is exclusively for his wife.
Never again will I come between you and him. I have come
Only to prove my innocence to him. He suspected me needlessly.
I also wish to offer you all the wealth I possess,
For which I have no use. I am here to beg your pardon
For the past, for the misery you have suffered on my account.

KANNAGI

The woman is presumptuous too! Do you dare offer me sympathy?
Do you dare offer me tainted gold as compensation for your sins?
Do you dare call me sister? Do you not know my station,
My surname and my virtues by birth? Do you think
You can purchase my pardon with your ill-gotten wealth?

MADHAVI

You insult me needlessly, my dear.
In the eyes of the compassionate almighty we are both
Unfortunate women paying penalties earned in former lives.
Birth and station in this world are not taken into account in the next.
As for virtue, I surely acknowledge yours,
And realise that I cannot expect you to see any in me.

KANNAGI

A miserable courtesan, virtuous!

MADHAVI

Yes, strange as it may seem, I have virtue.
Whatever others may say, my life has dedication.
I am devoted to the noble art of dance
And my heart has been constant in its love.

KANNAGI

For another woman's husband!

MADHAVI

Will you understand helplessness? If we could but control
Our hearts as easily as we do our hands and feet in dance,
Then every woman would be an angel, and this world
An earthly paradise. In my weakness I found strength.
If I had yielded to the tempting offers of other men, my fame
Would have been greater. I was constant and true to my lover
Out of my devotion. Don't you call that virtue?

KANNAGI

You stuck to him only because of his wealth.

MADHAVI

How simple a judgment from a woman wronged!
I had the wealth of the city of Puhar for the asking.
But all that I have is all that he gave me.
I know it is all yours. I wish to restore it to you,
The rightful owner, whenever you command.

KANNAGI

Answer me this.
Did you not sing faithless songs of longing and pretend
You were in love with someone else?
If you were as sincere as you claim and loving,
Why did you lie to him with such conviction?

MADHAVI

I had no ties recognised by custom to keep him by my side.
And when there are no ties, a woman is in constant danger
Of her man leaving. Every other woman is a rival,
Especially one that is beautiful, and the suffering wife,
The emblem of sacrifice looks more attractive from a distance.
You feel the pain of jealousy where no cause exists.
We were more possessive than a husband and wife would be.
Bonds of love that seemed pure and divine became shackles
From which he longed to get loose. I was in agony.
Jealousy was the only means of keeping alive his love for me.

KANNAGI

Are you saying he was tiring of you?
That the passion was flagging?

MADHAVI

No, it did not appear so. It was guilt, I think,
A wounded conscience. There were times when he used to sit
For hours and not utter a word, but gaze into the emptiness
That seemed to envelop him. Even our daughter's pranks
Failed to amuse him. Many were the times I longed to ask him
About you, but he would not share his thoughts with me.

KANNAGI

Let me confess, I have often wondered about you,
What you were like, what charms you possessed, the arts
You practiced, the love you bore for the man I claimed as mine.

MADHAVI

I wondered about you too. If we had only known each other
As women first, we could have learned to share the man
We both loved, and made him doubly happy and contented.

(Kannagi calls for Devanti and prepares to leave. Devanti enters and waits.)

KANNAGI

My mind is listening, but my heart rebels.
You are the cause of all my misery and I hate you still.
How can I ever share my only man with another woman?
But your words ring in my ears.
And your thoughts, strange as they sound, seem pure.
You have a ready answer to all my questions. Stay awhile and rest.
Meet my husband if you like, and let him decide your fate.

(Mathari comes in, very agitated, and whispers to Devanti. Kannagi turns to her.)

What is it my friend? You seem agitated, and my lord
Has not returned yet from the city of Madurai.
If you have news, do not hide them from me.

MATHARI

I bring you news. Prepare to hear it.

KANNAGI

Is it about my husband?

MATHARI

He was apprehended, accused of being a thief...

KANNAGI

Who dares to accuse him so?

MATHARI

He was accused, caught with the stolen goods, convicted and sentenced...

DEVANTI

There must be some mistake. It cannot be true.

MATHARI

He was executed at the king's command.

DEVANTI

It must have been idle street corner talk, someone else
Was executed, another stranger to this city.
They thought it was my lady's husband. *(She turns to Kannagi)*
Do not listen to her, madam. I shall go myself and find out the truth.
I am sure there is a mistake. It cannot be.

MADHAVI

Who told you about this? Did you see the execution?
Did you watch the trial? What proof do you have?
How do you present such a dreadful tale as a matter of fact?

MATHARI

How I wish it were not so! How much I wish that my tongue
Had been cut off before I repeated it! I should have died
On my way here, rather than bring such a sorry tale
To end your happiness for all time. But I fear it is true.

KANNAGI

My husband!

MADHAVI

My lover, my life!

KANNAGI

Is this the fate of one so bold, so true,
One too proud to accept the help of his own parents?
To die accused of being a thief with no defence...
Oh unjust king! Unjust kingdom! Oh fate! Oh fate!
We tempted you when we came to this accursed city.
If only you had stayed with Madhavi and left me
In my unhappiness. This horrible death is too cruel,
Undeserved, unjustified.

MADHAVI

You were so full of life. You gave life to others
When they were in fear of death. None returned from your doorstep
Empty handed. Thousands sing your praises, remember you in prayer.
Could not their blessings protect you from your fate?

DEVANTI

How did it happen? How did you know? What else do you know?

MATHARI

When I left you some time ago, I met my husband in the streets.
People gathered and talked of this unusual theft by a stranger,
How bold he had been, and how angry the king was
That his queen's precious anklet should have been stolen.

DEVANTI

Anklet? The queen's anklet?

MATHARI

That was what we were told.
A stranger approached the king's jeweller and offered for sale
The queen's anklet, saying that it was his wife's and they had come
From a far-off land in search of a new life.

It seems the jeweller reported it to the king,
Who sent his guards immediately to recover the ornament
And punish the thief by instant death.

DEVANTI

How did you know it was my lady's husband?
It could be any stranger, from any town.

MATHARI

We heard it talked about again and again.
The repeated description of the stranger and the anklet
Were ominous and led only to your lady's husband.
We went immediately to the jeweller's house where we saw...
Oh, I cannot bear to say it!

KANNAGI

Please tell us what you saw. The heart
Once broken cannot be further damaged.

MATHARI

I saw it there before me. It was your husband's body bathed
In his own blood. The head severed by a cruel axe had rolled away,
And idle spectators were walking past
Talking of a thief and his just punishment.

DEVANTI

Is the king's jeweller so vile, the king so incompetent, his guards
So foolish, that they cannot tell a thief from a noble, honest man?

KANNAGI

My husband, you left me once for another.
For whom have you left now? Which heavenly angel has
Enticed you to another world?
And is this unjust king a mere accomplice in such an act?
You promised me at dawn today that you would be back
Before nightfall. For how many sunsets shall I wait this time?

MADHAVI

You left me for your wedded wife. For whom
Have you left us both now, my beloved?
You would not hurt a single enemy in your life.
Why did you choose to hurt your lovers in your death?

KANNAGI

Felled by a mere assassin,
Why did you venture out of our home?
Simple-minded, to be tricked by the very first rogue
You met, why did you leave our beloved Puhar?
If you were so foolish, so ill-informed about this woeful kingdom
And its immoral king, what made you choose this city?

MADHAVI

When the cursed axe fell on your neck,
What were your thoughts, my love? Was the blade too sharp,
The blow too accurate, to leave any time for thought?
Or did the messenger of death hack you over and over again
In a crude, cowardly way? What were your thoughts then?
Did you think of me, of our brief but blissful love,
Of our silly pranks, happy duets, nights on the beach,
Expeditions on the river? Did memories flash by?
Did you think of a daughter and her clever chatter?
Did you think of my faithlessness, if it was true, or only imagined
In a love quarrel? Was there even a fleeting thought of a woman
In another part of your life, or were the last moments
Too precious to be wasted on her?

KANNAGI

Did I leave my home, my parents and my friends and everything
I had known and loved merely to follow you to your cremation?
No, my lord, I shall follow you far beyond the blazing pyre.
I shall search every corner of heaven and hell
And claim you as my husband even in death.

MADHAVI

I loved you more than any other on this earth. Now you are gone,
My love will be cremated with your remains. Let it be consumed
By the leaping flames. Let the rising smoke spread over
The entire earth. Through your love I shall learn to love the universe.
Every living thing, creeping or crawling,
Bird or flower, frog or serpent,
They will be equally dear to me, for they possess
The divine pulse of life that once was yours.
My feet will no longer dance to the gay tunes
That once attracted men. My body will not
Cause distracting thoughts by its gait. My eyes
Will not carry on a silent conversation as bait.
With all this put away forever
I shall serve all living things.

MATHARI

My dear lady, we all suffer with you.

KANNAGI

Is this the fabled land of hope and glory
Praised in song and verse where philosophers abound,
Where the land is prosperous and the rains do not fail?
Is this the city ruled by a king steeped in wisdom,
Inhabited by civilised people where honesty is rewarded
And trickery swiftly punished?
It is a jungle where wild beasts roam to satisfy their hunger;
Where there is no law, only cruel, selfish, greed; no justice,
Only the wishes of a tyrant King; no warmth for the unfortunate;
No compassion for guests. This is the state praised
In song and verse by lackey minstrels. We have come here
Not to make our fortune, but to meet our doom.

MATHARI

My dear lady, we are all grieved that such misfortune
Should overtake you. I am doubly grieved that you should meet

Your wretched fate under my roof. But your anger,
Though natural, may be unjust.
The anklet was the queen's they say.
No one else has the wealth to own such an ornament.

DEVANTI

Ignorant woman! Do you dare to suggest that our lord
Would stoop to such tricks as practised only in this kingdom?

In the land where the sacred Kaveri flows,
Nourishing the land and nurturing its peoples, there are
A thousand merchants more wealthy than your miserable king.

KANNAGI

What cruel destiny, what manner of sins committed
In our former life, what retribution for unavenged wrongs,
Which gods that we failed to propitiate have driven us to this cruel fate,
I know not. This woman here, my friend and protector,
Who gave me shelter in a friendless city and welcomed me
With open arms, even she suspects my husband.
The title of thief, repeated by the ignorant, confirmed
By the king's execution, sung by minstrels hired by the king
Will stick to his name for all time.
But I shall defy them all.
I shall prove to the world he was innocent.
I shall not snap the marriage string on my neck, nor demean myself
Wearing white, being pointed out as a carrier of bad luck,
As one whose chastity failed to protect her husband in his hour of need.
I shall not be ordained into a widowed life. I do not recognise
His death. I proclaim now before all present here
That my lord was innocent and was done to death by foul means.
I swear that I shall restore the truth from the web of falsehood
Before the sun descends tonight.

I kneel before my god in submission, but my prayer is a demand.
I expect you, oh god, to attend to me swiftly.
As a chaste and virtuous wife, equal in love and sacrifice
To all the heroines of our holy books
I demand that the heavens should give me proof
Of my husband's innocence.
(The rumbling sound of thunder is heard)

MATHARI
It is a sunny, cloudless sky
Yet we hear thunder. There is no rain and we see lightning.
Pardon me, divine lady, for suspicions
Even for a moment about your husband.

DEVANTI
Your call has been answered. All the world will soon know
He was innocent. There has been a cruel miscarriage of justice.

MATHARI
I shall bear witness to the miracle we have just seen.
I shall proclaim to the inhabitants of this city that your husband
Was wrongly done to death.
But first I must make arrangements for the funeral.

KANNAGI
I have no more tears to shed. I will not light the funeral pyre.
I will go directly to the king's palace.
I have a mission to carry out.

MADHAVI
There is no going back on the fact of death. We know
The gods have proved him innocent. Let us be content with that.
Your anger has divine sanction. Do not let it loose needlessly.

KANNAGI
If I am driven to silence I shall be an accomplice to the injustice.
My husband's death must be avenged
As much for my anger as for the anguish of all righteous women.

INTERLUDE: KANNAGI'S DESTINY

Kannagi remains kneeling. The others withdraw. If there is a dance sequence, emissary angels of Indra, the god of fire, may bless Kannagi with floral offerings and then carry her away. If there is no dance, the percussion group may play before Kannagi and around her and escort her away at the end of her prayer. Sutradhar and Nati provide the link.

NATI

Was it wise, Madhavi seeking out Kannagi? The meeting, face to face?

SUTRA

If it had to be, it had to be.

NATI

It is not the done thing. They have their different spaces, the courtesan and the wife.

SUTRA

The playwright thought it necessary, so they met.

NATI

Adigal Ilango himself?

SUTRA

The one who wished to present the tale on stage today. He thought it necessary.

NATI

So they met. I'll tell you something? At the end I was glad they did.

SUTRA

So was I. It was a good meeting, was it not?

NATI

Woman to woman. Defying all caricatures of women in rivalry.

SUTRA

Two tall women!

NATI

She could not meet Kovalan, though.

SUTRA

She could not. It was too late.

NATI

What a horrible death for Kovalan!

SUTRA

Even the great goddess of Madurai could do nothing about it.

NATI

Tell them about it. *(Refers to the audience)*

SUTRA

Kannagi demanded an explanation from the presiding goddess of the city of Madurai. How did this great injustice take place? Was this the way she protected newcomers to the great city?

NATI

The goddess explained that Kovalan had to die because of sins of commission in a previous life.

SUTRA

He was known as Bharata then. He had abandoned virtuous conduct and turned into a cruel rake.

NATI

Bharata had a merchant called Sangaman beheaded, a totally rash and unjust act.

SUTRA

Sangaman's wife, Neeli, killed herself, but not before cursing Bharata and calling on the gods to deliver the same fate to him.

NATI

Once set on course, no power could alter the destiny for Bharata, which was fulfilled in his next life as Kovalan.

SUTRA

Kannagi might have resorted to the same course, cursed the King and ended her own life.

NATI

But she did not. She sought nothing less than a revolution was in the order.

SUTRA

And the gods were with her in her resolve.

NATI

Indra, the god of fire himself.

SUTRA

No less. The cleansing of the city of Madurai could be accomplished only with the help of Indra.

NATI

And to think it was all because of a crooked palace jeweller!

SUTRA

That is one way of looking at it.

NATI

And a scheming minister.

SUTRA

Wait! You could say that they were also doing only what they had to do.

NATI

Their little bit in the grand design.

SUTRA

Intertwined with the destinies of Kovalan and Kannagi.

NATI

If the jeweller had not stolen the queen's anklet himself...

SUTRA

With his privileged access to her jewellery room...

NATI

If the jeweller had not been the thief himself...

SUTRA

We would not have a last scene to perform!

NATI

But first, we must have the confrontation with the king. Kannagi must meet the king.

SUTRA

And the queen. Kannagi is determined to confront the king in his palace, but the matter concerns the queen as well.

(Nati and Sutradhar withdraw)

ACT III

SCENE 1

The queen's chamber at the palace in Madurai. The queen is waiting impatiently for the king. He enters.

QUEEN
When did I see this gentleman visitor last?
Let me count the hours, days, weeks. Or is it months?

KING
I know, I know. I stand accused.
I have neglected a household duty, but not abandoned it.

QUEEN
Not any household duty.

KING
But the all-important one of
Attending to the queen at sunset.

QUEEN
And after. You are so full of the cares of state
That you have no time for a mere queen.
It is said that you are the unchallenged lord of this land,
That your enemies tremble at the mention of your name,
That you are so wise and just the wild beasts in your forests
Do not molest men on legitimate business.
I have so often heard your poets declaim
Your slightest wish as the supreme desire of your subjects.
Your thoughts are their commandments,
Your will is law. And yet, is not your time your own?

KING
The work of a ruler is never finished. There is no one

To whom I can delegate my authority.
I alone am responsible to god for the acts of those who
Govern the land, for they are carried out
Under my name. I have to remain above all
But remain within reach.

QUEEN

In the moments you spare for me, your mind is preoccupied.
You hear my words without listening.
Your conversation is distanced and half-hearted. Your ministers
And your problems of state follow you
Into the sanctuary of our private chamber.

KING

It will be hard for you to understand, my dear.
My task is severe in demands.

QUEEN

Try to convince me.

KING

For a start, I have to know everything about all
So that I may be constant in my vigilance.
The clever scheming of selfish courtiers, the flattery
Of those who wish to keep me in ignorance of my weaknesses,
The harmful advice of unfaithful ministers
are all my constant enemies, of whom I must beware.
The protection of the realm from foes outside
Or from disruptions inside is a sacred duty
That I shoulder without rest.
Above all, I have to guard against
The tyranny of my own unbridled power.

QUEEN

You are a god to your people, are you not?

KING

That would be presumptuous.

QUEEN
A demi-god then.

KING
I have the responsibilities, certainly, but unfortunately
Not the powers or the wisdom of any kind of god.

QUEEN
Many are the days that I have sat
By the fountain in the garden and waited
For your visit. I have watched my rippling shadow
In the pool fade and disappear with the sunset.
Many are the nights I have sat by the window
And counted the stars, saying to myself
My love will surely come before I have counted
A hundred. How often have I numbered
All the stars in the firmament in vain!

KING
Today I am early,
Before the sun sets and before the stars are lit.
Today I have given orders not to be disturbed.
I shall devote the entire evening to pleasing you
And entertaining myself.

QUEEN
How strange that sounds coming from you.
If I were of a suspicious nature,
Or of a jealous temperament, I would think
You had a mistress hidden somewhere
In one of your numerous offices of state. But tell me more
About your late evening duties.

KING
I cannot rely on the reports of my courtiers,
Or even my ministers, for their practiced blabber
Is only what they know I like to hear. They carefully hide the rest.
So, I often walk the city streets after dark, disguised

As a merchant or a beggar, and listen to people talking,
Deciphering what they really think about me.
The price of street gossip is foregoing
The pleasures of being with my queen every evening.

QUEEN

And what public wrong or private grievance
Have you set right today?

KING

It is both public and private.
Public, because a clever thief from another land
Has been caught and executed. Private,
Because the grievance of my queen has been set right.
Your eyes show interest. Shall I proceed?

QUEEN

My wise king is clever too. He knows that his queen is curious.
But the queen detects a matching gleam
In the king's eye. Perhaps he is eager to tell the tale.
In reply the queen says yes, you may proceed.

KING

You will recall, how can you forget, a precious anklet
That was mysteriously lost some days back.
It caused you much grief. Shall I continue?

QUEEN

Stop teasing me like a newly married groom
And get on with it.

KING

Well, if such is the queen's wish.
The anklet has been recovered from the thief.
The king is thus doubly satisfied.

QUEEN

Have you got the anklet?

KING

Here it is. It is the one you lost, I believe.

QUEEN

The king, after all, is a man.
How can a woman expect a husband to recognise her ornaments,
Or even notice them when they are worn?

KING

An ornament is not made to draw attention
To itself, but to the body wearing it.

QUEEN

So, my king does have an eye
For detail, shall we say?

KING

There can be no ornament of such grand design,
In such purity of gold and exquisite craftsmanship,
Except on the ankles of a Pandyan queen.

QUEEN

I cannot believe you have really got it back. I am so pleased.
How did you catch the thief?
How did he get past all the palace guards?
What punishment did he get? I have more questions.

KING

You were in such rage when it was lost.
Does your pleasure at its recovery compensate adequately?

QUEEN

Of course I was in rage! Precious jewellery
Was missing from the queen's chamber,
And all the king's forces were rendered incompetent.
Nobody knew who the thief was or where to find him.
Is that a matter for congratulations?
But now he is found and punished too.
Tell me how it was found and who found it,

So that I may reward him properly.

(There is commotion outside, followed by an urgent knocking on the door)

KING

Who is it? Who dares to disturb the king
When he is with his queen?
(The knock on the door is repeated)
Come in!
(The minister enters in distress)

MINISTER

It is I, your Majesty, begging your mercy and your pardon.
I would not dare to disturb your privacy
Unless it was of genuine importance.

QUEEN

Have the king's commands no respect in this palace?

KING

What is it?

MINISTER

A woman stands by the palace gates and demands
An immediate audience with the king.

KING

I see. I am not aware of any royal command
That it is the business of the king to find out
What a woman needs if she stands by the palace gate.
Can you not pacify her if she is aggrieved?
Give her alms if it is charity she needs?
Or if she needs the protection of the state from the cruelties
Of a roguish husband or a tyrant father, can you not arrange it
Without the king's consent? Have you not learned
The elementary duties of your office?

MINISTER

She is no ordinary woman, your Majesty.
Her eyes though filled with tears are balls of fire.
Her voice is soft, but her words harsh,

Ringing through the streets like a terrible curse arrived.
The people are afraid of her and speak in whispers in her presence.
She swears vengeance on this realm and on the ruler,
Yet no one dares to hold her back. The guards tremble at her sight.
Holy anger surrounds her presence. She is possessed
By a powerful spirit. There is none
To resist her anger or her demands.

KING *(To the queen)*
You see how I am kept busy, my dear.
A distracted, unhappy and probably mad woman
Chooses to raise her voice
And the minister of the king is struck with fright.
The palace guards tremble at her sight, he says.
So, the king has to forfeit his privacy, grant an audience
Immediately and find out what the complaint is and set it right.

MINISTER
Believe me, sir, this woman is a messenger of evil.
She will not reveal her mind to anyone but you.
I am sure she has some vile designs. That is why
I have come in all haste to ask for your advice.

KING
The minister is supposed to advise the king, I believe.
There is a convention in this state to that effect,
And yet, you come here to ask for mine.
Has your mind been emptied of all experience and wisdom
That you do not know how to act? You do not answer.
The verdict is empty. Bring the woman here.
Let her say what she wishes in our presence.

MINISTER
Do not see her, your Majesty!
Give me the order to imprison her or at least
Send her away beyond the borders of our state.
For she utters blasphemies against your sacred person and against
The justice of your rule.

KING

You ask for my advice and then presume to give it yourself.
The woman surely has great influence
To upset your powers of reason. She must be
Interesting, even if not in her senses. I will grant her request
If only to see her for myself and to hear her speak.

QUEEN

Please do what the minister says, my lord.
She seems an undesirable element. More likely a pest
Set to disturb our evening. Perhaps she deserves the fate
That has befallen her. Remember, this evening is mine.

KING

Do not upset yourself, my dear, I promise you
Some unusual entertainment.

MINISTER

Strange things have been happening in the city, sire,
It is a disturbed state. All work has been suspended.
The merchants have closed their shops. The craftsmen
No longer ply their trade. The chatter of the women by the riverside
Has ceased. The Brahmins chanting their hymns have fallen silent.
The Buddhist monks whose eternal calm is never disturbed
Seem perturbed today. All are apprehensive, of what
They do not know. They dare not talk aloud.
They stand in groups in the public squares and in the streets
And exchange signs and whispers.
Only thieves and rogue characters move about boldly,
While honest men are nowhere to be found.
There is panic everywhere.
No reasons given, no complaints made, no one accused,
The air is full of sorrow, a feeling of impending doom.

KING

All this because of one woman who stands at the palace gates!

MINISTER

Yes, your majesty! Her words are arrows piercing
The hearts of men. Her rage is a fire that consumes
Everything it falls upon. Men follow her in trance,
With fear, but reverence, ashamed of themselves,
For she accuses them all of betrayal.
Yet, unable to resist her fiery presence,
They gather like moths around a flame.

KING

You proclaim she is evil, but imply she is divine.
How is that possible? If she is a heavenly spirit
And brings her curse upon this city,
Do you think we can avoid it by imprisoning her?
Yours is not the counsel of a minister.
Advice should be given after calm consideration
Of all the factors involved, without emotion
Or passion clouding judgment. You do not appear fit
To advise now. You are driven by a fear of the unknown.

MINISTER

Your Majesty, this is not a case that can be judged
Without fear. The woman inspires nothing but fear
In all around her, uncontrolled, unrestrained.
She walks the streets like a fearless, unconquered foe in an alien land.
Please let the army deal with her.

KING

My friend, the army takes charge only when
The ministers are bankrupt of all wisdom, and justice
Cannot be enforced by law. But what madness is this?
A woman comes to the palace gates and demands
Justice from the king, and the minister of the state

Requests that the army should deal with her!
There is something mysterious in all this.
If her demand is just, she shall have it fulfilled,
Whatever the cost. I shall see her immediately.

QUEEN
No, my lord.

KING
I should not see her?

QUEEN
Do not give her audience.

KING
You will have to give me a reason,
A counsel wiser than the minister's.

QUEEN
I ask as a queen.

KING
The king seeks a reason so that
His people know him as reasoned and reasonable.

QUEEN
It was a dream.

KING
The queen had a dream.
That will be the preamble to the king's verdict
Before a woman out of her senses is put away.

QUEEN
Call it a vision, then.
A premonition, a woman's intuition:
This woman may be the face of ruination.
I beg you, listen to the minister.

KING
All men must act by comprehension.
A king no less.

QUEEN

What a woman senses
A man cannot always comprehend.
(There is commotion at the entrance to the chamber)

SCENE 2

KING

Am I not the guardian of my people, the fountain of justice where every citizen drinks his fill? *(Kannagi has entered, followed by the leader of the palace guard. She stares defiantly at the king.)*

KANNAGI

Are you? Are you indeed the guardian?
The upholder of law, destroyer of evil, protector of the innocent?
Have you been ordained by God to rule this state?

GUARD

We tried to stop her, sire,
But she would not be stopped.

KING

Never mind, let her go on.

KANNAGI

Are you a descendant of the renowned Pandya lineage?

KING

I am a king of Pandyan descent. I am also a king by my own right,
By the valour of my armies, by the justice
Of my rule and by the affection of my subjects.

KANNAGI

Then why do you hide yourself in your wife's chamber
When there is justice to be done
And injustice to be undone?
Why is your palace so heavily guarded?

Why do your ministers show valiant effort
To frighten me with foolish threats?
Is this the justice of your rule? It is clear
You are no king, but a tyrant and a thief!

MINISTER

You are not in the streets anymore, stranger,
Casting a spell on a hapless mob.
Be careful how you address the king.
Accusing the monarchy with arrogant utterances!

KING

Young woman, it may be that you are distracted,
You might have suffered at the hands
Of some foul villain. But that is no cause
To accuse us of being tyrants.
You will receive justice
If you deserve it, and any wrong shall be set right
Insofar as it lies within our mortal power.
However, if you desire justice from the king,
You should show the respect that is due to him.
Your face appears noble, your carriage cultured.
You speak from the heart, but your words are harsh.
What is it that you desire?

KANNAGI

My husband has been murdered wrongfully
And I have come to demand the justice
That he failed to receive in your city,
And to take revenge on the one who caused his death,
The king of this land.

KING

That is no way to demand justice from a king.
But still, explain yourself. Who are you?
Where do you come from? Who was your husband?
How did he come to die? What cause have you
To burden us with his death?

KANNAGI

I am the daughter of a merchant prince
In the great city of Puhar. My name is Kannagi.
My husband was Kovalan. There, I have taken his name.
We came to your accursed city in search of fortune.
Driven from our home by fate, though of noble birth,
We came to set up a trade and start
A new life with a fresh purpose.
I had an anklet.
It was an anklet of incomparable beauty
And immense value, in price and in sentiment.
Do not look surprised. You cannot know
The craftsmanship of our beloved land.
My husband took the ornament into the city
To have it assessed and seek a suitable price for sale.
It would provide the start to our venture.
He was directed to the best jeweller
In the city of Madurai, the king's jeweller.

KING

Was it not our jeweller that reported
The thief to the palace?

MINISTER

It was, my lord. He recognised the anklet at once.
He knew about the theft.

KING

He had presence of mind detaining the thief
While the palace guards rushed to make the arrest.

KANNAGI

He was not arrested to be accorded a just process of enquiry
As accepted in all civilised reigns. He was charged,
Accused and handed a verdict in the same breath. In the next
He was murdered on the spot. They called it delivery of justice.

KING

Is it not justice in your land to punish a thief?
We regard it a grave offence.

KANNAGI

Unjust king! You did not kill a thief, but an honest man
And so became a thief yourself.

KING

Your rash and foul utterance may be excused
Because of your grief, drawing on our patience
As our mercy has no bounds.
But your husband was caught with the anklet in his hands.
In a country where there are no thieves and no cause for thieving,
Any infiltration must be exterminated quickly.
Delay encourages rapid spread of the contagion.

KANNAGI

What proof did you have against him?

MINISTER

The anklet was found in his possession. When questioned
He admitted to possessing it. By these words
He accused himself. That was evidence enough and more.

KANNAGI

Does that hold water in courts of justice in this wretched city?
How does possession make one a thief?

KING

Does not the possession of stolen property
Make the possessor a thief and a villain?

KANNAGI

You make too many connections, in too much haste.
The queen to the anklet, the anklet to theft,
The theft to my husband. What if the anklet
In his possession was neither stolen nor the queen's?

MINISTER

An ornament of such value could belong

To none other than the queen.

KANNAGI
What if the anklet was mine?

KING
Impudent woman! The anklet was made
By my jeweller who recognised it immediately.
Does not the maker know his work when he sees it?

KANNAGI
Foolish king! Do you think a thief clever enough
To steal from your well-guarded palace
Would turn stupid overnight
And try to sell a stolen ornament to your jeweller?

MINISTER
The thief was caught with the stolen anklet
And that was that.

KANNAGI
What if the jeweller himself was the thief?

MINISTER
The jeweller is an honest and trustworthy man.
He has been long and loyal in our service.

KANNAGI
I see it clearly now. The jeweller a convenient accomplice
In the crime. The king the trusting fool.
The minister the master villain of the act.

MINISTER
If you do not mind your tongue, woman,
I shall order you to be removed by the guards!

KANNAGI
Just as you stopped me from entering, I suppose!
But let me ask the unfortunate queen now,
When was your anklet stolen?

QUEEN
About ten days ago.

KANNAGI

Ten days. That was nine days before we arrived
On the outskirts of Madurai. *(The Minister snorts)*
There are ample witnesses.

MINISTER

That is easy for a clever thief. He might
Employ other men to do the dirty deed.
He might bribe the servants of the palace.

KANNAGI

Bribery? In the palace of a Pandyan king?

MINISTER

The evil influence of foreigners.
He might receive the stolen goods outside the city
Entering later only to close transactions.

KANNAGI *(Ignoring him, addressing the king)*

When did you find out about the theft?
Who told you of it first? What action did you take?

KING

My jeweller rushed to the palace this morning,
Sought my audience urgently and informed me that a man
Was waiting in his house with an anklet, wishing to sell it,
The one that was missing from the palace.

KANNAGI *(To the queen)*

He knew it was missing?
Had the jeweller been informed of the loss?

QUEEN

Not by me directly. There has been no visit
To the palace by him since the theft.
The palace authorities must have informed him.

KING

I thought he had been informed by you.

KANNAGI

Blissful ignorance! Does the king wish to enquire now
How the jeweller knew about the theft?

MINISTER

That does not matter in the least, your Majesty,
The theft was known to all palace staff.
The jeweller would know too. He came to you
As soon as he saw the thief and the stolen ornament.

KANNAGI

What if he had not been informed by anyone?
After all, he was not at the palace since the theft.
He would know of the loss then by being the thief himself.

MINISTER

Enough of your wild and reckless fantasies!
The jeweller, like every honest servant of the king,
Was only being dutiful in reporting the thief.

KANNAGI *(To the king)*

What did you do when you were told by the jeweller
That the thief was waiting in his house?

KING

We sent our guards with him to locate the ornament,
To make sure it was in the thief's possession,
To confirm he claimed ownership of it
And then to execute him. Justice had to be swift.
The leader of the guards will tell you the rest.

GUARD

The thief was waiting in the jeweller's workshop, see.
The jeweller pointed him out to us. I went up to him,
Asked him to show me the anklet, which he did, see,
And claimed it was his wife's.
But I knew it belonged to the queen, see.

KANNAGI

How did you know that?

GUARD

As a loyal and obedient guard, conscious of my station, see,
I have always looked at the queen's feet while I spoke to her.
Not at her divine face, see.
I recognised the anklet, all right.

MINISTER

Well spoken, my friend. Proceed.

KANNAGI

Did you charge him of the theft then?

GUARD

Oh, no, I could not do that.

KANNAGI

Why ever not?
Being on a mission to apprehend a thief?

GUARD

We are trained, see. We mix caution
With cleverness of action. We were forewarned
By the jeweller that the thief moved
Suspiciously in the city. He was a stranger, see.
He might be armed, or have an armed band nearby,
Ready to spring at a signal. So I played it cool like, see,
And pretended to be sent by the king. If he was interested
In selling, we could talk about the price, I said.
I had to get close enough, see.

KANNAGI

You were not ashamed to kill a man without stating
A charge, backed by proof. You struck a cowardly blow
While his back was turned to you taking out the ornament.
Is that how you maintain the honour of the king?

GUARD

What I said to myself too, lady, when I first saw the man.
His face was straight, see. Not the face of a thief.
He told us of his folly in his native land, and how

He came to be in the sorry state of having to sell
The jewels that belonged to his wife, see.
But he was clever, see, cleverer than us.
He had sised the stranger up. He assured us the man was a villain
Who combined the art of robbery
With a clever tongue and disguise, and warned us, see
Not to be taken in. What's more, being from a foreign land,
He could be using magic, see.
We had to strike him down before his suspicions were aroused.
We were reminded then to carry out
The orders of the king, see, which were
To recover the ornament and kill the thief.
It's not for us to judge or ask why.

KING

The action of my guards might appear hasty
At first sight, but they are to be lauded.
The fact remains that the man possessed
The stolen property, and so had to pay the penalty of death.
Now, woman, be satisfied that our rule is just.
We shall do what is in our power to alleviate your grief.
For it is not our intention to punish the innocent needlessly.
And we shall see that you do not suffer
For the crimes of your husband.

KANNAGI

Alleviate grief?
Can you bring my husband back to life?
I am here to accuse you of murder and demand justice.
Do you think I am here for charity?

KING

The proof, woman!
You must prove your husband to be innocent.

KANNAGI

Why should I prove him to be innocent
When you have not proved him guilty?

MINISTER

Do not quibble with words, woman.
He had the queen's anklet in his hands.

KANNAGI

The queen's anklet, did you say?

KING

Yes. Happily it is restored to her.

KANNAGI

The queen's anklet, let me see it.
(The queen hesitates. The king motions to her to show it.)

QUEEN

Here it is. *(She unclasps the anklet from her foot and holds it out.)*

KANNAGI *(She takes the anklet and examines it)*

Do you claim this as your own?

QUEEN

Of course!

KANNAGI

A lie! This anklet was my mother's gift to me.
I remember every line of gold, every figure
And every stone that is set in it.
By the law of your land you are a thief
By being in possession of it.

KING

Hold your tongue, woman!
We have been very indulgent with you
Because of your grief. We have tried by several means
To convince you of your husband's guilt.
You have lost your balance and are closed to reason.
You cannot see the weakness in your lover.
Your words are not those of a petition to the king,
But the arrogance of a disruptive rebel.

We cannot tolerate any more of your rants.
(*To the guard*)
Take her away!

KANNAGI

One moment, king! You have had the upper hand so far.
You failed to give the benefit of doubt to my husband,
And then found clever words to counter
My questions without answering them.
Your words are backed by the strength of your army
And by the craftiness of your ministers.
My husband is dead and his voice is stilled forever.
He cannot be heard in self-defence. But I am here still.
I am bound by an oath. I swear now on my chastity as a wife,
And on the honour of my dead husband
That this anklet is mine. I shall prove it presently.
I shall not myself deliver the justice that you have so well earned.
I shall hand you over to a council of gods.
Countless generations will condemn you
And your unjust rule as ignoble. You will sink
Into oblivion as a weak and vicious king,
Unworthy of his ancestry, who to please his wife
Had an honest man murdered.

KING

The proof! The proof! Or else
You will suffer the same fate as your husband
For your impertinence.

KANNAGI

What if I were to give you the proof?
What will you do then?

KING

If you show us beyond the shadow of a doubt
That I killed a man innocent of this crime
Then I too shall prove to you that though I failed

To rule like a king, I shall die like one.
I swear by the honour of all my ancestors
That I shall execute by my own hands
The punishment of death on myself. Further,
If I hesitate and delay the execution of my vow
May the gods themselves strike me down!

QUEEN

My lord! What rash and senseless words are these!
That woman is evil to the core. She merely
Takes advantage of your goodness.
You are not obliged to listen to her.

KING

The queen's anxiety is well placed.
I appeal to her to recall her own obligation
To trust the king's judgement.

MINISTER

You have spoken in haste, sire, in justified agitation.
But this woman is possessed, sire.
Withdraw your words before it is too late.

KING

My minister too! Then I am assured that there is confidence
In the land in the king's justice.
Do not be afraid, my friend. If she does prove me guilty,
I must die by my own law. But if she does not,
Then my fame shall shine all the brighter
For future kings to follow.
(Turns to Kannagi)
But if you should fail to prove
Your husband's innocence and my guilt,
Then you shall pay the penalty
Of being a false accuser of an honest man,
Being a traitor to the king, and being an arrogant
Rebel in pursuit of an ill-conceived cause.

KANNAGI

How can you be aware, foolish king, that the script
For your imminent doom is already written?
Only one person has seen it before its playing.
I have seen it played before me long before this day
And I see the scene unfolding before me now
In the same detail, moment by moment.
When you are dead by your own decree,
There will be death and destruction in your glorified city.
It shall burn for a fortnight at a stretch without respite.
On the last day, I will meet my husband on a lonely hill
And fly away with him in a heavenly chariot.
Only then will the fires cease,
For then my anger shall be appeased.

QUEEN

Listen to her! These are the ravings of a mad woman
Who has lost her head.

MINISTER

Let me take her away, your Majesty! The crowds are gathering
Outside the palace in mischievous curiosity.
They are getting unruly. Any further tolerance of this woman
Will be taken as a sign of weakness. It will result in rioting.
There may be looting and arson,
The fires the woman threatens.

KING *(Very agitated)*

The proof! Where is the proof?

KANNAGI

Ah, the king is agitated now. He is no longer foolishly confident.
He is afraid of those men, his beloved subjects as he calls them.
He is fearful of the justice of which he boasts so much!
He sees the sword of justice in his hand
With two sharpened edges. There is an edge facing him.

Suspicion is gnawing into his soul. Was it a mistake, he asks.
He is getting nervous. Where is his confidence now?
His foolish boasts and the display of power?

KING
Do not think you can taunt me, woman.
Whoever you are, good or evil, right or wrong,
Self-appointed priestess or the devil's agent, give me the proof.
If I have made a mistake, if I have failed as a king,
I shall still die nobly.

KANNAGI
Yes, poor man, you have made a terrible mistake,
And you shall pay for it just as my husband did with death.

KING
Then let it be quick. I order you now
Not to keep me waiting any longer.

KANNAGI
Your suffering is my victory. Should I not
Prolong it for effect? What is the hurry?

KING
The proof! Or I shall kill you with my own hands!

KANNAGI
You have a conscience, after all.
Though weak in judgement, you are not foul.
You are but a victim of your fate in your failure.

KING
Ignorant woman or ignoble, know this.
All my life I have given my people justice
That is unwavering and seen to be done.
If I fail this once, I am prepared to pay the price.
But I must be shown where I have failed.
Must I beg you now to show me?

KANNAGI
When the bullying fails, you beg. You are now

A worm that I can crush under my foot. Your death will be
Neither heroic nor epic as befits a king. It will not be
Triumphant, as in the death of a martyred enemy.
You will die a mere coward's death.

KING
If you will not let me have the proof,
Then we shall both die. The world
Shall know that I killed a woman. *(Draws his dagger)*

KANNAGI
This is the anklet
That you say was recovered from my husband?

KING
Yes! *(To the queen)* Is it not?

QUEEN
It is. The stolen ornament was returned to me.

KANNAGI
What stones did your jeweller put inside
To make your anklet jingle as you walk?

QUEEN *(Aside)*
I knew it! I half suspected it! Oh god, my god,
Save us! Let her be mistaken.

KING
Answer the question, my dear. What were the stones?

QUEEN
Stones, my lord?

KING
The stones inside the anklet.

QUEEN
The stones inside. Why, pearls, my lord.
The anklet has pearls inside.

KANNAGI
Pearls! Miserable pearls that every peasant woman

And fisherman's wife has for playthings in my home!
Are those the stones fit for a queen of the Pandyan kingdom?
Now, pay attention, all of you.
I call upon the gods of all the worlds
And all unborn generations to bear witness
To this act of mine. I proclaim that this anklet
In my hand, which you claim as yours,
Has no pearls at all inside.
I say it has only rubies of the purest strain.

(Sutradhar and Nati have entered. He is carrying the arati lamp. She carries a flower basket. Kannagi takes out a matching anklet.)

I should know. Here, do you see?
The matching anklet for the other foot?
Miserable rulers of a wretched land, look again!
And tell me what you see.

(She breaks open the anklet. Nati scatters red rosebuds from the basket in her hands.)

Precious rubies, red as the innocent blood you shed.
Rubies the size of rosebuds, found only in my blessed homeland
Never to be seen in your court or kingdom.

(There is stunned silence. The king recovers and strides to a corner. He holds his dagger in front of himself. The queen rushes to him.)

QUEEN

My king, my king!

KING

I am no king. I am a villain. I am a murderer.
I must die. *(He hesitates)*

(There is a crash of lightning. The king falls upon his dagger. The queen turns his body over, takes out the dagger and kills herself. The minister and guard rush to their side and kneel.

Kannagi drops to her knees and prays, the second anklet still in her hand. Sutradhar and Nati stand protectively above her. The minister and guard watch in awe from one side.

The light in Sutradhar's arati goes out. The cyclorama comes alive with the leaping flames of Madurai city on fire, as in the first scene of the play. Nati gives the flower basket to Kannagi, who walks towards the burning city, scattering flowers as she exits.

Sutradhar and Nati remain on stage.)

EPILOGUE

The minister and guard stand. They are joined by Sutradhar and Nati.

GUARD

What will I say to the family? I killed an innocent man.

MINISTER

She was wronged. I knew as she approached me that she had a case.

GUARD

I knew when I saw the man he was innocent. It was his face, see.
He was noble and upright.

MINISTER

I begged the king to send her away, did I not? Would he listen?
All this could have been avoided.

NATI

Avoided? Was it in your power?

MINISTER

His deed, for a start. He it was that killed a visitor from another city.

GUARD

I was carrying out orders! As a minister you did not give the right advice to the king when he most needed it.

SUTRA

The king? The queen? Was it in their power to alter the course?

NATI

Each of you did what you had to do. You were neither wise nor foolish,
Only faithful to your path.

GUARD

And now, this...The city in flames, houses crumbling, people cremated before their natural deaths.

MINISTER

At least we are safe within the walls of the royal palace.

SUTRA

Are you?

(There is a loud crashing sound)

GUARD

Loyal and faithful to our paths, are we not to be spared?

NATI

All of Madurai is to perish. All its people and all that they possess. Only the truly innocent may be spared, the children, the feeble and disabled, meek animals, and the truly chaste, such as Kannagi herself.

MINISTER

What is to become of her?

GUARD

Where does her path take her?

SUTRA

A chariot with wings awaits her at the top of the hill.

NATI

She will be united with the noble Kovalan in her new celestial home.

SUTRA

The gods have created for her a new position alongside themselves.

There is a role given to her.

NATI

Go now! Seek out your loved ones. Be united in your end.

SUTRA

Leave the palace. It will be the first to be turned to ash.

(The Minister and Guard exit.

There is a mighty roar as the flames get brighter.)

NATI

Henceforth, Kannagi, the chaste mortal wife, shall be known throughout the universe as a deity, and revered as Kannagi, the goddess of faithfulness.

SUTRA

Madurai burns. Let us rejoice. For out of the ashes shall arise a new Madurai, kinder and gentler in spirit, worthy of the goddess residing there.

Fade out

Close of play

Kurukshetra Burning!

An adaptation from
Smashana Kurukshetra** by **Kuvempu

FOR

SRINIVAS G KAPPANNA

CHARACTERS IN THE PLAY

Dhrutarashtra: *(Also spelt Dhritarashtra). King of Kuru kingdom with its capital in Hastinapur. He is blind.*

Gandhari: *The queen. She chooses to blindfold herself and give companionship to Dhrutarashtra.*

Kauravas: *The one hundred sons of Dhrutarashtra and Gandhari.*

Duryodhana: *The oldest of the Kauravas, and the leader of the clan. He is a famed warrior, not without virtues. Also referred to as Kaurava in the play.*

Pandavas: *Cousins of the Kauravas, sons of Pandu, with his kingdom in nearby Indraprastha. The three prominent warrior sons are Yudhishtira (also known as Dharmaraja), Arjuna and Bhima. The two others, Nakula and Sahadeva play other important roles in the tale.*

Kunti: *The mother of the Pandavas.*

Karna: *The first son of Kunti, not by Pandu but through an invocation of God Surya. He is abandoned as an infant and brought up by charioteers and is thus regarded low in caste, a non-kshatriya. He is befriended by the Kauravas and is very close to Duryodhana.*

Schooling: *The Kauravas and Pandavas receive schooling in martial arts and warfare from the same gurus, notably Drona and Bhishma. When war breaks out the Gurus throw their lot with the Kauravas. Arjuna and Karna are seen to excel in the martial arts.*

Draupadi: *Daughter of King Drupad. Krishna makes her his sister and arranges her marriage to Arjuna. She is claimed by Arjuna as wife in an open contest of archery held to give away Draupadi. Later, she is compelled to accept all five Pandava brothers as* *husbands.*

Sanjaya: *Charioteer and companion of Dhrutarashtra and Gandhari, blessed with a divine vision of seeing things at great distances. He narrates the happenings in the great war to the king and the queen.*

Vidura: *Originally a wise minister in the combined Kuru kingdom, he walks away from the Kauravas, lives a humble life and becomes a devotee of Krishna.*

Asvatthama: *Mighty warrior in the Kaurava camp, loyal to Duryodhana, famed for his midnight slaughter in the Pandava camp.*

Krishna: *The son of the Yadava chief, Vasudeva and his wife, Devaki. Hence, known as Vasudeva Krishna or Vasudeva. Considered an incarnation of Vishnu in Hindu thought.*

Characters in the play in order of appearance

Old Woman

Dwapara

Kali

Krishna

Kaurava (Duryodhana)

Kunti

Chorus: *An ensemble of about six women and six men who play either a Chorus Group or the individual parts shown below:*

• Three servants of Emperor Kaurava • A mother in search of her soldier husband • Her girl child • Two spectre-devils on the battlefield • Vidura, Krishna's disciple • Dhritarashtra, the blind patriarch-king • Gandhari, his queen • Sanjaya • Yudhishtira (Dharmaraja) • Draupadi • Arjuna • Bhima • A dying soldier • Asvatthama • Sahadeva

Note: *The characters of Dwapara and Kali at the start of the play form a dramatic device in Kuvempu's play. Dwapara is the guardian or timekeeper of Dwapara Yuga, the third of four epochs in Hindu mythology. (Supposedly 864,000 years.) The epoch ends with Krishna's departure to his heavenly abode.*

In the play Dwapara regretfully hands over charge to Kali at the commencement of the current epoch, Kali Yuga, sad at the gruesome end of his Yuga. Indeed, in popular usage the term Kali Yuga connotes an era of degradation of human values. Kuvempu's optimism and faith in mankind is seen in a young Kali in the play who is confident that mankind will rediscover its genius.

Time: *Overnight, at the end of the eighteen-day war*

Place: *Various parts of the Kurukshetra battlefield, littered with corpses*

INTRODUCTION

MOST READERS AND performing groups will already be familiar with the great epic Mahabharata, all the characters in the tale, and all the events culminating in the great eighteen-day war. The death and destruction is so vast that picking up threads is as good as a new beginning for the entire land. They will also be familiar with the words and phrases of Sanskrit origin used occasionally in the text.

For the benefit of those with less familiarity, especially readers outside India, a short introduction and a glossary provided at the end of the play may be useful.

Synopsis

The epic Mahabharata war has ended. For some it is a triumph, the end of an era of injustice. For others it is the beginning of another long journey in a never-ending cycle of the rise and downfall of human civilisations. At the start of every such journey are the unavoidable troubling questions about the human propensity for war. The same human intelligence that is the source of all creativity in building a civilisation also finds the most ingenious methods to destroy its own creations. Whether one is proclaimed victor or vanquished, there is the inescapable task of accounting for the deaths of hundreds upon thousands of men and women, on the battlefield and in circumstances now euphemistically called collateral damage. When all are reduced to the same state of lifelessness, and from there to the same pile of ashes blown to the winds, we cannot help asking who really won, what really was achieved, and who may prescribe the true state of dharma. Kuvempu chooses the spectacle of the battlefield turned into a vast carpet of corpses as the setting for this play. The change of guard from Dwapara to Kali between the two aeons is used as a vehicle to raise the difficult questions about the sanctity of war and mankind's unending quest for the battle to end all battles. Krishna's questionable role in the battle is addressed with a rare combination of wit and sympathy. Kuvempu's humanistic philosophy of life and his optimistic faith in human goodness comes shining through.

The playwright

Kuppalli Venkatappa Puttappa, the first winner of the Jnanpith award from Karnataka, was born on December 29, 1904, in Hirekodige and brought up in Kuppalli, both villages in Shimoga district. Kuvempu came to Mysore for his education. Starting his academic career as a lecturer in Kannada at Maharaja's College he became a professor and a principal, and retired as the Vice-Chancellor of the University of Mysore.

Kuvempu strode the world of modern Kannada literature like a colossus, starting a whole new school of thought in poetic tradition and bringing unprecedented glory to Kannada in the linguistic and literary sphere. He was prolific as a poet and produced over 30 major collections of poems in a period spanning five decades. His creative intellect also expressed itself brilliantly in his various plays, novels and critiques. In addition he created a significant body of children's literature and translations.

This adaptation

Bangalore Little Theatre (BLT) was privileged to be invited to perform at a theatre festival organised to celebrate the Golden Jubilee of the formation of Karnataka State. The choice of Kuvempu's play for a festival of this kind was straightforward. This play simply had to be presented to the rest of the world in the English language. However, it was clear that mounting the production was going to be a formidable task. It would require great courage and even greater perseverance. BLT is very grateful to Karnataka Nataka Academy and, in particular, the President at that time, G Srinivas (Kappanna), for the encouragement and support provided through the project.

The director of the production, Vijay Padaki, also undertook the task of the adaptation in English. It was done through techniques of action planning and improvisation, using Professor Prabhu Shankara's available translation. The main features of the adaptation are worth mentioning here.

First and foremost, we had to strike the right balance between fidelity to the rich literary quality of the poetic script and the needs of actionability on stage. This also meant achieving a brisk pace, to be aided by a crisp syntax.

Second, given the epic structure of the play, it appeared most appropriate to incorporate the narrative style of the Greek Chorus into the script. Most parts in the adaptation are thus played by an ensemble that switches between individual parts and the Chorus. Simple white gauze masks served the purpose for the Chorus.

Third, since the entire play unfolds at different points of the Kurukshetra battlefield, now littered with thousands of corpses, the décor for the production relied heavily on innovative lighting. The corpses were, simply, a vast quantity of jute (hessian) bags (spread irregularly in a stretch stage Left to stage Right of the stge and kept underlit.)

Finally, the adaptation took the liberty of incorporating an interpretation of its own into the script. This was done after a great deal of experimentation and reworking of the basic idea, to make sure that it was congruent with the playwright's intentions and basic philosophy of the original play. The performing group felt very strongly that while any war or armed conflict is tragic enough in itself, the heaviest burden of the war is borne by the womenfolk. In the aftermath of every war are women who remain to bear the tragic impact with resignation–the mother who loses a son, the wife who loses a husband and scores of women who must submit to the conquerors. In BLT's production of Kuvempu's play the character of the old woman represents a continuing tragedy throughout history. To convey the timelessness of this tragedy, we had her begin each of her scenes with a lament. These are half sung and half chanted, but rendered with great feeling. The laments were chosen from great dramatic works spanning three thousand years:

1. Hecuba in Euripides' *Trojan Women*
2. The beggar woman in Lorca's *Blood Wedding*
3. The mother in Brecht's *Mother Courage*

FIRST PERFORMED

At Karnataka Rangabhoomi Namaskara, the festival of Kannada plays in English organised by Karnataka Nataka Academy **October 2006.** First produced by Bangalore Little Theatre October 2006.

Old Woman	SUMAN SRIDHAR
Dwapara	SHASHANK PURUSHOTHAM
Kali	RAHEEM DAREDIYA
Servants	DEEPAK GANGADHAR, SANTOSH SAMUEL, MAYANK RUNGTA
Mother	BHAMINI N
Child	SITARA MENON
Demons	NISCHAL PAI, CHINMAYEE DUTTA
Krishna	RAJEEV GUPTA
Vidura	BADRINATH AD
Dhrutarashtra	MAYANK RUNGTA
Gandhari	NISCHAL PAI
Sanjaya	JAYAPRAKASH
Dharmaraja	ANAND RAMPRASAD
Arjuna	BADRINATH AD
Bhima	SANTOSH SAMUEL
Draupadi	RASHMI
Soldier	JAYAPRAKASH
Kaurava	GULSHAN DEVAIAH
Asvatthama	DEEPAK GANGADHAR
Sahadeva	MAYANK RUNGTA
Kunti	PRIYA RAO
Chorus	BHAMINI N, RASHMI, CHINMAYEE DUITTA, NISCHAL PAI, SITARA MENON, SANTOSH SAMUEL, MAYANK RUNGTA, BADRINATH AD, JAYAPRAKASH ANAND RAMPRASAD, DEEPAK GANGADHAR,
Lighting	ANANDA RAJU, PRITHAM KUMAR
Stage	KANCHAN BHATTACHARYYA
Sound	ANAND RAMPRASAD, VIJAY PADAKI
Property	DEEPTHY SEKHAR, MALTESH BADIGER, CAREE OWENS
Costumes	DIVYA JAIN, GULSHAN DEVAIAH, VIDYA MASAND
Make up	K RAMAKRISHNA, UMESH
Choreography	GAYATRI KUMARSWAMY, MADHUSMRITI SHUKLA
Designed and Directed by	VIJAY PADAKI
Assistant Director and Script	NAYANTARA ROY

Many thanks to Prof Prabhu Shankara in Mysore for permission to use his available English translation of the original play as the base for this adaptation.

PROLOGUE

The play opens with a tight spotlight (Down Right of stage) on an Old Woman seated on the floor. She is crouched, her face is not seen.

Light cross-fades to cyclorama. The Chorus is silhouetted. It comes to life with a choreographed depiction of the end of a battle. Some fall, others lead off victoriously.

Cross-fade to Old Woman (DR.) A long wail from her. A chorus of four women join the Old Woman, huddle behind her...

Cross-fade to cyclorama. Dwapara appears Up Centre.

Both areas held. The Chorus (CH) taunts Dwapara.

CH 1

Dwapara!

ALL

O Dwapara!

CH 2

Your Golden age is ending, Dwapara!

CH 3

The age of wars and slaughter.

ALL

Unnatural deaths.

CH 4

You have presided over many wars, Dwapara.

ALL

Great many wars.

CH 1

The war to end all wars.

CH 2

The mother of all wars.

CH 3

The war on evil.

ALL

By many other names.

CH 4

At the end of every war, Dwapara, did you see a huddle of women left behind?

ALL

Look at her, Dwapara!

CH 1

Do you recognise her?

CH 2

From another war, another age.

CH 3

In every war. In every age. She wanders from age to age.

CH 4

It has never ended, Dwapara.

ALL

Listen to her, Dwapara!

(Spot DR on the Old Woman and huddle. Old Woman sings Hecuba's lament.)

Lift thy head, unhappy lady, from the ground;
Thy neck upraise; this is Troy no more,
No longer am I queen in Ilium...
Brought to nothing after all...Ah me!
What else but tears is now my hapless lot,
Whose country, children, husband, all are lost? ...
Ah, the high-blown pride of ancestors! How cabined!
Now what must I suppress, or what declare? ...
Ah, woe is me! The anguish I suffer lying here...
While ceaselessly my tearful wail ascends.
For even this is music to the wretched,
To chant their cheerless dirge of sorrow.

(The performing group is welcome to choose an alternate rendition of the lament.)

(Cross fade to Dwapara Up Centre. The Chorus exits. The Old Woman remains in her position.)

SCENE 1

DWAPARA

How is it that this Kurukshetra of the great Bharata war
Wears the silence of a cremation ground today?
The blare of the war trumpets piercing all quarters,
The deafening charges of warriors in assault,
The clanging of swords punctuated by war cries of valiant fighters –
The sounds I heard every day are heard no more.

Where are the waves upon waves of twangs
From the bowstrings of archers? And over them
The thunder of chariots bearing elite forces of warriors?
Where is the lightning ferocity of consecrated weapons
Covering the sky with shooting sparks?
Where are the showers of arrows piercing the clouds,
Soaring past the gates of heavens above?

O the other side, the lord of the serpent banner was a lion
Leading his eager pride of warriors in attack.
Where has that lion buried himself today?

Where is the howl of Bhima, valiant son of Vayu, whose mighty mace
Knocked down enemies like dried leaves on withered trees?
Where is the Panchajanya conch, with its shrill blare
Driving panic into the hearts of the Kaurava hordes?
What silence has swallowed up the neighing of stallions
Proudly rearing their necks as they carried their riders in the charge?
The trumpeting elephants raising their trunks high as they rolled onward?
Kurukshetra!
Till yesterday it was the playground for heroic deeds.
Today it is a graveyard for spectres to play on.

What are battlefields, but vast graveyards?
And what is a battle but a massacre foretold? What is victory?
It is the gloating of survivors and the lament of the vanquished.

Must it be so in every age? Is this the legacy I transfer to the next age?

(Cross fade to DR. The Old Woman picks herself up and sings the last part of the lament as a reprise, directing it at Dwapara. She exits. Dwapara continues.)

At the very end of my reign, O Lord, Lord, should it be a graveyard
To offer me this mute farewell from my reign?
Should I wash my feet in the blood of champion warriors?
Must I tally how many noble spirits have fallen,
And how many brave young men have laid down their lives?
Acharya Bhishma, Karna, Drona, Abhimanyu—
The legion of great heroes, reduced to ashes in the flames of war.

The high spirited Kaurava emperor, a victim of base trickery,
Lies helpless with a thigh smashed. Karna, too, has met his untimely end
And naively believing the falsehood from the son of Yama
Drona has become the victim of a pupil turned adversary.

Descend, o shroud of darkness!
Come down from the depths of the clouds and cover this graveyard.
Heed the lesson from the setting sun.
Unable to bear the distressing end of the Kuru dynasty
He has chosen to sink into the western ocean.
This is Kurukshetra no longer, but the Dwapara graveyard.

KALI

Dwaparadeva!

DWAPARA

What a dreadful, cruel and melancholy scene is this!
There is death and destruction as far as the eye can see.
And the ear catches only its mocking laughter.
The wreckage of golden chariots, the heaps of dead elephants,
The hordes of spectres playing with freshly recovered skulls,

The packs of jackals tearing at the innards –
The great deluge has arrived at just the end of my age.

KALI

He is lost in a deep melancholy. He does not hear me calling.
Never have I seen Dwapara so overcome, forgetting himself.
O Dwapara!

DWAPARA

Silence itself weeps uninterrupted.
The creeping darkness sighs and groans.
The last lamentations of dying soldiers,
With limbs broken, bellies burst, heads split open,
Rise now to frighten the God of Death himself.

KALI

Dwaparadeva!

DWAPARA

Kalideva!

KALI

How is it you are alone? Standing rooted, lost in thought?
You do not hear even when called.

DWAPARA

Has it come to this,
That Dwapara should meet Kali in this graveyard?

Presiding deity of the coming age,
Are you to be crowned at a cremation ground? What do I show
As the product of countless years of human achievement?
What can I offer as my proud handiwork?
Shall I conduct you through this vast graveyard?
Shall I present you the corpses of warriors who died fighting?
What auspicious wealth is left for me to bestow upon you?

KALI

Dwaparadeva, I beg you to compose yourself, not to be so agitated.

I will gladly receive whatever you give me and set about my task.

What is your lapse, pray explain?

After all, that which we call the Eternal brought forth a visible creation,
Sustained it for a while, and then chose to make it invisible again.
Why should you, the presiding deity of one age
Be perturbed over its dismantling?
The universe itself emerged from a creative void.
It has returned to that void. In obedience to another law
It will take some other form and emerge once more in another age.
The divine course of creation is in its cycles of evolution and dissolution.
Why grieve over it? It is the treasure seen in a dream,
Vanishing upon waking. It is not proper to grieve over it.

DWAPARA

Kalideva, all that is destroyed, can it ever return?

KALI

Of course! Can there be any doubt about that?

DWAPARA

All the great heroes...?

KALI

Yes, all of them.

DWAPARA

Brahmacharis like Bhishma, son of the heavenly Ganga?

KALI

Yes, they will appear, men like him and many excelling him.

DWAPARA

Will masters of archery like Drona reappear?

KALI

Men and women of great talent who will invent thunderbolts
Belching out flaming trails as they wander among the planets
And reach for the stars beyond!

DWAPARA

And givers of charity like Karna?

KALI

Yes, my dear brother, they will appear without fail.

DWAPARA

In might, in compassion, in dignity, will high-minded leaders
Like the Kaurava emperor ever rise again?

KALI

Yes, indeed. Why doubt it?

DWAPARA

Blessed indeed are you, privileged to rule over such an age.
Yet, Kalideva, do the scriptures not predict
That people of your age are destined to be stunted?

KALI

So be it, then! They will mount the shoulders of their forefathers
Who were destined to be of great stature in an earlier age
And become taller than them. Will they not have a wider vision, then?
Is the Dhaulagiri peak not higher than the Himalayas?

Why waste words? Death is the foundation for new life,
Destruction the inspiration for new creation.

DWAPARA

Do you hold then that the Kali age is to be greater than the earlier ages?

KALI

I shall not proclaim anything just yet, but I have faith in its inherent merits.

This age can build the grandest edifice for itself
And reach the highest levels of accomplishment
By building on the foundations laid by all past ages.

DWAPARA

O Kalideva, may the heavens bestow on you the good fortune
To realise your noble vision. I may now depart in peace.
I must visit the lord of the Kauravas before he breathes his last.
He was truly the man of the age.

He has shown for all ages what great strengths lie in the human soul.
He has shown this through his valour and firmness of purpose.

Allow me now to transfer to you the presiding authority for the new age.
And then take your leave.

KALI
I bow before you in humility. May your experience be my guiding light.
(There is a short ceremony of Dwapara handing over his staff or sceptre to Kali. A large number of flickering lights appears on the cyclorama.)

KALI
My dear brother, what are you gazing at?

DWAPARA
Look, out there Kalideva. What do you see?

KALI
A horde of fireflies? They are lamps, hundreds and thousands of them.
The darkness of night has given birth to lamps.

DWAPARA
Look again, Kalideva. Look closely.

KALI
They are getting bigger now. I see human forms behind the lamps.
They are torches and torch bearers, moving about in the darkness,
This way and that way, stopping, stooping, straightening up, moving on.

DWAPARA
The loved ones of warriors, who died fighting –
Some for the Pandavas, some for the Kauravas.
They cannot tell the difference anymore. It is a long search,
Seeking out a dear one, reduced to a nameless corpse.

They are themselves reduced to ghosts in human shape.

KALI

All the sorrows of birth and death have converged here tonight,
From all families and all households.
What a monumental congregation it is turning out to be.

DWAPARA

This is the reward for the martial cravings of men.
Clothed in godly principles by their heroic warriors, they are upheld
In battle cries to the last breath. The graveyard bears testimony
To the valour unleashed from mighty warriors
As they lash themselves forward with those principles.

SCENE 2

Three servants of Emperor Kaurava are looking for him. They are covered by a single large shawl-like cloth and move about in unison, and speak as one body with three voices.

Beware, beware!
Don't rush forward rashly in the dark.
In this gory mire are buried arrowheads.

(Pointing upwards)
This way.
Look, there is a warrior with a crown lying here.
It could be our master
Have you gone mad? Every corpse you see you blab is our master.
He, who was frightened by a bear,
Sees a bear even in a black rock.

Alas! I don't know how we can find the Kaurava Emperor
Among these heaps and heaps of corpses.
Treading upon corpses at every step
We are turning into corpse eaters.

Arrowheads at every step, both my feet are in tatters.
What a battlefield!
What a massacre!

Until today I never knew what a battlefield was.
It is so terrible.
This graveyard is far more terrible than the fighting.
Whoever thought such things could happen?
Whoever imagined that our master would suffer defeat?

What can anyone do when fate comes into play?
Let us at least put in our last services to the master
And earn some *punya* (probity).

Can we ever find on earth another noble soul like our master?
Who can match him in compassion?
Who will show such boundless kindness to his servants?
He was a true father to us.
With him gone we all become orphans, begging for our living.

Listen. One day, late at night, I was laid up in bed, groaning in pain from an unknown ailment. It was as if my end had come. At that time of night someone knocked on the door. My wife cried out 'Who's there?''It is I. Open the door,' came the reply. When the door was opened I saw our master. He had come in disguise, unaccompanied, without his guards. I felt the joy of a devotee who has seen god himself. And my ailment vanished!

What does it matter whether our master has lost or won, fallen or risen?

What does it matter whether he is in heaven or hell?
Our master is always our master.
His mind is our mind.
His fate is our fate.
Come on. We must find our father.

(The servants exit. Four members of the Chorus huddle UC against the cyclorama as mourners. Two of them become the Demon spectres in the next scene. The Mother and Child appear.)

CHILD

Ma, where are we going in the dark?

MOTHER

To the graveyard, my sweet. To find the person who brought you into this world.

CHILD

Where is he? How far do we have to go?

MOTHER

That's what I am trying to find out, my child.

CHILD

Ma, look! Who is this man?

MOTHER

Somebody I don't know. Somebody I know has a sweet child like you at home.

CHILD

Why is he sleeping here? Why isn't he home?

MOTHER

What can I explain to this child who does not know what life is.

How can I say 'My dear, true heroes have no home, except the battlefield?'

This man who offered his waking life to the call of war is now sleeping the sleep of death.

CHILD

Will he not wake up some time?

MOTHER

No, he will not, my child.

CHILD

If he never wakes up, he will not speak again, will he?

MOTHER

No, he won't.

CHILD

He has a child like me, you said. Won't he take her in his arms and play with her again?

MOTHER

No, my sweet, no. No more will sweet thoughts spring forth from his mind, for his tongue is lifeless. Tenderness for his children, love for his wife, affection for relatives, compassion, mercy, kindness – no more will these noble feelings rise from his heart. He cannot laugh. Neither can he weep.

He feels no happiness. Neither can he feel sad.

O lord, lord, isn't life's sorrow far better than death's silence?

My child, this man is now in the land from which no traveller returns to report.

That land is now his home. He is now neither father nor husband to anybody, not an older brother or the younger, not a relative, not a friend, not a foe.

CHILD

What is he then, Ma?

MOTHER

He is a corpse, a dead, rotting corpse.

CHILD

O Ma, my father, who we are looking for – has he also become just like this man?

(*Mother hugs Child tightly, weeps*)

SCENE 3

The two demon-spectres rise (UC), towering over the deserted battlefield. (They can be puppet figures fabricated on tall bamboo poles. The two actors speak the lines from behind the poles.)

D 1

Akka, I am still scared that dreaded Duryodhana will come after us brandishing his mace. When humans set themselves to the business of killing, they excel even the Goddess Mari.

D 2

Cast off these false fears. Where is Duryodhana? He lies by the Vaisampayana Lake, his thigh smashed by the deadly blow of Bhima's mace.

D 1

The wicked Duryodhana! Serves him right!

D 2

That was only due to the sport of fate. I tell you, Bhima might well have been in the same plight. I stood there and watched the mace combat. Duryodhana is not the vanquished. Bhima, having won, is not the victor.

D 1

Akka, What is this madness of humans? It seems to overtake even our devilry.

D 2

True, true. Such a huge crowd has besieged this graveyard, we do not have room even to stand.

D 1

They have become squatters in our graveyard.

D 2

Killing has become so common here. It can be maddening even for us.

D 1

You must admit that we have never seen such heroism in any battle before this.

D 2

Or such massacre. What a mad lust for killing these humans have. I can't help feeling some disgust.

D 1

Akka, look there!

D 2

What is it?

D 1

It is something moving. Is it one of us, or another human?

D 2

It cannot be one of us. No demon has a real body! It is some old woman, isn't it?

D 1

How firm she looks, even in her old age. Why does she stoop again and again? What is she looking for?

D 2

Ah, she must be looking for her son. She is not disturbed by the sight of rotting corpses.

She carries a mother's love in her heart. It is sacred to her. It protects her, and drives away the corpse eaters. Oh, she is coming in this direction. Quick, we must get out of sight!

(The demons disappear. The old woman enters, groping her way *with her staff.)*

WOMAN

The farther I trudge, the vaster seems to grow this graveyard! I suppose it is natural that as one grows older and older, what seemed such a small earth in youth should grow larger and larger! Woe is me!

(She sings the lament from Lorca)

They are opening the coffins now
And white linen waits, spread on bedroom floors
For the weight of bodies with torn throats.
No bird shall awaken
And the breeze carrying their cries in her skirt
Shall fly with them over black treetops
Or bury them in soft slime

(She continues)

I cannot understand what this murderous sport these children are playing today! My boy, my boy! You came running to the hut every evening to recount the battles of the day even as you gobbled up the morsels I placed in your hand. Why are you so late today? I cooked a special dish for you and then waited till nightfall, staring at the path you always take. 'He'll come now, he'll come soon, he'll be here in a moment.'

The darkness of night has closed in upon the earth and upon my heart. What shall I do now? Where shall I go? O my child, my Narayana, where are you? Come to me! Make this grandma happy! Who else is there in my life? Narayana, my child! Narayana!

(Krishna appears, accompanied by Vidura. Seeing him, but not recognising him, the old woman inquires)

WOMAN

O my children, can you show me where my Narayana is?

KRISHNA *(Gently)*

Who is your Narayana, ajji?

WOMAN

What sort of ignorant child are you that does not know my Narayana? Is there anyone, on this side or the enemy side that does not know the valour of my Narayana?

KRISHNA *(Pretending to remember)*

I know, grandma, I know. Forgive me. Your Narayana is lying further up in this very direction. Go and see him.

WOMAN *(In surprise)*

Lying? Why is he lying?

KRISHNA

I don't know, ajji. As I was coming this way, I heard him calling out to you.

WOMAN *(Stretching out her hand)*

Come here, child. Please help me up. *(Krishna raises her with respect)* What magic there is in your touch, my child! All my weariness is gone. A new strength has flowed into me.

KRISHNA

The nearness of youth brings forth youth, ajji.

WOMAN

May good attend you, my child!

(The old woman exits)

VIDURA

Vasudeva, what is this sport of yours? This Kurukshetra graveyard has become today a gateway to salvation.

KRISHNA

Vidura, there is no leisure today. Listen:

If anyone utters any one of my countless names at the moment of death, even unwittingly, I will give him my very self, whoever he may be, and under whatever pretext he may call my name. Today I must remain by the side of the dying, and release them from the bondage of birth and death. I will make a festival of dispensing salvation!

VIDURA

Will you bestow the same benediction *o*n the vicious as well as on the virtuous without any distinction? Will you dispense salvation to all alike?

KRISHNA

Foremost devotee of mine, listen again:

There is no man of virtue on this earth who would not set foot on the wrong path ifcircumstances so conspire. On the other hand, there is no vicious man in all creation who might not light upon the right path if circumstances are helpful. Moralityis bound by space and time. Can it be a guarantee to salvation by itself which is beyond both virtue and vice? Short-sighted mortals are ignorant of ultimate reality, that which is enthroned in the innermost self.

They abuse me, and try to push me away. If I do likewise, it would be a betrayal of truth. I have neither friend nor foe. All are alike in my eyes.

VIDURA

The *Veda, Sastra*, the *Agama* and the *Purana* – they all explain the distinction between virtue and vice, heaven and hell, morality and immorality, sin and sanctity. They lay down the right and wrong in conduct. Why do they do so?

KRISHNA

Vidura, the Vedas and the *Sastras* represent one part of me. They are not the whole truth. My heart is much larger. There is room – even happiness – in my heart for sinners whom the Vedas refuse to harbour, whom the Sastras do not permit even to approach.

There is no one I shun, there is room in me for all. Listen to this secret: Morality, Truth and Dharma are ornaments placed on me, they are not fetters that bind me.

I am greater than all the petty laws, to be relished more than dry principles, more ancient than the most ancient moralities! The universe is my stage. I create in it the players with such distinctions as kings and ministers, subjects, soldiers, generals, men of virtue, the wicked and the sinners. When the play has ended, they must all go at once.

If the thief in a play is thrown into prison, how can it be a play?

(Krishna moves on, and Vidura follows him)

SCENE 4

Dhrutarashtra and Gandhari enter, led by Sanjaya. They are looking for the Kaurava Emperor who has been vanquished by Bhima in the mace battle.

SANJAYA

O King Dhrutarashtra, you who are without sight are indeed blest today. The burden of pain caused by the four remaining senses can only be lighter than the pain caused by all the five.

DHRUTA

Do not give me false consolation, Sanjaya. The pain, that the eyes do not feel, doubles the pain the ears do. O Fate, why did you not create me with deafness added to my blindness?

GANDHARI

Sanjaya, this morning you came to this battlefield with my son. Show him to me now. Where is he? My son, my son, what does it matter what you are to others? You are a good son to me. To God you may be weak principled and given to blasphemy, to Dharma an outcast, to Faith a betrayer, to men of virtue a sinner, and to Bhima the arch-enemy. To me you are my darling son!

How did I hurt you? Are you burning with indignation that your father deserted you, and your mother blamed you for it, that your friends are dead, and the Guru's son has left you? Did you die that you may kill me?

SANJAYA *(To himself)*

I can neither console them, nor remain silent. To console the bereaved is to overwhelm them. Grief should burst out in tears; that alone can bring solace. Dry moralising is useless on a graveyard! *(Aloud to Gandhari)*

My lady, I have dispatched messengers to locate the jewel-crested crown of the Kuru line. *(Turning to Dhrutarashtra, with compassion)* Come on, O King, let us move on. Let us meet your son who has fallen fighting, before he breathes his last.

DHRUTA

Sanjaya, you are the light before my eyes, you are my staff. Lead me on. I will follow.

(All three exit)

SCENE 5

Dharmaraja, Bhima, Arjuna, and Draupadi enter, seeking Ghatothkacha, Abhimanyu and other relatives who have have *fallen fighting. Draupadi soon moves away from the group to a corner and remains silent through the scene.*

DHARMA *(Bitterly)*

This is the fruit my dharma has borne! Bhima, son of Vayu, behold the garden of Dwapara scorched to ash in the fire of your might!

BHIMA *(Mocking)*

Yes, indeed! We forget that the garden was the sinful den of *adharma.* It has been purified by the flames of *punya.*

ARJUNA

What is the need for a prelude of massacre for dharma? Can dharma not be brought to a land without the bloodshed of war?

BHIMA

Go and ask your Krishna, he will school you. He will convince you that before any evolution can be completed, there must be much dissolution. The path of change by preaching needs centuries. The path of change of heart through counsel needs ages upon ages.

But for the path of change by will, a single battle suffices! The futility of endeavour of an entire era has been ended in the space of eighteen days. The virtue acquired by the fulfillment of purpose is far greater than the losses that distract you. The Ganga washes away any sin in the endeavour. Our beloved Draupadi will vouch for this. Feebleness of spirit is not for heroes.

(A part of the Chorus brings in a dying soldier and lays him down in one part of the stage. They then position themselves above Bhima.)

SOLDIER

Water! Water!

DHARMA *(Looking in that direction)*

Whose cry is that?

BHIMA

It is some soldier, dying!

DHARMA

When a man is crying in distress should not another comfort him? Such a man is a god indeed. Should he fail, he is a veritable demon! *(Dharmaraja goes to the soldier and kneels by his side)*

SOLDIER

Water!

DHARMA

Arjuna, go at once and fetch some water. *(Arjuna exits)*

BHIMA

Elder brother, ask him first who he is, from which side, whether he is one of us or a Kaurava.

CHORUS

Bhimasena, The time for hatred is over. Shed your rage at least now.

(The Chorus speaks)

CH 1

In the graveyard, and at the moment of death, what does it matter who a person is?

CH 2

All belong to the God of Death, our people and the enemy's people.

ALL

They are all his victims. All!

CH 3

Must you be so ruthless?

CH 4

Enmity and friendship, ambition, gain, envy, loss, the conflicts in their wake

ALL

They will all sink into nothingness.

CH 1

They will be the same in being nothing.

CH 2

They are all embraced in the deep blue of Heaven's magnanimity.

ALL

All same in being nothing.

BHIMA *(To Draupadi)*

O Krishne, Did you hear that? The cruel one is I, it seems. They have all become gods of mercy. Had I thrown away my mace during this war and taken up mercy as my weapon, what would have been the fate of these merciful people?

DHARMA

Our last refuge is indeed mercy! Is mercy not the very image of the Supreme Being? Younger brother, like the cooling showers that descend from the heavens, mercy flows spontaneously from magnanimous hearts. Mightier than the royal sword is mercy. By turning foes into friends, it turns hate into love in them.

CHORUS

Softer than the heart of God is mercy.

CH 3

Does it not steal the heart of God Himself? It blesses him that confers it, saves him that receives it.

CH 4

So vast is the wealth of mercy that its possessor is ever rich. Whether used now or later.

ALL

Whether he lives or dies.

DHARMA

To those who have it and give it freely, it is the gateway to salvation. And to those who receive it without rancour it is the stairway to heaven.

BHIMA

All this I have heard ever so many times.

(Arjuna enters with water. Dharmaraja gives it to the soldier. The Chorus begins to carry the soldier out, Dharmaraja leading. They pause before Bhima.)

SOLDIER

Who are these? Accursed Pandavas? Woe! At the very last moment of my life I have sinned against my Master, the Kaurava Emperor, drinking water given by the Pandavas! Forgive me, my Master! Forgive me!

BHIMA

This indeed is the hero after my heart! As in life, so in pain and death, he can tell friend from foe, unforgiving till the end. He is the true hero! The rest are all fakes!

SCENE 6

A pool of blue light serves as Dwaipayana Lake. The sky of the Dwapara a geoverhead, which spreads like a vast blue canopy, is studded with the stars of that age.

The Kaurava king, his thigh smashed, drags himself to the bank of the lake. He grieves over his agony and his shame. Asvatthama stands before him.

KAURAVA

Go away Asvatthama. When I cannot help myself now what service can you or anybody else render to me? I came here alone, and alone I will depart from here. Go, go away!

(Asvatthama salutes the Emperor with folded hands and moves away reluctantly. Kaurava calls out to him.)

KAURAVA

Wait! *(Asvatthama returns)*

ASVATTHAMA

Your wish, my command.

KAURAVA

Wish! The wish of the graveyard! Will you carry out this last wish of mine without confusing yourself once again? The last time, if you care to remember, it was the slaughter of women and children, animals and their young, mistaking them for the Pandavas.

ASVATTHAMA

I will do anything for redemption.

KAURAVA

I must rely on you to try. Will you cremate Karna with me? Karna and I on the same pyre. We lived on this earth together, we reigned over the empire together. We lost it all together. In death, too, we shall be together, and find some joy. It is my last desire that we should be consumed by the same fire! Our ashes must not be any different. Will you fulfil this one wish of mine without bungling it?

ASVATTHAMA

I will go at once. *(Exits)*

KAURAVA *(To himself)*

Trusting you all, I only deceived myself!

O Bhishma, my Acharya! All of you offering allegiance to my side, you were there always, yes, but only in body, and only for the bread. Not because you loved me, only for the bread. I know that well. You were on my side for appearances. To them you gave your hearts and your minds.

At the first lame excuse you gave me the slip, one by one, and I was left to suffer this defeat, the smashed thigh, and the shame. Camouflaged in the guise of dharma, all of you tricked me!

(Enter Dwapara)

DWAPARA

O Emperor!

KAURAVA

Who is it mocking me with the title of Emperor?

DWAPARA

Emperor of the Kuru line, it is I, Dwapara.

KAURAVA

Noble Dwapara, I have no court now to offer you a seat. Pray do not approach me.

DWAPARA

O King of kings, you have lived a full life without bowing to anyone. Is freedom itself not the greatest empire? Could there be a greater emperor than the free soul? You will always be an emperor!

KAURAVA

What brings you here?

DWAPARA

My reign ends today. I have come to seek your leave and bid you farewell.

KAURAVA

Why seek my leave for that? There are the Pandavas, and there is Dharmaraja. And there is that Krishna! They are the emperors now!

DWAPARA

As long as you live, you alone are the Emperor! To me you are still the Lord of the Kuru line! Permit me to say farewell. I have already transferred powers to Kali. May I take leave of you now?

KAURAVA

Farewell, Dwapara. I too prepare for my departure.

DWAPARA

We shall meet again! *(Exits)*

KAURAVA

We all depart, only to return once more!

(A pause. He then bursts out.)

Dharma! Adharma! Who are the devotees of dharma, and who are the violators? Ah! That Krishna! Is he not the very founder of dharma? The great protector of dharma?

That base cowherd! Uncouth, uncultured! Granted I am a betrayer of dharma, what about the Pandavas? What sort of dharma did they uphold? Pleading with sweet tongues they teased out the secret of Bhishma, and killed him. They hatched cowardly plots, and called them battle strategy! Acharya Drona – as much their mentor as ours – he was dispatched to the other world by sheer deception!

And Karna...*(Breaking down)* My beloved, trusted Karna, son of Surya, whose supreme valour even the immortal gods adore – they killed him by trickery, openly, for all to see. And then it was my turn. Against all rules of single combat, they knocked me down by striking at my thigh. These wretched creatures are the devotees of dharma, and I am its violator! Where else would this treachery come from but the scheming mind of Krishna? The foremost Guru of the art of deception!

O wretch Krishna! Krishna! Krishna!

(Krishna Appears)

KRISHNA

King of kings, here I am!

KAURAVA *(Looking up in surprise)*

Who are you?

KRISHNA

I am Krishna.

KAURAVA

Villain! Have you come here to see me in my hour of humiliation? And mock at me?

KRISHNA *(With a smile)*

Lord of the Kauravas, Did you not beckon, addressing me by my name?

KAURAVA

I cried out, you wretch. It was not a beckoning! I cried out in rage, in agony, I did not call out to you. What do you suppose? Poor me! I prayed, I begged this noble soul: 'O Murari, O ocean of mercy, come thou and save me!'

Go, take the same path that brought you here, and let me be. Get out, you villain, go! Do not linger in a place uninvited!

KRISHNA

Patience, Emperor, patience!

KAURAVA

Do you taunt me, you knave, calling me Emperor? Are you not the scheming foe who destroyed my empire?

KRISHNA

Am I? Was it not yourself who destroyed your empire? Am I the villain? Who acted out of envy and spite, and deceived the Pandavas on the pretext of a game of dice? Who provoked Dharma by the outrage on Draupadi in an open court, before all assembled? Who lit up the flames of war? When I begged you to give up a tiny bit of land to the sons of Pandu what was your response? Scorning the wise counsel of all elders, you threw oil on smoldering coals. You are the cause of your own ruin, O king. Behold the tragedy of Kurukshetra through your folly.

KAURAVA

O pestilence! You sorcerer, foul demon, thirsting for blood from the victims of war! Who is the corpse-eater that gobbled up all the heroes of my army? O evil incarnate, that very day when you came from Vidura's cottage to my court, you had already set about preparing the funeral pyre. Every step you took was in deceit, leading us all to this graveyard. And now you prattle on about righteousness.

KRISHNA *(Within himself)*

Enough of this play! The time has come to break the spell. *(He fixes his gaze upon Kaurava and speaks in a divine voice)*

O hero Kaurava, truth-seeker Kaurava, enough now! The play is over, the curtain is drawn. It is time to break out of the charm. Awake! Open your eyes! Do not ever forget that you are but an actor. *(Peace and serenity spread over the countenance of Kaurava. Krishna smiles upon him.)*

Come, the stage manager and the actor should be leaving the stage together to return to the green room. Is the spell broken? Has the dream lifted?

KAURAVA *(With a smile)*

Guru of the Universe, it is the power of your mantra. It was indeed a golden dream, but what a terrible dream it was! O Stage Manager, did I perform my role to your satisfaction?

KRISHNA

You are an actor's actor, O Kaurava. There is no one to match you in the art. I lost my heart to it myself.

KAURAVA

What do you think of Karna's act? Was it not excellent?

(The Chorus enters. A fade out of the star-studded sky begins.)

KRISHNA

He comes next only to you. In that last battle of his he really excelled himself. As I watched him my heart swelled with pride and joy.

KAURVA

Are you not after all the Supreme Artiste?

CHORUS

Where has the star-studded sky gone?

CH 1

And Kurukshetra, the vast blanket of death, where is it now?

CH 2

Where are those heart-rending cries of distress?

KRISHNA

After the dream has lifted, can there be any substance in it at all?

CH 3

Look! Gandhari and Dhrutarashtra are coming this way.

CH 4

Led by Sanjaya. It is time to close the play now.

ALL

Sign off the play in a befitting manner.

KRISHNA

I go. I will meet you again...there!

(*Krishna exits. The Chorus carries Kaurava away to his last resting place. Sanjaya, Dhritarashtra and Gandhari appear in procession. They snake through the scene and exit without speaking.)*

SCENE 7

Krishna and Vidura are in conversation.

KRISHNA

Vidura, I have just met Emperor Kaurava. What a Man! Will I ever meet his match anywhere?

VIDURA

A man of unshakeable resolution! But who are those coming this way?

KRISHNA

It is Sahadeva, and that must be Lady Kunti with him.

VIDURA

She seems to be looking for something.

KRISHNA

How wonderful, that a graveyard should bring people together like this.

VIDURA

What might be her need?

KRISHNA

The mother who cast away her baby son from its cradle has come to claim him back.

VIDURA

What do you mean? Who has she come to see?

KRISHNA

Who else but the matchless Karna? Matchless in valour, matchless in charity.

VIDURA

Karna, Kunti's son?

KRISHNA

You would not know. You will learn more later. Let us not be seen as she pours her heart out to the other son.

VIDURA

A day of endless revelations.

KRISHNA

Also a day of reckoning for many. This way, we must not be seen. *(Sahadeva and Kunti enter. She is looking for the corpse of Karna. Sahadeva knows the secret of Karna, but does not show it.)*

KUNTI

Child, what an accursed womb is mine. That it once bore the scorching ground itself – how strange that today it is distressed by a mere funeral pyre.

SAHADEVA

Mother, who are you looking for? Will you not tell me? I may be able to find him for you. Is he a warrior of rank, or an ordinary soldier?

KUNTI

A celebrated warrior indeed, my child, a hero of world-wide fame. One who excels the Sun God himself. In war he was the terrible Kalki himself. Yet, in peace, he dispensed unmatched charity.

SAHADEVA

Is it...Karna?

KUNTI

Yes, my child, Karna. My Karna, the child of my maidenly love. My first son, the oldest of you brothers.

SAHADEVA

Mother, how can...

KUNTI

Child, do not add torture to an already wounded womb. Take me to Karna. Pray show him to me at once.

(A pause. Sahadeva moves to a corner of the stage and points out a corpse to Kunti, then steps away. Kunti approaches the dead Karna.)

KUNTI

Woe, my child! Has it come to this at last? That I who bore you and then cast you away in the river, must come to caress your cold skin on the cremation ground? Oh Gurudeva, Oh Durvasa, forgive the sinner who let you down. The boon you bestowed upon me – look at the path it has taken!

(To Karna) Did I bring you forth only to turn our beloved land into a graveyard? My child, my child, do not think of your friend, the Kaurava lord, as the one who laid out this feast for Mari on the Kurukshetra field. If you can only see my hand in it! O Mother Ganga, might I not be the real cause? Will you pass this way and see what has become of the child I placed on your palm? Can you not save him once more today? Child, child, why did fate choose to punish you this way for the first sin that your mother committed?

You came into a world of princes, and I sent you away from there, to grow up among charioteers. Forgive me, child. Oh God, forgive my folly. My darling child, you do not know this. It was the day the Pandavas and Kauravas came face to face to show off their skills in archery. I watched you with pride, but in secret, and with my head lowered. And then, one in the group of warriors gathered there insulted you. He mocked your charioteer stock. I raised my head by instinct, but held it back again. I could have spoken the truth and claimed you back, but I did not...Oh, I did not! I suppressed my mother's instinct, and... *(She cries out)* Krishna! I listened to you, Krishna! It was your counsel that marred my life further, and I put my child to death. In obedience I passed on your advice to my son, 'The arrow used once must not be used a second time.'

I extracted a pledge from him. In unquestioned obedience, the braveheart that he was, he put himself to death. It was I! Accursed is my motherhood, it was I that sent him to his unholy death.

O my son, can you accept even now that your mother was deceived? A guileless, helpless woman? But you have deceived me too, by leaving me. Oh my darling Karna, why did it have to be this way?

SCENE 8

The Old Woman is seen wandering. She sings the lament from Brecht.

With all its luck and all its danger, the war is dragging on a bit, Another hundred years or longer, the common man won't benefit Filthy his food, no soap to shave him, the regiment steals half his pay But still a miracle may save him, tomorrow is another day... The thaw sets in, the dead remain...

(She stops to rest)

WOMAN

What is this devilry? So many people moving about on this gloomy field, and none to pay the slightest attention to another fellow being.O Narayana, where are you? Speak to me!

Who cares for old folks? It was different when my child was with me. Knowing there was a soldier in the making they came often to look us up. Even the generals came, those with the honey tongues, patting us on the back, luring us with promises. They lectured too – on patriotism, allegiance to the master, duty and dharma, and such other lofty philosophy. Finally, they took you away from me. I allowed myself to be beguiled by them. Where are those exalted principles now? It was all a trap, a snare laid to catch simple gullible folks, and to lead them as sacrificial offerings in the quarrels of the feuding rich. *(The Mother and Child enter, still in search)*

CHILD

Mother, I can't walk anymore

MOTHER

Just a little longer, dear. Do you want me to carry you? *(The Child stays away. The Mother spots the Old Woman.)* Who's there? Ajji, why are you sitting there all by yourself?

WOMAN *(Seeing the mother)*

My dear woman, I have searched and searched in vain for my boy, Narayana. I am dead tired. Where else must I search? There is no one to ask, no one to tell. But tell me about yourself, my dear.

Why have you brought this child here to this graveyard, and at the dead of night?

MOTHER

Ajji, there is no one else but us in our hut, no one to care for this child. I have come here seeking my husband. But all I see in this vast field is heaps and heaps of corpses, nothing else.

WOMAN

To which party did your husband belong?

MOTHER

He belonged to the Pandava army. And your son?

WOMAN

He was with the Kaurava Emperor.

MOTHER

Ajji, was your son a foe of my husband?

WOMAN

Who is a foe to whom? Am I your foe?

MOTHER

Of course not! What an idea!

WOMAN

Poor people like us are utterly helpless, my dear. If the Pandavas and the Kauravas fight over land, our children are forced to take one side or the other, and out of false pride, fight and kill one another. What enmity can there be between my son and your husband? We are both in the same distress, my dear. Come along, let us move on together. We have company now. *(They move on. The mother stops and screams, pushing her child back. The old woman rushes to her side.*

WOMAN

Oh, horrible! Two corpses locked in embrace, killing each other.

MOTHER

Oh ajji, look! This rogue has stabbed my husband to death! Ohhh!

WOMAN

Aahhh! Your husband has spiked my son to death!

MOTHER

Accursed be the Kauravas!

WOMAN

Accursed be the Pandavas!

SCENE 9

The funeral pyre of thePandava party in one part of Kurukshetra. Bhima, Arjuna and Dharmaraja are gathered, stricken with grief. The bodies of Abhimanyu, Ghatothkacha and others are on the pyre. At the sight of Ghatothkacha's body on the pyre, Bhima is filled with boundless grief.

DHARMA

Bhimasena, complete the task on hand. Whatever happened is in the past, has happened. Of what use is this grieving? Light up the pyre. *(Bhima wails)* O Bhima, if you wail like this, how can you carry out the duty of consoling others?

BHIMA

Elder brother, I have now understood the depth of grief of Gandhari and Dhritarashtra. *(Arjuna is also overcome with grief)*

DHARMA *(To himself)*

How can men be heroes without first being *sthitaprajna?* They mistake mere anger for valour. Once their anger dries up, their valour evaporates. Without the intoxication of an emotion they are immobile. I will light up the pyre myself. *(He stops)*

Who is it coming this way? Mother Kuntidevi! She escorts a body prepared for the pyre. *(Four members of the Chorus bring in a body of Karna and place it on stage. They position themselves around Dharmaraja, Arjuna and Bhima. Kunti and Sahadeva remain on the other side of the body.)*

DHARMA

It is Karna! What is the meaning of this?

KUNTI

My child, Yudhishtira, pray cremate Karna on the same pyre.

DHARMA

Mother, the cremation fire has neither mercy nor envy. Yet, the men who light the fire will want to know what this means.

KUNTI

My darling son, I cannot say anything more. You must fulfil my desire.

BHIMA *(Furiously)*

What are you saying, Mother? How can we cremate this destroyer of our family? Look there! Those are Abhimanyu and Ghatothkacha. It was this wretch that murdered them!

CHORUS

Away! *(Kunti weeps)*

CH 1

Remove the carcass of this beast.

CH 2

Dharmaraja, if you are unnerved by her weeping, it will be the hour of the deluge.

ARJUNA

The fire that consumes Abhimanyu must not touch Karna. What is Karna to us?

CHORUS

The friend of our foe!

CH 3

The one who used trickery and sent our children to their early death.

CH 4

Abhimanyu! And Ghatothkacha!

KUNTI

O my children! Bhima! Arjuna! I pray to you with folded hands, on my knees, fulfil my desire if I am indeed your mother!

BHIMA

It is because I respect you as my mother that I have to say this.

KUNTI

Do not see me as your mother alone. Think of me as the mother of Karna too. Show me kindness. Do not argue, my sons.

(Asvatthama enters)

ASVATTHAMA

O Dharmaputra Dharmaraja, I come here to fulfil the last wish of a dying warrior. I trust that you, all warriors yourselves, will readily accede to the wish. Just before breathing his last, the Kaurava emperor summoned me to his side and commanded me to cremate Karna along with him on his pyre. You will accept that it is the dharma of the living to fulfil the wishes of the dead.

BHIMA

Take him! It is indeed your dharma to cremate this Karna.

KUNTI *(To Asvatthama)*

It is my desire that Karna should be cremated on this pyre of ours. Do not come between me and my wish.

ASVATHA

Mother, It must be Kaurava's wish first. And then my own pledge. With folded hands I pray you, send Karna with me.

BHIMA

Why delay? Take him away!

KUNTI

O Bhima! Will your heart not give in for a moment even for your mother's sake? *(The Chorus carries the body of Karna away, Asvatthama following. There is a long wail from Kunti.)*

Karnaaa!!! Did I bear you only for this ignoble end?

(Turns to Sahadeva) Why are you silent, Sahadeva?

DHARMA

What is the meaning of this, Sahadeva? Mother in her woe says she bore Karna...

SAHADEVA

Forgive me, elder brother, Karna is indeed the eldest of us all. *(Dharmaraja is speechless)*

BHIMA

Utter falsehood!

KUNTI

I alone, sinner that I have been, will now suffer alone. A stranger in your midst. For generations to come the world will not find anybody to blame for the tragedy of Kurukshetra, but they will condemn me as the sinner who sent her own child to death.

DHARMA

Mother, what have you done?

ARJUNA *(In private anger)*

Krishna! You lied to me, didn't you? You made me kill him, didn't you?

SCENE 10

Six to eight members of the Chorus enter in a choreographed move from R, as the Old Woman wanders across the stage from the opposite side. They try to stop her playfully. She tries to weave her way through. The Chorus leads the Woman to a spot DL and seats her. She watches as members of the Chorus merge into one large body, transformed into the terrifying Rudra form of Siva.

RUDRA

All charities, all vows must come here at last to rest. All vices, all virtues must at last turn to ashes. The canopy of the heavens, the bountiful earth, the boundless ocean must meet their end here at last. Time and space, birth and death, all things living and non-living must come here at last to fulfil their end purpose.

(Krishna enters from UR through the cyclorama area, watches Rudra and steps below him.)

KRISHNA

Mahadeva!

RUDRA

Vasudeva, is it you?

KRISHNA

Yes, indeed, it is I. You seem absorbed in the final scene of the tragedy.

RUDRA

Yes, indeed, O Stage Manager! Has your play come off well?

KRISHNA

With ready help from you! How could it ever fail?

RUDRA

You are the Guru! There is such great beauty in your art. And such terror in the drama. It calls for all the nine *rasas*. It is perfect!

KRISHNA

With you to inspire the author, the tragedy is sure to be a success!

RUDRA

Vasudeva, what play will you compose next?

KRISHNA

The epic drama of the Kali age! The prologue will be set tomorrow, the first day in the age of Kali.

RUDRA

O Cosmic Poet, tell me the plot, quickly, describe the scenes to me.

KRISHNA

Here are a few prominent ones. Look there, Bharatvarsha, the garden of the Upanishads... And in the garden, Gautama the Buddha, dispeller of superstition...

Near him, Ashoka, the most compassionate... Moving westward, Jesus, the Saviour of the oppressed ...

Enlightened Greece, the mighty Roman empire, the many civilisations of Europe, and a Britain that turns great with science and its myriad applications in technology.

There's Arabia and the Prophet Mohammed. And in the sub-continent there, the appearance of Shankaracharya and his path to self-realisation. The Mughal Empire, showcased by the great diversity of cultures, held united by the tolerance among faiths. Karnataka, Vijayanagara, the poet Ranna...

Revolutions...the overthrow of empires. The invention of gunpowder and flying machines...the great wars drawing many nations into them...the horror of gigantic bombs...mass destruction... The resurgence of Bharatvarsha...Ramakrishna Paramahamsa...

(The figure of Rudra turns into members of the Chorus once again. Optional: The Chorus and Krishna bow to a figure of Ramakrishna Paramahamsa, revered by the poet-playwright Kuvempu.)

Ahimsa and satyagraha...the Mahatma...the inspiration for freedom movements across the world.

And yet, the persistence of human greed...the demons of poverty, impoverishment, subjugation.

(The Chorus is Rudra again, who trembles in rage, raises a war cry. Kali enters with his sceptre.)

KALI

Patience, patience, O Rudra! Do not be prejudiced. Do not close the great Epic in haste. It is as yet incomplete, still unfolding. Behold the future promised.

Peace on earth, goodwill among all peoples, prosperity without waste, gains without losses, lives lived to full potential, in tranquility with nature.

Look, look further into the future, the far, far future. The happiness of the earth is rooted in the earth's common people. There is laughter from children at play. There is opportunity for all, in study, in sport, in artistic pursuit, with no tally on colour of skin or birth station, or language or faith. Girls equal boys in number and in achievement. The shackles of our own making break down, slowly but surely, one at a time. The world looks to us once again for inspiration. There is music in the air, sweet, melodious, divine music. The people of the land learn to look after themselves once again.

(Rudra dissolves into the Chorus again. The Chorus and Krishna celebrate Kali's arrival, and bow in admiration to him. Krishna takes leave of Kali.

The Chorus forms a couch to carry Krishna away reclining. They exit in joy. Kali sees them off and turns to go himself. He sees the Old Woman seated in the corner. Kali goes up to her, raises her to her feet, and gives her his sceptre for support. They walk out together.)

Rapid fadeout

Close of play

GLOSSARY

Ajji — Grandmother. Also affectionate term for an elderly lady.

Akka — Elder sister. Also a suffix to a woman's name for respect.

Punya — Holy merit, earned merit.

Vedas — A large body of religious texts originating in ancient India. The texts constitute the oldest layer of Sanskrit literature and the oldest scripturesof Hinduism. There are four Vedas: the Rigveda, the Yajurveda, the Samaveda and the Atharvaveda.

Upanishads — A part of the Vedas, they are ancient Sanskrit texts that contain some of the central philosophical concepts and ideas of Hinduism, some of which are shared with religious traditions like Buddhism and Jainism.

Sastra — A Sanskrit word that means precept, rules, manual, compendium, book or treatise in a general sense. The word is generally used as a suffix in the Indian literature context, for applicable knowledge in a defined practice. When condensed into a set of practices it is called a *sutra.*

Agamas — A collection of principles and guidelines of several Hindu devotional schools, handed down traditionally. The term literally means tradition or 'that which has come down'.

Puranas — A vast genre of encyclopaedic Indian literature about a wide range of topics particularly myths, legends and other traditional lore.

Rasa — Literally means 'essence'. It connotes a concept in Indian arts about the aesthetic flavour of any visual, literary or musical work that evokes an emotion or feeling in the audience but cannot be described.

Dharma — Signifies behaviours that are considered to be

in accord with the order that makes life and the universe possible, and includes duties, rights, laws, conduct, virtues and 'right way of living'.

Adharma	Antonym of *dharma*. It means 'that which is not in accord with the dharma'. Connotations include discord, disharmony, wrongness, unnaturalness, evil, immorality, wickedness, and vice.
Sthitaprajna	A state of equanimity that combines calmness and intelligent vision. The state that Krishna induced in Arjuna on the battlefield when he was riddled with doubt and torn in emotional turmoil.
Krishne	Moniker for Draupadi, meaning the chosen one of Krishna, who makes her his sister and arranges her marriage to Arjuna. It may also mean the dark one, referring to Draupadi's complexion.
Gurudeva Durvasa	A rishi who became a Guru to young Kunti and taught her the Atharvaveda mantras by which she could invoke the presence of any god and beget their children. She sought Surya and conceived Karna through this boon.
Mantra	A sacred utterance, a sound, a syllable, word or phrase, or group of words believed to have psychological and spiritual powers.
Dwapara	A character created to represent a sage and chronicler overseeing the Dwapara eon, one of the *yugas* in Hindu thought.
Kali	A character created to represent a sage and chronicler overseeing the Kali eon. The *yuga* is explained in the introduction to the play. The character of Kali presents the poet-playwright's humanistic and positivistic world-view.
Murari	Another epithet for Krishna
Dwaipayana	The lake where Duryodhana cooled himself and rested when the war was lost. The final combat with Bhima was when he was tracked down there.

The Echo

An adaptation from the novella in Kannada
Chomana Dudi** by **Shivarama Karanth

FOR

MALAVIKA KAPUR

A TRIBUTE

The play script is dedicated to the memory of Kota Shivarama Karanth, in whose great body of work the early novella *Chomana Dudi* has a prominent place. The added significance is the historical fact that an extended field trip was the turning point in Karanth's life. The experience opened his eyes to the harsh reality of bonded labour in the rural areas, a far cry from the romanticised ideas we have of life in the Indian village. This play script came out of a long conversation we had sharing ideas about ecology and sustainability. It is an original product in itself, undertaken in the Play Development Programme at Bangalore Little Theatre Foundation. Yet, the author unhesitatingly acknowledges the inspiration provided by the Kannada novella, as explained in the Notes below, and his gratitude to the ready encouragement given by Shivarama Karanth himself for the play script.

Vijay Padaki

CHARACTERS IN THE PLAY

The characters may be seen as placed in three concentric circles. At the centre are just three characters: Choma, Belli and the Drum. The drum is Choma's trusty companion, and may, therefore, well be seen as a character in the play. It is left to the ingenuity of the performers to treat the drum as either an inanimate object with a voice or to be played by an actor imaginatively. I have viewed Choma's tale as an intense father-daughter relationship, their human yearnings and natural aspirations kept suppressed within a societal system not of their making.

In the second circle we have the main characters linked to the lives of Choma and Belli. These are Sankappaiah, the landlord, Biruma, the owner of the toddy shop, Manuel, the supervisor of the coffee estate and, finally, Michael, the owner-manager of the estate, although appearing briefly. Also in this circle are other members of Choma's household. His older sons, Chaniya and Guruva, are seen on stage. Kala and Neela, younger brothers to Belli, are not seen. Biruma is seen onstage only in the prologue. The household includes the dog, Badu, and two bullocks. The imagery around the unseen boys and animals is a crucial challenge for actors.

In the outermost circle are characters who criss-cross through the tale and add substance to it in their own way. One actor can play all these parts.

'I have great faith in the ingenuity of actors to devise means of reducing the very large cast of characters in order to make it possible to perform....'. That quote is from Agatha Christie in her 1952 introduction to *Witness for the Prosecution*. It is certainly true of a great deal of contemporary drama. I also saw *The Echo* fitting into the Storytelling Theatre programme of Bangalore Little Theatre, to be performed by just two actors.

The Echo unfolds through nine scenes in one continuous flow. It is constructed to have only two to four characters on stage at any given time. If the performing group wishes to have an intermission it can be between Scenes 6 and 7.

SCENES

Scene 1: Introducing Bhogana village
A series of vignettes and crossfades to establish the character of the village and Choma's family.
Scene 2: Choma and his family
The bullocks and his dream of becoming a farmer. Choma's debt at the plantation.
Scene 3: Bonded labour
Choma's older sons leave for the plantation to clear the debt. The journey and their arrival.
Scene 4: The plantation
The reality of life in the plantation, the lure of drink. The brothers' quarrel and the decision of the younger one not to return.
Scene 5: Death of the older son
The older son returns with news of the younger deserting. Death of the son.
Scene 6: Choma's wail
Forces ranged against him. Life without dreams of farming fulfilled.
Scene 7: The plantation's grip
The debt at the plantation remains. Choma's daughter and a younger son go to clear the debt.
Scene 8: The daughter at the plantation
The daughter's awakening and her falling into traps. Her escape and return to the village.
Scene 9: The fate of the untouchable
Celebration of daughter's return followed by tragic death of younger son. Last recourse to conversion for dignity. The gods do not want a release.

The stage and set are as simple, humble and stark as the lives of the characters in the play. Yet, they acquire a sharpness every now and then under appropriate lighting, and in the way the characters inhabit the space, as if standing out in defiance and crying out to be seen.

A differentiation in levels might help. The highest level, perhaps (Up Left) may be the plantation management space, along with the manager's desk. The lowest space, (perhaps Down Right) may be for the hutment where Choma and his family live. They have been there for generations. Perhaps there is a tree near the hut, a favourite spot for Choma and his drum. An intermediate level may serve the needs of multiple scenes, with several different characters. A cyclorama with a platform below it can serve many useful purposes.

INTRODUCTION

THIS IS AN English language adaptation of a Kannada classic, developed at the Academy of Theatre Arts, Bangalore Little Theatre Foundation.

One of the earliest challenges was the choice of a suitable title for the play in English. The title *Chomana Dudi* in Kannada is beautifully wrapped in layers of connotative meaning. It seems impossible to find a single word in English that captures the multiple shades of *Dudi*. I finally settled for the aural quality of a wail that returns as an echo every now and then and refuses to be wished away.

Starting acknowledgement

Although Kota Shivarama Karanth was already known and revered as a colossus in Kannada literature in the seventies, my first encounter with him was in his environment activism avatar. I was part of the founding Faculty of Indian Institute of Management in Bangalore, and studying social movements that brought diverse individuals and groups together, rallying around issues of significance. It included understanding tribal cultures and the constitutionally guaranteed rights to them. It was through Karanth's profoundly holistic view of society that I first understood the necessary and inevitable connections across literature, storytelling traditions, poetry, music and performances on the one hand and the so-called development issues that we had got accustomed to examining in glass jars in academia.

Karanth's personal accounts on circumstances leading to *Chomana Dudi* led to invigorating new insights. I decided then to dramatise the novella from this perspective. When I first approached Shivarama Karanth with this thought his response was that it was a good idea. Years later I had the opportunity of a leisurely chat after a meal. He fully understood the two caps I had worn all my life, one in the theatre and the other in management, with a special interest in large development programmes. He gave the project an enthusiastic thumbs-up.

I started work on the play soon after that meeting. The first ten pages were dissatisfying. I tore them up and put the project aside. This happened three times. Even as I was trying to understand what was going wrong, the calendar read 9 December 1997. He was no more. I had not produced anything of substance to show him before he passed away. I was angry with myself. I was also very sad.

It was the time when the Royal National Theatre in London and Bangalore Little Theatre were engaged in an important exchange project. It helped to take my mind off the project. I returned to the idea every year, but the momentum was lost.

Towards the end of 2013, I picked up my old notes, revisited the novella, saw the landmark Kannada movie once again online, and had longish discussions with friends steeped in Kannada literature. The embers began to glow again. And then, it was really a re-reading of ecological case studies that got me to put pen to paper again. And fingers to the keyboard. I grasped, at last, what was missing in my previous attempts. I shall not inflict these ruminations on the reader here. Instead, I shall simply share with the reader the few guideposts that I adopted in picking up the abandoned project and bringing it to closure, this time in a continuous burst of writing. Here goes:

- It is, first and last, a play. It was an entirely different and original product, accepted as such by Karanth himself. It must satisfy the requirements of a good play. It must not end up as a transfer of the narrative prose (very descriptive and without doubt very beautiful) into the mouths of characters on stage.
- The construction of the play will rely on the creation of images, some seen, some to be imagined, that will compensate the absence of narrative prose. It must rely on good acting – and action – to accomplish this.

- The spoken word has to be kept clipped and parsimonious – not using two sentences to say what can be said in one, as attractive as the original prose might be.
- The number of characters on stage has to be limited. The novella has a score of delightful cameo characters. They are essential to the prose and film traditions. Drama on stage? We must aim to do more with less, the most with the least. We must also keep the constraints of a performing company in mind. A small cast, working with a minimalistic stage, would make it attractive for performance by many.
- A case in point is the decision not to have Choma's two younger sons, Kala and Neela, appear on stage. This was not an easy decision. The two boys can bring a certain springiness to the scenes. (And amateur drama companies love to accommodate their children on stage!) On balance, however, I felt the value added by their presence was not as much as the acting challenge to create their presence without their being there.
- The script had to maintain complete fidelity to the essence and content of the prose, but it had to go beyond the narrative to create the needed sense in the spoken word.
- Finally, in the case of this play script, I felt it best to retain the linear flowin the novella. The story is spread over two years, over three annual temple festivals. As tempting as it might be for a dramatist to play with back-and-forth time frames, Choma's tale appears to acquire a deeper meaning as it unfolds through the two years.

I am quite aware of the possibility of raised eyebrows to the approach taken in this adaptation. They are more likely to be from those who are berthed in literary traditions. Kannada dramatists (and dramatists world-wide), on the other hand, with their evolved theatre craft, are more likely to find sense in this adaptation for the stage.

SCENE 1

Introducing Bhogana Village

In the dark, the sound of a thunderstorm. Build up to huge claps of thunder, followed by rain. Slow fade out.

After a few beats of silence, the long wail of a dog. Then a slow, steady rhythmic beat of a country drum.

Lap dissolve to the beat of a temple plate cymbal, arati, temple bells.

Lap dissolve to gaggle of voices in a festive crowd.

Fade out and lap dissolve to the drum, now louder, more strident. Gradual reduction in tempo to the original. Slow fade out, but a fatigued beat, irregular in rhythm, kept through the following scenes, serving as a preview or overture.

- *The lights fade in on the cyclorama to silhouette a line of villagers returning from the temple festival.*
- *Crossfade to Belli, huddled in sleep on the floor, her face buried between her knees. She stirs. She is tired, worn out, and temporarily unable to draw on the reserve of stoic determination that has served her at other times. She goes back to sleep.*
- *Crossfade to tree outside the hut. Choma, overcome by fatigue and drink is at the drum, not letting go.*
- *Crossfade to cyclorama. A pair of oxen silhouetted, tied to a tree*
- *Crossfade to toddy shop. Biruma is pouring out a glass of the drink to a customer.*
- *Crossfade to cyclorama, a group of men undertaking a journey, led by Manuel.*
- *Crossfade to Choma as before.*
- *Crossfade to Belli. Manuel is standing over her. She stirs, rises hesitantly.*

The drumming stops abruptly. Blackout.

The lights fade in on the landlord, Sankappaiah, at his verandah. Choma enters feebly, pays his respects, and squats on the floor before the landlord. Long pause. Fade out.

Cross fade with a tight spot on the drum. A voice on the audio system.

DRUM

When did I come into Choma's life? He does not remember. He cannot remember. He might, when his head clears. *(Pause)* It is usually clear in the morning. You cannot expect it to be clear after sunset. Nobody expects that of Choma. *(Pause)* No one in the village can tell when I came into Choma's life. He has me. He beats me very hard every night. He beats me for long hours. He has no wife. He has me. I don't complain. He needs me. When the anger is spent, and the lightness of head takes over his body, he beats me with anguished, telling strokes.

He has a family of course, as dear to him as he is to them. Do they remember their mother? Does he? *(Pause)* I was there when she came into his life...into this very hut that they made their home. Under this very tree they sat as he caressed his drum and showed her how it responded to his touch. *(Pause)* I did not mind when he left me under the tree to attend to matters more demanding. *(If an actor is to play the Drum, he appears at this point. He goes up to the drum and stands staring at it, even as the audio track continues.)*

But this is Choma's story. Not mine, nor that of his wife. Choma's tale. A long saga for some – those who delight in taking note of every twist and turn through every journey, beginning to end. A short and simple tale for others, with only an end...the end known from the beginning. It does not matter where we begin. Life in the hamlet of Bhogana has not changed much since I first came here. Set deep in a hillside forest, the little village has not more than two hundred people living there, in about forty homes. You will not find Bhogana village on a map. Who cares about a tribal village and its people? Except those who have learned to thrive on the wretchedness of others. Oh yes, there are some who care. *(The actor playing the Drum picks up the drum and attaches it to himself as designed by the performing group. The audio track continues.)*

There is so much I can tell you about Choma, about Choma's village, about the forest in which the village exists, the people here, the people in the world outside who are tied to this village...the way the lives of all these people criss-cross. And Choma, his life, his family, those who left, those who remain...his dreams. Ah, we do not have the time. We cannot do full justice to the story of Choma in the little time we have...*(The actor takes over from the audio track at this point)*

That master storyteller who created Choma has passed on. Can anybody tell the story the way he did? It has been left to me. After all, I was Choma's constant companion.

(Cyclorama. Silhouette of a line of villagers returning from the temple festival, a few flaming torches among them.)

DRUM *(Continuing)*

There is an annual festival in the neighbouring village of Panja. It is a temple festival. People from villages all around gather there. It is the only temple in these parts. It is the only festival in the year.

The villages are empty the whole day, from before dawn to well after midnight. Everybody is in Panja to see the idol taken out in a chariot and taken back to its place in the temple. What idol? Which deity? They do not all know. They do not care. It is a god that calls out to them once a year. Thanks to the idol's outing there is a festival in Panja. There is a fair, there is music and dancing, there are all kinds of fancy things sold in the temple square and on both sides of the street. Of course there is a sumptuous lunch served by the temple. On this day there is no cooking in any home in any village. They return only at night, tired and worn out. So they make the most of the temple meal.

Choma, too, went to Panja, his family with him. That was four sons and a daughter. They enjoyed themselves like all the others, dancing and making merry as much as custom permitted. They returned earlier than the rest of the villagers. There was no food at the festival for them. Custom did not permit untouchables joining the others at the meal. He sat by himself, under this very tree, while Belli prepared the rice gruel for all. Belli, his daughter, was like a mother to all her brothers. I gave Choma company outside.

(A fade out begins. The drum fades in.)

He played with me all evening, sitting under this tree. He poured his heart out to me. What would he do without me?

(Rapid fade out. Drum in full.)

SANKA *(He is seated in his verandah)*

What would he do without me? Life in this village...What can you expect in a tribal village? We are all poor people. Only, some people are poorer than others. *(Choma enters feebly, pays his respects, and squats on the floor before the landlord. A pause.)*

This is Choma...He is one of those. Born poor, he will remain poor all his life. He will die poor. He works the land here – my land. He has a family of six to feed – two boys, one girl, two more boys – no wife – one dog they call Badu. He also has a pair of oxen. He takes very good care of them. I have asked if he will sell them to me. He will not entertain the thought. Choma and oxen! For what? That hut where the family stays – dog, bullocks and all – the hut may be his, but the land? The land is mine. What is he going to do with the oxen? The Muslim butcher at the edge of the village – he made an offer too. He can tell a good load of meat when he sees one. But Choma...

The oldest son is the same age as me. He is his father's son. I am who I am. *(He tosses Choma two bags of grain.)*

SANKA *(Continuing)*

I pay him in kind. That's half a seer of rice for his day's labour. And a seer and a quarter of paddy. They will pound it and winnow it and get another half seer of rice from that. *(Choma picks up the bags gratefully and starts to leave.)*

You could say it is sufficient for a family of six to hold body and soul together. He does not ask for more. It will do for now. It will meet his immediate need.

(Crossfade to Biruma. He is at his toddy shop.)

BIRUMA

He should be here any moment now. Always the first at my toddy shop, just after sunset. Totally religious about it. He believes firmly that the day he does not have his drink he will drop dead. That has not happened so far. He never has the money for the toddy. He pays in kind. That is all right in the village. If people pay for the drinks by giving something that is useful, why not? A bag of rice, some firewood, some jaggery...a daughter, a wife...

You see the three large jars of toddy standing there. The best toddy is in the first jar. It is kept for those who know good toddy and can afford it. Choma gets his drink from the third jar. It is already poured into a bottle and kept there for him. What would he do without me?

(Choma enters feebly, pays his respects, drops a bag of rice before Biruma and squats on the floor.)

Dot on time. Not more than five minutes since the sun disappeared in the western sky.

(Rises to get a bottle of toddy for Choma, places it before him.
Crossfade to Belli. She is at work.)

BELLI

I must keep dinner ready before dark. No lamp is lit inside our hut. Why? What precious things do we have inside that need a lamp? What can we possibly do inside that needs light? When we need fire, we get it from the landlord's house. We eat outside and then go in whenever each of us thinks it is time. We eat whenever each thinks it is time. I make sure the little ones eat early. Kala and Neela, I make sure they get something to eat. They have been sick a long time. In this village the menfolk drag little boys to the toddy shop. They start early. Not Kala and Neela, though. They have been spared. The older ones, yes. Chaniya and Guruva probably go to the toddy shop every now and then. Probably on the sly. They would not like to be seen drinking by their father. He would not like to see them there.

My father, he is different. He must have his drink every day. But he makes sure there is some paddy saved for the house before going to the toddy shop. As if I don't know that he gives away the rice to pay for his toddy.

Sometimes he takes away baskets I have woven for sale at the weekly market. They fetch him an extra glass or two. When he drinks he casts off all the cares and burdens of this cruel world. All he has as precious company is his drum.

People in the village say things about him. Behind his back. Choma and his drum, they say mockingly, and they laugh. All he ever wants in this life is his toddy and his drum. They cannot understand.

He is my father, after all. He has given me life, brought me up. Whatever I am is because of him. I look after him. What would I do without him?

(Crossfade to drum. Soft drumming in the background. Choma enters, walking unsteadily. He passes the drum, knocking it down. The drumming stops abruptly. The drum remains in a tight spot.)

DRUM

He will be back. I do not mind this little offence. It is not serious. It is not by intent. He needs me. He will be back.

(Rapid fade out. Drum in full. The sound of a thunderstorm, followed by rain. Slow fade out.)

SCENE 2

Belli is at work. She is preparing a batch of rice gruel and attending to smaller chores at the same time. Choma walks in and sits. Belli pours ladles of the gruel into a bowl and hands it to Choma.

CHOMA

I have been thinking...

BELLI

Yes?

CHOMA

The time has come.

BELLI

You are right. We have to do something about the hut. The walls have too many tears and openings. The battered old roof does not keep out either the wind or the rain. We are sleeping out all the time. The downpour last night...

CHOMA

I was not thinking of the hut.

BELLI

Oh...

CHOMA

Our two bullocks.

BELLI

Even they were drenched inside the hut.

CHOMA

They are now more than ready.

BELLI

You are going to sell them at last?

CHOMA

No. I have not raised them to be sold.

BELLI

You are not going to...

CHOMA

I will meet the landlord today and ask him.

BELLI

He is sure to snub you.

CHOMA

I have worked it out. All I want is a small patch of the field at this end. He can rent it out to me. I will pay for it. One *maund* of rice should be a good price as rent.

BELLI

No! You must not do anything so stupid. He will never listen to you. He can never accept you as a farmer. He will mock you and abuse you! (*Choma is speechless. He starts to sob.*)

CHOMA

I wanted to be a farmer when your mother was alive. It did not happen. I thought at least her children would see me as a farmer. And I have to hear this from you! You dash my hopes...Why have I hung on to the two bullocks? To hear this from you! (*Belli softens and sits next to him. Choma is sobbing.*)

BELLI

You are weeping. I have never seen you... Not since the day Amma went away. I never knew... (*Belli is helpless. She does not know how to console Choma. She rises, picks up the drum and sits before him. She begins to play the drum. Choma snaps out of his state and snatches the drum from her. Belli is relieved. She rises.*)

BELLI

There! I know you will not do anything foolish. I have to leave now. The women going into the forest for picking must have left by now. I will catch up with them. We can talk about this in the afternoon. (*Belli leaves hurriedly. Choma sits still for a moment and then begins caressing the drum. Gradually he starts beating a rhythm on it.*)

(*Crossfade to Sankappaiah. The sound of the drum reaches him.*)

SANKA

Ha! Rather early in the day for this. Dhamadhama-dhakadhaka-dhamadhama-dhakadhaka – over and over, on and on. What could it be? Only two possibilities. He is either in a good mood and has started drinking early. Or he is in a bad mood. And is drinking early. I say it is a good mood. *(The drumming stops)*

He has stopped. That means he will come here any minute now. And make excuses about his late-coming. He should have been in the fields by now. All the other workers are there already. Late! It is not the first time he is late.

(Crossfade to Choma. He is seated where he was, the drum between his legs. He is looking up at Manuel towering over him.)

MANUEL

Choma.

CHOMA

Yes...

MANUEL

You are Choma.

CHOMA

Yes, sir. *(Rises)* And you are...

MANUEL

Twenty rupees.

CHOMA

Twenty? Rupees?

MANUEL

You owe twenty rupees to the planter.

CHOMA

I owe him twenty rupees?

MANUEL

You borrowed money. You think it was a gift? *(A long pause during which Choma begins to understand the demand.)*

CHOMA

The coffee plantation...Kalasa...

MANUEL

Aah, you remember!

CHOMA

It was long ago. My wife had just died, and I needed...

MANUEL

You needed money. You borrowed money. From the planter.

CHOMA

It must have been a small amount. About five or six rupees.

MANUEL

And security.

CHOMA

Security?

MANUEL

Who will give money to a miserable untouchable like you, huh? What security? Only the bones in your body. You were to clear the loan by working on the plantation.

CHOMA

It was a long time ago.

MANUEL

You did not return. You stayed back here.

CHOMA

It was just five rupees.

MANUEL

It is twenty now. Rascal! People like you, all rascals. Take loans and never think of paying them back!

CHOMA

Twenty rupees...

MANUEL

I will be here on Saturday. Be ready to start for the plantation.

(Manuel leaves. Choma is frozen, dumbfounded. The sound of a dog barking offstage, followed by the voice of Belli.)

BELLI

The bullocks are straying back home from the field! Be sure to tie them up when they get there.

CHOMA *(To himself)*

I will sell the bullocks. I will have to sell them after all.

(He sits in despair) How else can I pay off the twenty rupees? *(The sound of a dog barking again)* Badu! Good dog! Bring the bullocks home. Good dog! You know those are no ordinary bullocks.

(He rises, inspired) No! They are not to be sold! I will find another way to pay off the planter. I will find a way.

(Crossfade to Sankappaiah)

SANKA

He should be back from the fields by now. Funny fellow! First he is late. Then he rushes in here, picks up his spade and basket and rushes out like someone possessed. All the others stopped nearly an hour ago. He is still there, digging and clearing, digging and clearing. All that silt from the monsoon torrent – until it is cleared there can be no cultivation there. He has not taken a break the whole morning. Aah, there he is.

(Choma enters, wiping his brow, and squats before Sankappaiah. A long pause. Sankappaiah pushes a piece of tobacco and a betel leaf with lime on it to Choma with a stick. Choma accepts the gesture gratefully and begins to knead the tobacco in his palm with the lime. Sankappaiah watches Choma for a while and finally speaks.)

SANKA

Your bullocks. *(Choma looks up expectantly)*

Have you pledged them to some god or what? *(No response)*

No? You have some other plan? *(No response)*

Why not harness them for ploughing here? *(No response)*

You know my bullocks are old. They may not be fit enough this season. Your bullocks – you can sell them to me. Or they can remain your own, but left here in my shed. *(No response)*

Bullocks are not kept for show, are they? They are meant for ploughing, yes or no? They are needed for ploughing here. *(No response)*

If you say yes, I will not look anywhere else. I will pay you cash straight away. You can name the price. We can ask another person to fix the price if you like. *(No response)*

Say something. Are you on some *maun* (vow of silence) or what?

CHOMA

How can I deny you the use of my bullocks?

SANKA

So you will give them to me.

CHOMA

I cannot sell them. I have a wish. A dream.

SANKA

What dream?

CHOMA

Only you can make my dream come true.

SANKA

What dream?

(Handing Choma his wages of a bag of rice and a bag of paddy) Here, you have worked hard today. You can be sure there will always be work on this farm for an old hand like you. Now, forget all your dreams and run off to Biruma's toddy shop! *(He laughs. Choma laughs along politely, but does not move.)*

What? Still sitting there?

CHOMA

About the oxen.

SANKA

Yes?

CHOMA

I wish to till the land myself with those bullocks.

SANKA

You wish to...

CHOMA

Sire, you have so many tenant farmers on your land. Can I not be one of them? I will till it myself.

SANKA

Choma, you know who you are – an untouchable. How can you ever think of being a farmer?

CHOMA

Give me a small plot, sire, even barren patch, and I shall take your name with reverence for the rest of my life.

SANKA

(Thoughtfully) There is a lot of barren land. Maybe...I have to think about it. I cannot give you an answer without consulting our mother. *(Sankappaiah goes indoors. Choma touches the ground with his head and raises his arms heavenwards in anticipation of a divine boon. He then hears the loud shriek of a woman offstage followed by spitting. Choma is frozen. Sankappaiah steps out, shaking his head.)*

SANKA

It cannot be done. Our ancestors never ever leased any land to an untouchable. It is not possible to change that now. *(Choma lowers his head to the ground once again, this time sobbing. Sankappaiah watches. Manuel enters and pays his respects.)*

SANKA

Choma, you better leave now. *(Choma raises his head, stares at Sankappaiah, not noticing Manuel.)*

MANUEL

Choma! *(Choma rises in fright)*

Sankappaiah, sir, may I ask what this son of a whore is doing here?

SANKA

He works here. He is a landless daily wager.

MANUEL

This rascal owes our planter some twenty rupees. Has he come here begging you to bail him out?

SANKA

No, he is here because –

MANUEL

I hope you will not make that mistake. When will a wretched untouchable like him ever repay a loan? In which century? Son of a whore!

SANKA

Choma! Do you owe the planter money? *(Choma does not answer)* Did I not give you work here on the condition that you had no debts anywhere? Well?! (*Choma leaves hurriedly, in fear. The two men laugh.)*

SANKA

Look at him scurry. He has left his wage behind! *(Calling after him)* Choma! Your rice and paddy! How can you go to Biruma's shop with empty hands?!

(Crossfade to the drum)

DRUM

Choma had not known sorrow like this in a long, long time. Not since his wife had been taken away by the evil spirit of *Guliga Bhoota*, throwing up blood and dropping lifeless. It was not the abuses. Untouchable, bastard, thief, son of a thief, son of a whore – these were routine, the words floating around people like him all the time, from the time he was born. It was not the debt to the planter either. He would find a way to be released from that, although he knew that once his neck was in the clutches of a debtor there really was no way out. Not for himself, not for his sons, god knows for how many generations. But not being leased a patch of land to till...It was a blow that had knocked him down. Why did Sankappaiah have to consult the mother? Could he not make up his mind himself?

He waited in the wooded area till Manuel and the landlord went indoors. He recovered his two bags of wages and went to Biruma's shop – wretched, angry, dejected, confused. Biruma was closing his shop, but when he saw Choma approaching with a large bag he waited. Sankappaiah had added a bonus seer of rice for Choma's hard work. Biruma weighed the rice and announced a smaller quantity in his usual sly manner. Choma did not care. He wanted the drink. *(The actors may have the following narration accompanied by mime in front of Biruma's shop if they wish to.)*

DRUM *(Continuing)*

When the drink arrived he gulped it all down at once. When Choma demanded some more, Biruma added water to the dregs in the jar and thrust a bottle before him. Choma asked if there was something to eat. Biruma glared at him, closed his shop and walked away. Choma yelled after Biruma, but knowing that it was useless he broke into a dance in front of the shop. He danced till he dropped exhausted. He woke up well after midnight when there was a thunderstorm. Cursing the downpour, he staggered homeward, the path lit now and then with the flashes of lightning. *(A slow fade out on the drum. The voice continues.)*

DRUM

Belli had a pot of gruel ready for Choma. The two younger brothers were already asleep. She had dozed off waiting for Choma's return. (*By now the stage is dark. The following conversation takes place in the dark, perhaps with occasional glimmers, accompanied by sounds – gusts of wind, pots, pans, etc.)*

CHOMA

Belli! Where are you?

BELLI

You are here. I was worried...You are drenched...Ohh, you have a fever...Sit down here.

CHOMA

Something to eat.

BELLI

Here...It has turned cold, but let me pour it into a bowl.

CHOMA

No need, give me the pot. What about you?

BELLI

Go ahead. Have as much as you want...Now you must rest.

CHOMA

I am all right.

BELLI

The fever is very high. Let me find something to cover you.

CHOMA

Naah...

BELLI

Where are you going? Don't step on the children.

CHOMA

Aah, here you are! *(He begins to beat the drum. It is stopped abruptly.)*

BELLI

Here! Give it to me! It is way past midnight. The children are asleep. You must be out of your senses, drumming in the middle of the night!

CHOMA

I am not drunk, Belli. Don't talk to me like that.

BELLI

You must lie down, now. Here, cover yourself with this. Go inside and lie down. *(A pause and change of tone)* I hope you remember you are getting a visitor in the morning – that supervisor from the plantation.

(Fade in on drum)

DRUM

Belli did the right thing, don't you think? Drumming in the middle of the night! With high fever too! The next morning... Everybody was out, busy with the day's chores. Belli had taken charge. The older boys attended to the landlord, the younger ones fetched the bullocks, left out in the rain, shivering. They were given a rub down and released to graze on their own.

Belli herself had so many things to do. She had begun to see the oxen as a burden. Choma was still asleep, the fever even higher now. When Belli reached home she went in directly to attend to Choma. Manuel arrived just then.

(The scene alternates between the drum and the entrance to the hut here onwards)

MANUEL

Choma!

(Belli appears from inside)

BELLI

Sir...

MANUEL

I have come for Choma

BELLI

Sir, my father is running a high fever.

MANUEL

Fever? So suddenly? He was fine yesterday. Has he called the fever by his side because of my visit?

BELLI

Sir, can you please come some time later?

MANUEL

Thieves! Scum of the earth! Gutter swine! Bastard offspring of a bastard race! You dare to defy me with your filthy lies! *(By this time Choma has staggered out)*

Aah, here is the prime bastard himself. So, you have a fever!

CHOMA

You don't have to shout at her, sir. Shout as much as you want at me. Here, clench your hands around my neck. That way you will feel the fever I am carrying.

DRUM

The supervisor saw that Choma was weak and calmed down. He explained to Choma that he was just doing his job. He had to collect the debt – either in cash or in labour. He had enquired with Sankappaiah if he would be willing to pay up on Choma's behalf and hold him as labour instead. The landlord was not inclined.

Choma stared in disbelief as Manuel continued.

MANUEL

Sankappaiah has offered a solution. If Choma gives him his bullocks he might consider a suitable arrangement.

(Chaniya and Guruva, Choma's older sons, have joined the group in front of the hut.)

CHOMA

The bullocks...they do not come into the picture. You want your twenty rupees? I will get it for you. Leave that to me.

MANUEL

Have it your way. But you have to show me soon.

CHOMA *(Pointing to the sons)*

You see these two boys?Do you see how big and strong they are? Bodies of iron. The two of them together can take care of my bond in half the time.

MANUEL

If they are ready to come.

CHOMA

Do they have a choice? Did I have a choice?

MANUEL

When can they start?

BELLI

Right away. Let me just give them a good meal first. *(She sends the two boys in)* They were ready for this. They want to go.

CHOMA

Are you satisfied? You came looking for one. You are getting two.

MANUEL

They can be at the plantation till the debt is cleared.

CHOMA

Do not pay anything more, just take care of their two meals a day. Send them back as soon as the debt is cleared.

DRUM

The boys were excited about the journey to the plantation. They had never been any further than a village or two nearby. And the neighbouring village of Panja for the temple festival.

There was not much preparation needed. The boys had no clothes other than what they wore. Choma pulled out a woven basket and put some of his old clothes in them.

He then took off the blanket that Belli had put on him and put it into the basket. As eager as the boys might have been to set off with the plantation supervisor, the thought of leaving their ageing father and loving sister slowed them down. Their eyes turned misty. And that brought tears in the eyes of the two others. Choma called the three children together and they sat down. Choma spoke to the sons.

CHOMA

Work honestly. Work hard. Be done with the debt I have imposed on you as quickly as you can. Come back soon. You will never have to think of the plantation again.

Guruva, keep your tongue under control. Don't be rash. Speak with respect to the supervisor and the planter. Keep out of bad company. Keep away from the toddy shop. It's bad enough that I took to drink. You don't have to live a beggar's life. The two of you must live with your heads held high.

Chaniya, I will find a bride for you before you return. Here, you keep this ring of mine. It will protect you. It will be useful if you happen to be in trouble and need money. *(A long pause)* You will come back soon. Clear the debt and come back soon.

DRUM

Choma had run out of words. They sat still and read each other's minds. They wiped their tears and sat a little longer. At a nod from Belli the two boys rose and left quietly. Belli moved closer to Choma and put her arm around him. They sat together a while longer.

I knew the time had come. He would rise and reach for me.

(Fade out. The sound of drumming.)

SCENE 3

The sound of drumming continues.

The lights fade in on the cyclorama to silhouette a line of villagers on a journey. Chaniya and Guruva have joined others in the long trek to the plantation.

Light on Belli in a corner, held low. She is huddled on the floor, her face buried between her knees. She stirs. She goes back to sleep.

The drumming stops.

Light on the drum. Choma is lying next to it, asleep. He rises, walks up to Belli. Seeing her huddled he takes off his sheet and covers her with it. He sits next to her.

Spot on drum.

DRUM

The journey to the plantation was long. It was taxing. Small groups of fours and sixes joined the party along the way like thin rivulets till the number had swelled to over a hundred. We could write a whole story on the journey alone – the awe-inspiring beauty of the forests, the hills, the streams. Those who have not been to South Kanara will never know the true meaning of what is penned in words by the writer of this tale. It is a land to gladden the hearts of the hardest of mind, and to unleash the poet in them.

For the newcomers, like Guruva and Chaniya, it was a picnic. They were in high spirits, at least the first two days. The old-timers did not show the same enthusiasm. They were well prepared for the hardships on the way, as well as the hunger, the cold and the illnesses that hit many of them. They knew the hell that awaited them at the plantation.

There was a death on the journey. A sickly child succumbed to a fever. It was sad and demoralising, but not unexpected. The journey was interrupted briefly, and the group moved on. Eyes burning, legs swollen, backs bent, they moved on. Every time they came to a stream they cooled off their bodies as best as they could.

There were toddy shops along the way. Chaniya and Guruva grew up from the occasional drink on the sly in their village to open drinking in seasoned company.

Finally, after four days and three nights on the road, across hot plains, through steamy jungles, and over a range of hills, they arrived at the plantation. They were paraded before Michael Sir, the owner of the plantation, and then sent off to the labour lines, the long row of rooms that looked like an elongated cowshed.

A new life was opening for Chaniya and Guruva. For the others it was a return to the life they had known only too well. It was a life from which they had no escape.

More about the plantation later. Here comes my master now. He looks lost. He needs some comfort.

(Choma enters slowly, picks up the drum and sits down. He caresses the drum without playing it. He begins to talk to himself.)

CHOMA

God will take care of my two sons. I should not be brooding about their absence. They will be all right in the plantation...We have two mouths less to feed...There are the two other boys, Kala and Neela. They are not so sick now. They are growing...There is Belli...Belli, Belli, I have so much more to do for you. I will, I will. My promise to your mother...There are my two bullocks. God was great sending them to me as two lost calves in the forest...He must have wanted me to be a farmer...I close my eyes and I see a plough before me. If I cannot till my own land, there is no reason why I should do it for a landlord...I can go to that government officer and ask for a piece of land. It will be dry and hard, but it will be my land...My own hut on that land...I will work that land and grow whatever it can give us...There is the forest. We take care of the forest. The forest will take care of us... *(To the drum)* I have you...Haam!

(He gives the drum one or two sharp beats, rises and enters the hut. The sound of drumming continues. Sankappaiah's voice is heard offstage.)

SANKA

Choma! Choma, rascal! Choma!

(Entering) Bad enough your keeping the whole village awake beating that drum through the night, you want to go deaf with your own drumming! Choma! *(The drumming stops. Choma emerges and immediately drops to the ground before the landlord.)*

SANKA

So...you are down with a fever. You are resting. Belli came to say that you are weak and sick.

CHOMA

It is the fever from the rain, sire.

SANKA

But you are strong enough to beat that drum.

CHOMA

It was also the loss, sire. With both the grown up sons gone to the plantation...My heart was down.

SANKA

So you went to Biruma's shop to drown your sorrow!

CHOMA

How could I go there, sire? With what would I pay him?

SANKA

My question, too. If you don't come to work, you have no earning. With what will you pay for all your daily needs? Unless you have been sitting here and weaving baskets or something like that! Four baskets for eight bottles of toddy!

CHOMA

No, sire, I have just been...

SANKA

There is a lot of work to be done before the monsoon breaks. Fields to be fenced, bunds for the drain, a new shed for storing bamboo shoots. Do I have to come here to tell you? Make sure you are there tomorrow when the sun rises. *(He turns to go)*

CHOMA

I will be there, master.

(Sankappaiah smiles and tosses Choma a wad of tobacco)

SANKA

Tomorrow. At sunrise.

(The cyclorama. We see Choma working furiously, digging, shovelling, shifting head-loads of earth...Looking heavenwards.)

(Sankappaiah's verandah. Choma enters and sits. Sankappaiah enters. Choma bows.)

SANKA

Well done, Choma! Which spirits did you call to your side when you went to the fields? You were possessed. Nobody will believe how much you have done between sunrise and sunset. And to think you were sick till just a week ago! *(Choma has remained with his head touching the ground)*

What is it, Choma? You want something extra for the day's work? *(Choma looks up and nods in the negative)*

What is it then? Speak up. You know I understand your difficulties.

CHOMA

One small piece of land...A lease...The land will remain yours... Just enough to grow ten seers of paddy.

SANKA

Ohh, Choma...You and your farming!

CHOMA

My bullocks...

SANKA

And your bullocks!

CHOMA

Sire, it is not to show off that I am a farmer.

SANKA

You need more income? I know that. With two sons gone, there is less coming into the house. I know.

CHOMA

Just one small piece of land.

SANKA

Let me think it over. There is no hurry.

CHOMA

Before the monsoon comes down...

SANKA

Let me think it over. *(Choma rises, his face brightening. He straightens himself and walks out with a new found optimism. Sankappaiah sees him go.)*

SANKA

I pitied him. I would much rather lease land to him than the others who make promise after promise, but have excuse after excuse in not paying up the rent. I like the rascal. But my hands were tied. There was no way I could help him out without the family's consent. Without my mother's consent. They would have none of it. Certainly not in this family. An untouchable as a farmer! They would never hear of such a sin. Even people of lower castes would turn against the family if an untouchable was leased land for farming. I waited it out for a few days, and then broke the news to Choma. Of course Choma was disappointed. He turned away and hid his face. I could make out that he was crying. I gave him some advice. I told him that no man can stretch his legs more than the length of the mat. I told him there was no point in weeping over what fate had reserved for him and his people.

Choma did not report for work the next day. He sent word that he had to be away visiting a sick relative.

(Crossfade to a small desk and two chairs. Choma and a peasant are next to it.)

PEASANT

I was like you. In the village right next to yours. I could not bear it any longer. So I came here. My family joined me two months later.

CHOMA

And you are a farmer now?

PEASANT

Not a lowly labourer anymore. I have my own plot of land to till.

CHOMA

The church gave you the land?

PEASANT

They got a lot of land for their work with people like us. The school, the hospital, the wells...

CHOMA

They are doing so much good work.

PEASANT

And they don't bother about what caste you are born in. Have you done farming? Or only coolie labour.

CHOMA

I have two bullocks of my own.

(The priest enters and goes to the desk. Choma bends to touch his feet. The priest straightens him. Choma reacts, not accustomed to being touched by a person of higher caste. The peasant exits at a signal from the priest.)

PRIEST

Sit down. *(Choma declines, remains standing)*

Do you know any others in this colony? *(Choma nods)*

Are you interested in shifting here? *(Choma nods hesitantly)*

There is no hurry. You can take your time to decide. There must be things you have to settle before you can leave your village. *(Pause)*

What do you think you can do if you come here?

CHOMA

I have two bullocks.

PRIEST

I see...You have experience working on the land.

CHOMA

If I can get...

PRIEST

It should be possible, it should be possible. We have no restrictions about any caste or creed. All are equal in the eyes of our god. Ask your friend, he will tell you. *(Pause)*

If you can stay till sunset, you can join all of us in the church up the road there. Your friend will tell you that it is very easy to give up your chains and start a new life. You accept the church, and the church accepts you. *(He turns to leave, stops)*

I will be available whenever you want to talk to me about it.

(The priest leaves. Choma is alone. He is troubled, but also angry, and does not know how to react to the idea of giving up the faith of his ancestors. The peasant appears and goes up to Choma, puts his arm around him. Choma pushes his arm away and storms out.

Rapid fade out. The sound of Choma's drum. This is soon overtaken by the sound of thunder and rain. There is lightning.

Light on the cyclorama. We see a pair of oxen silhouetted, tied to a tree.

Fade out cyclorama. Tight spot on Choma. He is standing still, looking behind him. He turns straight, very slowly, stoops, sits, and finally falls flat.

Belli is in front of the hut. She is worried.)

BELLI

The monsoon is here at last! The rain beats down mercilessly on the village, endlessly for six, eight, ten days. But who can complain? The forest is green, there is an abundance of leaves for picking, the fields are covered with water and ready for replanting the paddy. We have to put up with the rain coming into the hut, but that is nothing to complain about. It is the season for rejoicing.

Even Kala and Neela are joining me in the forest. They are well now, thanks to the merciful goddess. But, appa... He is not himself nowadays. Always gloomy, always staring ahead, not listening...As if his body is here but his spirit is wandering somewhere over the hills, miles away. *(Calling)*

Kala! Neela! Go to sleep now!

What can be keeping him out so late? I hope he has not had too much to drink. *(Calling)* I am going to look for Appa. Stay inside. Don't go out anywhere.

(Spot on Choma on the ground. Belli appears and stands above him.)

BELLI

Appa? *(There is no response)* Appa! *(She gets him to sit up)* Are you all right? How long have you been like this? How long have you been here?

CHOMA

Where?

BELLI

Come on, get up. We are going home.

CHOMA

Home? *(Belli leads him to the front of the hut. He sits. She enters the hut and brings out a bowl of gruel.)*

BELLI

Appa, you must have something to eat.

CHOMA

Eat?

BELLI

Have this, right now. There is some hot water left. I am going to get it for you to bathe. You are covered in mud.

CHOMA

Why?

(Belli goes into the hut. Choma puts the bowl away and stares ahead. Belli re-enters and sees him, puts the pot of water down and sits next to him.)

BELLI

Appa...You are not well. *(There is no response)*

Appa, it is no use. Farming is not for us. All the rubbing and scraping cannot turn a black dog white. We are not born in a caste that can be farmers. We are born as...

You cannot blame the landlord for not listening to you. He can only do what he must do. Even our own people...Have you thought about what our own people will do if you got a piece of land and start farming?

We are better off the way we are. All our needs are met. What more can we get by farming? Think about it...We are better off the way we are. *(There is no response. She holds his hand in hers for a while, puts it down and reaches for the drum. She stands.)*

BELLI

This drum, which has your heart planted inside it...Ask this drum if what I am saying is not true. *(She plays a few strokes on the drum)*

You will listen to the drum, won't you?

(Choma looks up. Belli plays again, now adding a few notes in song. She dances as she sings and plays. Choma rises and takes the drum away from her and begins to play it himself. She dances and sings. He joins her tentatively. Soon, father and daughter are both engaged in a dance.

Fade out.

Sound of distant thunder.

Fade in.

Choma is sitting motionless, exactly as he was when Belli brought him to the hut. Belli is asleep at the entrance. The drum is by Choma's side.)

DRUM

It was a stormy night. The storm inside Choma's heart was no less in fury, and had no parallel. He poured his heart out to me. I had nothing to say in return.

SCENE 4

The labour lines. On the cyclorama we see a long row of small rooms. Manuel leads a group onstage. They are carrying bundles and small trunks. Among them are Chaniya and Guruva. Manuel speaks to the imagined group.

MANUEL

This is where you will all stay! You can see that there are people in some rooms already. You can choose your rooms from those that are empty. The untouchables are all on this side. On that side is the path going up to the plantation – all the levels of the plantation right up to the top. We start work at six in the morning. Make sure you are on time. There will be cuts in your pay if you are late. Any questions?

CHANIYA

Where do we get water? *(Manuel glares at him)*

For drinking...for washing. *(One in the group points to a spot)*

MANUEL

There is a stream there. He will show you. If you keep your eyes open you will see for yourself. *(The others disperse, taking their belongings with them. Chaniya and Guruva remain with Manuel.)*

MANUEL

Your wage has been fixed at seven rupees each per month. It will go up to eight rupees after one year. You will be paid one rupee each at the end of every week. The rest will be adjusted against your father's debt.

GURUVA

What is the work we have to do, sir?

MANUEL

Whatever you are told. To start with, there is the care of the soil.

GURUVA

But the coffee plants are already full grown.

MANUEL

All the more reason for care. The ground under each coffee plant has to be dug, the soil turned over and mixed with manure. You follow?

CHANIYA

Yes, sir.

GURUVA

Yes, sir.

MANUEL

You will do what you are told.

(Manuel leaves. Chaniya and Guruva settle down.)

CHANIYA

Our group from the journey can take those three rooms there. Pomma can be next to ours.

GURUVA

The family from Kokkada can be in the room next to Pomma.

CHANIYA

They have become Christian, haven't they?

GURUVA

I don't know about that. They are our people.

(They freeze. A long pause. Crossfade to a small desk with a chair. A man is seated with his back to us, busy with some papers. Manuel is standing next to him.)

MANUEL

(Pleased) They will never clear the debt. As soon as they were paid at the end of the week they went straight to the toddy shop. That was then. Now, they must go there every other day. And the toddy shop is giving them credit freely. He knows his business! They are taking the credit freely too. What else? There is nothing left at the end of the month for anything else. *(Pause)*

We can expect them to remain with us for a long time to come.

(Crossfade to Chaniya and Guruva)

CHANIYA

It is different. What do you say? *(Guruva nods)* It is different. Do you think of home sometimes? *(Guruva nods)* Appa,Belli...

GURUVA

Kala, Neela...Badu...

CHANIYA

Appa played his drum, we danced, we sang...

GURUVA

We laughed. Badu joined, jumping about.

CHANIYA

All we have here is...All we have is the work and ourselves...Work, work, work from sunrise to sunset and then into this hole to rest our limbs...And then it is sunrise again.

GURUVA

At least they feed us. At least twice a day.

CHANIYA

The same ditch water meal after meal. I miss Belli's gruel.

GURUVA

Belli's singing.

CHANIYA

Who is there for company here? Just you and me.

GURUVA

There is Pomma, our neighbour.

CHANIYA

Pomma! He hardly talks.

GURUVA

Then there is the couple from Kokkada.

CHANIYA

The Christians!

GURUVA

And their daughter, Mari.

(They freeze. A pause. Crossfade to man at desk and Manuel.)

MANUEL

I have the accounts up to date. It shows the boys are close to clearing their father's...

(Crossfade to Chaniya and Guruva)

CHANIYA

Why are you so silent? *(No response)*

Silent and grumpy. Look at your face! What is it? *(No response)*

You are hiding something. *(No response)*

Manuel sir has promised a break of one month. We will be home soon.

Appa said he would find a bride for me! You think he might have found her by now? *(No response)*

You are not happy that I will get married?

GURUVA

Go! Go and get married!

CHANIYA

Ohohoho! You are upset that I am getting married, and you are not!

GURUVA

Appa wants you to get married, no? He did not say he wanted me to get married! Go and get married!

CHANIYA

Your turn will come. Just wait and see. It may happen even at the time of my marriage. You will see.

GURUVA

You don't have to take the trouble. Appa does not have to take the trouble. I am not a child. I can take care of myself.

CHANIYA

I see. *(A long pause. Chaniya looks intently at Guruva.)* The Christian family...Mari... You are not...

GURUVA

What is it to you?

CHANIYA

What is it to me?

GURUVA

What is it to you? You are already a bridegroom. Appa has found a girl for you. I will find whoever I like.

CHANIYA

But her parents...You know them! They have deserted their faith and have become Christian.

GURUVA

I know they are Christian.

CHANIYA

You are not going to bring Mari into our home!

GURUVA

What if I do?

CHANIYA

Will Mari give up her new religion and come back to our faith? Will you make her do that?

GURUVA

I don't know.

CHANIYA

Will you become a Christian?

GURUVA

I don't know.

CHANIYA

They have betrayed our gods!

GURUVA

You don't think our gods have betrayed us?

(They freeze. A pause.

Crossfade to desk and Manuel, by himself.)

MANUEL

One month's leave. Wage accounts done. Advances and dues noted. They could leave. One month's leave. They wanted to travel by bus. They had never been in a bus before. The plantation gave them a bonus payment for bus tickets. They had to change buses twice to reach the town closest to their village. They decided to change only once and walk the rest of the distance. Three nights on the road anyway.

(Optional: The actors may mime the following narration in front of the cyclorama.)

DRUM

When the party awoke after the first night Chaniya found that Guruva was not there by his side. He walked down to the stream, thinking he might have gone ahead there. He called out in all directions. There was no response. He found soon that the old couple from Kokkada and their daughter Mari were also missing. Chaniya continued the journey home by himself.

SCENE 5

In the dark, the sound of a temple plate cymbal, arati, temple bells.

Lap dissolve to gaggle of voices in a festive crowd.

The lights fade in on the cyclorama to silhouette a line of villagers going to a temple festival.

Belli and Choma are at Sankappaiah's verandah. Belli places two reed baskets at the feet of Sankappaiah.

SANKA

What is this?

BELLI

For you, master.

SANKA

Hmmm. You have returned to basket making. Good! I thought father and daughter were both lost to the village.

BELLI

How can you say that, master? We have done everything for you as always, we have toiled hard for you. It is the annual festival in Panja tomorrow, so I have been making baskets to take there.

SANKA

Yes, it is the festival of Panja once again. This village will be empty the whole day. Once again. *(To Choma)* I suppose you are all going too.

CHOMA

Yes, sire.

SANKA

You don't look happy about going to Panja, Choma.

CHOMA

What can I say, sire? We would be happier if the two boys were here to join us. God knows how they are. God knows when they will be back.

SANKA

You can offer a special prayer at Panja tomorrow for their early return. Here! I have a bonus for you. *(Dropping coins on the floor)*

For you and Belli. Half *anna* each. Go ahead, take it. *(They do)*

If Chaniya and Guruva were here, I would have given them the same amount. Oh, yes, there are Kala and Neela. Here, take one more *anna. (Belli and Choma bow in deep gratitude)*

Belli, make sure the boys get the money. It is for them, to be spent in Panja – not to be taken away by Choma for the toddy shop!

(Choma laughs. Belli is respectful. They leave Sankappaiah's verandah.

Choma's hut. It is dark. This scene should be played in near darkness, with the outline of the hut and the outlines of characters barely visible. Belli and Choma walk on. Choma sits outside. Belli moves in and out of the hut.)

BELLI *(Giving Choma a bowl)*

Here, have this.

CHOMA

What about Kala and Neela?

BELLI

They have had their share. They are half asleep already.

CHOMA

And you?

BELLI

I will get my bowl and join you.

CHOMA

Good.

BELLI

It has been a good day.

CHOMA

You think so?

BELLI

A good day. What do you say?

CHOMA

What can I say? I wish Chaniya and Guruva were here.

BELLI

They will come when it is time to come. They will not spend a day longer in the plantation.

CHOMA

Belli, when the boys return I will not let them go back there. Never.

BELLI

They don't have to go back. They must have settled the debt by now.

CHOMA

They must have. The two of them together, they must have settled the debt. I will not let them go out of this village again.

BELLI

We will all be together again. I will pray for that at Panja tomorrow.

CHOMA

Those plantation people...If they say we still owe them money I will sell the bullocks and clear the debt. But I will not allow the boys to go back.

BELLI

Go to sleep now. Go inside and sleep. You can sleep peacefully tonight.

CHOMA

You go in. I will be there soon. Let me lie down here for some time.

BELLI

Don't start beating the drum now. You must get good sleep tonight. We have to leave early for Panja tomorrow. It is a long walk.

(Choma lies down. Spot on drum briefly.

The voice of Chaniya as he approaches the hut)

CHANIYA

Belli! Belli, are you there?

CHOMA

Who? Who is there?

CHANIYA

(Entering) It's me. Chaniya.

(Choma rises and rushes to the entrance of the hut.)

CHOMA

Belli! Belli, wake up! The boys are here! They are back from the plantation! Your brothers are here!

BELLI *(At the entrance)*

Guruva? Chaniya? Wait let me get some fire outside. Collect some wood. I will bring some fire from the cooking stones.

CHOMA *(As he gropes for dried twigs)*

What happiness! The boys are back! Just in time for the festival too!

BELLI *(At the entrance again)*

Ayyo! There is no fire left there. We will have to sit in the dark here. Come, come, come, sit here. Appa, forget the firewood. Come and sit down. *(Choma feels Chaniya's shoulder and arm and speaks)*

CHOMA

This is Chaniya, I can make out. You sit here, next to me. Ask Guruva to sit there, next to Belli. She likes him more, no?

BELLI

Guruva! Come here to me.

CHOMA

Did you know it is the festival at Panja tomorrow?

BELLI

We are all going there. Now you will also be there!

CHOMA

The landlord gave us a bonus. Why couldn't you come before the sun set? He would have given you a bonus too.

CHANIYA

Belli...

BELLI

Haam!

CHOMA

Belli! Tell your brother about the bride I have chosen for him! *(Belli giggles)*

CHOMA *(Continuing)*

Now you are back, we will fix an early date for the marriage.

BELLI

You will recognise her when you see her. She is from the colony next to Panja. She will be there at the festival tomorrow.

CHOMA

Yes, you can see her there tomorrow.

BELLI *(Teasing)*

And you will keep staring at her! You will have no eyes for the goddess inside the temple!

CHOMA

I will talk to her father about a marriage date.

BELLI

Guruva! We will now look for a bride for you!

CHOMA

Guruva, child, you will marry within a year. I will start looking for a girl right away – from tomorrow.

BELLI

It will have to be someone very special, no?

CHOMA

Yes, yes. First we will make sure of the family and caste and what property they have.

BELLI

Guruva, aren't you happy? Don't you also want to get married?

CHOMA

Leave him alone. He is still a boy.

BELLI

Aren't you happy that you are home? Why are you silent?

CHANIYA

Belli...Appa...Guruva is not here. I have come alone.

CHOMA

Guruva...not here? Why is he not here?

BELLI

Where is he? When will he come?

CHOMA

Whenever he feels like it, I suppose. He thinks he is a grown man now, I suppose. These ideas get into the heads of boys the moment they have a moustache on the face.

BELLI

Appa! Guruva is not like that. He is a good son. The planter must have wanted him to stay back. He must not have given him leave.

CHANIYA

He has not come. He will not come...ever.

(Spot on drum. Held for a few beats. Fade out. Return to hut. The group is silent. Finally, Chaniya speaks up.)

CHANIYA

There is nothing more to say! That is the whole story. I can only repeat it as many times as you ask me to.

BELLI

It is not possible! Guruva is not that kind of a boy!

CHOMA

She is right. Guruva would never do something like that.

BELLI

I know. The two of you must have fought over something. Even here you were always picking a quarrel with Guruva.

CHOMA

Tomorrow! No Panja festival tomorrow. I am going after that boy. I will find him. I will go to Kokkada. I will find him. If what you say is true I will break his leg. If what Belli says is true, that you had a fight with him, I will return with Guruva and I will break your head!

CHANIYA *(Sobbing now)*

You will have to believe me in the end. Our brother...your son... he has run away with that Mari from Kokkada. *(A long pause. Chaniya and Belli are sobbing. Choma controls himself and speaks.)*

CHOMA

All right...He found a girl...He ran away. We can hope he will be happy. What do you know about this girl?

CHANIYA

The family is like ours. Same caste.

CHOMA

At least that.

CHANIYA

But they became Christians – I don't know when, but they are Christian.

CHOMA *(In rage again)*

I will never set my eyes on that boy again!

BELLI

How could he do this?

CHOMA

He can never step into this house again! Never!

BELLI

Didn't he know what he was bringing upon himself? Did you not think of informing Appa about what was going on? This house has lost a son!

CHOMA

Son! He has been swallowed up by the evil spirits roaming these hills. I thought I was blessed with four sons. I have only three. What difference does it make if one of them died or was taken away by the spirits? *(A long pause)*

Go inside and sleep now. Chaniya has had a long journey. He needs rest. Give him my blanket. Both of you – go in and sleep.

BELLI

You must sleep too.

CHOMA

I will. I will sit here for some time and then come in. The moon is rising over the hill. Let me sit here for a while.

(Belli guides Chaniya into the hut in the dark. Choma sits still. A few beats. A moon appears on the cyclorama. Choma rises quickly and strides towards the cyclorama.)

CHOMA

I will find him! I will bring him back! I will find a bride for him. She will be more beautiful than that Christian wretch Mari. I will bring him home!

(We see Choma silhouetted, a stick under his arm striding under the moon. Spot on drum.)

DRUM

Choma left looking for his second son. He had no idea where to go and how to look for him. He only knew he could not sit still doing nothing. He would find a way. He would find a lead. One lead would point to another. He would find Guruva. He had to make a start. He went looking for his son.

He left me behind. It was as if I had to look after the household in his absence. Little did he know that there was a tragedy building while he was away. He would lose his first son too.

(Spot on Belli. She is sitting by Chaniya's side, who is lying on his back, covered. Belli changes a damp cloth on his forehead.)

BELLI

This festival at Panja is not for us. We should all have been there together...Chaniya and Guruva back from the plantation, the debt cleared, a bride waiting to meet Chaniya...It was not to be.

DRUM

Who could have imagined the turn of events...First the news about Guruva, then, this!

BELLI

Now, this...Chaniya has had high fever all through the night and the whole day. He shivers and shakes as if he is in icy waters, but the fever... His head is blazing like the blacksmith's furnace... Appa is away...I don't know what to do.

DRUM

She did what she could do. She is a capable girl.

BELLI

Kala and Neela had a hundred questions. Where was Guruva? Where was Appa? Why couldn't they all go to the festival together? Why was Chaniya not talking to them? They wanted him to tell them stories from the other side of the world.

DRUM

She sent Kala and Neela off to Panja. She gave them a whole *anna* to spend as they liked. They took Badu along. She told the boys that the others would join them later in the day. She could then concentrate on doing something for Chaniya.

BELLI

I sat by his side, cooling his forehead. I waved two coconuts around him and kept them at the entrance of the village *bhoota*[1] shrine. I borrowed money from the landlord's wife and rushed to see Chinna, the village healer. He was the only person our people could go to.

DRUM

He knew that. He was not easy to see. It was never easy to get the needed spells and incantations out of him. Today he was away at the festival in Panja. She had to wait, her thoughts with the sick Chaniya all the time. When Chinna returned he was in a drunken stupor.

BELLI

I had to wait some more...For him to be able to sit up and listen to what I had to say. I placed the coin before him. He went in and fetched cowries and flowers. He placed them within a frame made of dried sticks and closed his eyes. He did not open his eyes till I coughed out loud. He then informed me that the destructive spirit of Panjurli was at work, and that to calm the spirit I had to place before him a special offering of a chicken, a pig and a generous quantity of rice.

DRUM

Oh, Panjurli! Please protect her brother! Belli shuttled between Chinna and her brother, growing weaker by the hour, but Chinna was supremely confident that offerings rather than medicines were the real cure.

BELLI

He is turning lifeless and pale...He is coughing up blood...

(Calling) Kala! Neela! Go and fetch Chinnappa here! Go at once! Tell him he must come here himself!

---

1 bhoota is a supernatural village deity.

DRUM

Chinna wasn't at home. He was at the toddy shop. The boys reached the toddy shop, but Chinna was in no mood to listen to them. He told them that it was an inauspicious time, and that nothing should be done till the next day. He would attend to their brother then. When the boys returned to the hut...Belli was covering Chaniya with a cloth.

(Belli is covering the body of Chaniya. Fade out to near darkness. Choma enters, addressing Belli.)

CHOMA

Belli! It is too late. Our Guruva has already married that girl from Kokkada. I looked all over, but could not see them. I was only told that they were married. It is too late. Guruva is lost to us.

(Notices Belli weeping) What is there to cry about? He was hot-headed, he went and got married on his own! To a Christian! He is not one of us anymore, that's all.

(Choma picks up the drum and starts to play it. Belli rushes to him, snatches the drum out of his hands and flings it aside. She shouts at her father.)

BELLI

Is this the time?! Drumming before a dead son! *(Belli drops to the ground and weeps uncontrollably over Chaniya's body. Choma is stunned. He stands over the body and raises his voice to the sky.)*

CHOMA

Panjurli!! You have forsaken us!!

(Rapid fade out. The sound of Choma's drum, beaten in frenzy.)

SCENE 6

Moonlight on the cyclorama. Choma and Belli are seated before the hut. Long pause.

Belli weeps quietly.

CHOMA

Mad! *(Belli controls her weeping for a few moments, but weeps again)*

All Madness! Your weeping will bring them back, you think!

BELLI

What else can I do? One of them dying before my eyes...The other gone, not even knowing his brother's fate...

CHOMA

Yes, gone!

BELLI

What do we do now?

CHOMA

There are two more boys. There is you. There is me. If we have to go, we have to go.

BELLI

Big talk! As if I don't know what you are hiding inside!

(Long pause. Choma turns away.) You have your toddy to drown in. What do I have?

CHOMA

You have your work, I have my work.

BELLI

Sankappaiah sent for you again.

CHOMA

I know.

BELLI

He wants to know why you have not reported for work.

CHOMA

He sent for me! I should report for work!

BELLI

I told them...I told them that the bullocks have wounds on their legs and cannot be brought for ploughing.

CHOMA

That is the truth.

BELLI

I did not tell them that you had beaten the bullocks and wounded them.

CHOMA *(Bitter)*

If I cannot plough my own farm with them why should they be offered for somebody else's gain?

BELLI

You think money and food will rain on us from the heavens? You think the landlord will invite us every day for collecting the leftovers of their meals from the leaves thrown outside?

CHOMA

We live!

BELLI

We live!

CHOMA

It is madness to weep! Bring the boys out! We will dance!

BELLI

The madness is in you! Dance! And at this time, well past midnight!

CHOMA

Bring the boys out!

BELLI

I will not! They are sleeping. Why must we burden them with our pain and sorrow?

CHOMA *(Roaring)*

Bring them out! They will dance! We will all dance! I say so! *(Rushing to the hut)* I will pull them up by their hair and drag them here!

BELLI *(Rushing to stop him, pushing him back)*

You will not! You can dance over my body if you like! You will not wake up those innocent boys! They cannot dance for you now.

CHOMA

If they cannot dance I will break their legs! I will dance on their bodies!

BELLI

Break mine first! Dance on my body instead. *(Calming Choma)*

Why must you take out your anger on them, Appa? God has left these two sons for you. You must take care of them. They are children.

CHOMA

God! Sons! He gives us children for what! *(Choma, overcome with dejection, sits on the ground, his face buried in his hands. He begins to weep.)*

BELLI

Madness! *(She sits by his side and comforts him)*

Go to Sankappaiah in the morning. Tell him you are sorry. He will understand. Tell him you are ready to start working.

(Fade out. Sankappaiah's verandah. Belli and Choma enter and stay at a distance. Sankappaiah signals to them to approach.)

SANKA *(Cold)*

You have not reported for work. *(No response)*

I sent for you, but there was no response.

BELLI

Master, he has not been...

SANKA

I am talking to him, your father. He knows how much work is pending on the land. We had agreed that he would bring his bullocks for that. We had agreed that he would be paid for using his bullocks.

CHOMA

Sire, what can I say? The bullocks are injured. Their legs are swollen and have wounds.

SANKA

Bullocks injured! Cooking up yet another story!

BELLI

Master, your man who came to call Appa saw the bullocks himself. He will tell you about the injuries.

SANKA

I see. Wounds, you say. Just like that?

CHOMA

They must have strayed into somebody else's land, sire. The people there must have beaten them with sticks to drive them out.

SANKA

Beating bullocks to wound them?

CHOMA

It looks like that, sire.

BELLI

To teach them a lesson. To teach Appa a lesson.

SANKA

An untouchable with bullocks! I have been telling him from god knows when to sell them off. He will get good money. He can clear all his debts and have enough left for other things. I offered to buy the bullocks myself. But will he listen to me? The pride in an untouchable!

CHOMA

Sire, you know what the bullocks...

BELLI

Master, what do you command us to do now?

SANKA

I can give him work. He doesn't have to work on the land with his bullocks. There is other work. He can bring down the coconuts. He can chop wood.

BELLI

Whatever your wish, master. He will do whatever work you choose to give him.

SANKA

He is not saying anything himself.

BELLI

Appa, it is all right. You can start work again. Our merciful landlord has taken you back. Just say yes to him.

SANKA

Look at his face! Like a corpse! Has he started going to the toddy shop in the mornings now? *(A pause)*

CHOMA

Thanks to our merciful landlord, I am earning enough now to be at Biruma's shop mornings and evenings!

SANKA *(Stunned)*

Get out of here at once! *(Choma remains motionless)*

You heard me! Now! Take your diseased body out of my sight. And don't ever step into any part of my land ever again.

(Choma stares at the landlord, breaks into a smile, stands erect, turns and walks out.)

BELLI

Appa! Master!

(We now see Belli shuttling between Sankapaiah's verandah and Choma's hut.)

Master! Please! I beg you on my knees, please forgive him! He does not intend any ill will, master! He is just not himself the last many days. Master! I am begging you...

Appa! What have you done! It was bad enough that you wounded the bullocks and had to lose the job of tilling the land, but this!

Master! Whatever might have been the madness that possessed Appa, it was only at that moment. You know he could not have meant anything bad. He is a good man...a poor man, but good at heart. He has always held you in highest respect. Nobody else commands the same respect as you, master. Please forgive him!

Please ask him for forgiveness, Appa! Swear to him that it was a mistake, that you are sorry it happened that way. He will forgive you. He is a good man at heart. Appa, you must!

Master, I swear upon the soul of my mother it is true. He is deeply sorry. He is in great despair. He realises his mistake. It was a moment of rashness that came out of all the tragic events in our lives. Who else do we have but you to look after us...to protect us?

Appa! He has softened! Now is the time to go to him and seek forgiveness. Don't look at me like that! We need his protection. You need him! Who else will give us work? We cannot survive without him.

Master! He will be all right. He is coming out of it. I have brought the two boys along. They are big now, ready to work now. I pledge them to you, master! The two of them and I...You know we are always there to serve you. Appa too. Just give him some time. He will be all right.

(Belli and Sankappaiah freeze. A few beats.)

SANKA

Let him come when he thinks he can come. Let him come and see me. We shall see what to do with him. The two boys and you can start work straight away. You can collect wages for all. Better than giving the money to him.

BELLI *(Kneeling with folded hands)*

Master! We should have known long ago that we were placed at your doorstep by god. We were blind, and could not see. We know now that god himself speaks to us through you. *(Belli walks back slowly to the hut. She stops at the drum and speaks to it.)*

BELLI *(Continuing)*

He has not picked you up in some time. He will, he will. He will beat you with a passion you have not known yet. He may hurt you.

(Fade out. The sound of Choma's drum.)

Intermission here if needed

SCENE 7

Choma's hut. Manuel is standing there.

MANUEL

Are people here all deaf? Or are they always drunk? Choma! Come out when I call you!

BELLI *(Stepping out of the hut)*

Who? Oh, sir...you, here?

MANUEL

Me, here, yes. Where is that good-for-nothing father of yours? Did he not hear me calling him? Or is he not coming out because he knows who has been calling?

BELLI

He could not hear you, sir, because he is not here.

MANUEL

Not here?

BELLI

He went out some time ago.

MANUEL

Went out, did he? He is not hiding inside?

BELLI

Sir, I swear to you...

MANUEL

All right, when will he be back?

BELLI

I don't know. He is not himself nowadays. He has been badly affected...by all that has happened.

MANUEL

What has happened?

BELLI

As if telling you will make any difference! When even crying out to the gods has not helped.

MANUEL

Your brothers – where are they? Have they also gone out? Not saying when they will be back? *(No response)*

Well?!

BELLI

Whatever happened to the brothers is something left behind, sir. It is sure they are not with us anymore.

MANUEL

One of them is in Kokkada, is he not? Married. I hear he has taken to farming. You must have been to the marriage. She is a Christian.

BELLI

We do not attend marriages of outcastes.

MANUEL

I see! One untouchable calls another an outcaste! As you please. That is your business. I am here for another business.

BELLI

What business can you have now in this village of untouchables?

MANUEL

Very simple. I am here to collect. Those two brothers of yours left without paying a piece of your father's debt. They came to the plantation, had a good time eating and drinking, and left. The debt of twenty rupees is now twenty-five rupees.

BELLI

Twenty-five rupees?

MANUEL

Twenty-five rupees. It is not a small amount. Who is going to pay off the debt? One brother has run off to be a farmer, protected by the church. It will have to be the other brother and anybody else from here. Two to three persons working honestly for nine months may be able to clear the amount. Or else...

BELLI

Or else?

MANUEL

It will be reported. It will go to court. The police will do what comes to their heads.

BELLI

If that also is to be added to our fate, so it will be. There is nothing we can do.

MANUEL

Of course you can do something to save yourselves. Send Chaniya to me when he returns. I will explain to him.

BELLI

Chaniya is not going to return.

MANUEL

He has run away, has he? The rascal! I should have known.

BELLI

Chaniya was called away.

MANUEL

I don't care who called him and where he went. He must report to me as soon as he is back. *(Belli is looking down and sobbing)*

There is no point crying about these things. It is business.

BELLI

Please stop tormenting us. As if all that has been heaped on us by the gods is not enough, now you...

MANUEL

You owe the plantation money! And you say I am tormenting you! All you have to do is to tell Chaniya to report to me.

BELLI *(Pointing)*

There! That tree where the dog is resting. Chaniya is there, under the tree. You may dig him up and take him with you.

MANUEL

(Dawning) I see...I will not trouble you any more now. Tell Choma I was here. I will come again on Friday to settle things. *(He starts to leave, stops, returns)*

I am only trying to help you. You must clear the debt for your own good. Any two of you can do that. It can be you. Why not? It will be better that way for all concerned.

(Manuel leaves. Sound of the dog barking. Belli remains frozen. Choma enters. He watches from a distance, approaches her, sits.)

BELLI

Did you hear what Manuel sir said? *(No response)*

He said he was coming back on Friday.

CHOMA

He wants to come on Friday. Let him come.

BELLI

You know why he is coming. Chaniya and Guruva cleared nothing of your debt in all the months at the plantation.

CHOMA

One must have spent all his money at the toddy shop. The other must have spent it all on that Christian girl. The witch! Well, let him go back to the plantation and clear the debt all by himself now. If he steps into this village I will break his legs.

BELLI

Guruva will not return to this village.

CHOMA

That will be good for him.

BELLI

He will not be going back to the plantation either. He is going to start farming very soon.

CHOMA

Farming? My Guruva? The gods smiled upon at least one of us! It is good it happened to Guruva...although an outcaste.

BELLI

All right, the gods blessed Guruva. That does not solve the problem of your debt. What are you going to do?

CHOMA

What can I do?

BELLI

You are asking me. If I try to make you see sense you shout at me.

CHOMA

I don't know what to think.

BELLI

Appa, listen to me. It is like this. The debt is still there. The debt has to be cleared. There are only two ways to clear the debt.

CHOMA

Two ways?

BELLI

We pay the plantation cash. Or we work on the plantation and pay it back as labour.

CHOMA

We can pay in cash?

BELLI

By selling the bullocks. No! Don't get excited! Think about it carefully, as if you were thinking about your own life.

CHOMA

It means there is no more life. I die.

BELLI

There is a new life, a life without debt. The gods decided to put you in a caste that cannot do farming. That is our fate. The gods did not decide we should live all our lives in debt.

CHOMA

I can be a farmer. I will be a farmer.

BELLI

Who will allow you to do that?

CHOMA

I will rent a piece of government land. They will give me a barren, rocky plot. I will show them what I can do with it! They will give me a corner no bigger than your two palms and my two palms together. I will show them!

BELLI *(Gazing at Choma)*

What for? For two handfuls of paddy? You can do that here, between the hut and the tree shading Chaniya's grave. Why don't you? You must stop dreaming and get your feet on the ground. You may talk big about making a rice pond out of a hill. The fact is we depend on those above for everything. From even before your time our people have eaten the salt from Sankappaiah's house. We are tied to the landlord forever. We are lucky he is a good man, very good at heart.

CHOMA

So...Pay off the debt from the money we get by selling the bullocks.

BELLI

Is that so difficult?

CHOMA

Sell the bullocks.

BELLI

I say sell them to the landlord. He will be pleased with you for that.

CHOMA

Sell them to the landlord.

BELLI

Before you beat them in rage again. Or kill them and feast on them. In your present state of mind you can do anything. *(A long pause)*

You have not spoken. Do you agree? I can take care of selling the bullocks for you. I will get a good price for them.

CHOMA

There is a better way. Instead of selling the bullocks you can put up this old man for sale! Sell me to the plantation if you like. No? You still want to sell the oxen? All right, tie me up and drown me in the river. Then you can go and sell the bullocks for the best price. After clearing the debt, buy yourself a grand sari and dance in the village square in it!

BELLI

So...We do not pay off the debt in cash.

CHOMA

You said there were two ways.

(Belli exits. Cross fade to Sankappaiah's verandah. He is seated making paan. Belli enters.)

SANKA

How is Choma? When can he honour us with his presence?

BELLI

Master, what can I say? He is behaving so strangely. I am trying very hard to understand his state of mind.

SANKA

You had a visitor.

BELLI

He took us by surprise. As if losing the two boys was not enough...

SANKA

Once they have their hands on your neck it is a grip of iron.

BELLI

We had no idea...The debt has remained unpaid. It has increased.

SANKA

The boys must have wallowed in drink all the time, far away from home.

BELLI

We don't know about that. All we know is that the debt has increased to twenty-five rupees.

SANKA

What else? The disease of all untouchables! Drink away till it is oozing out of the ears and nostrils and all other openings! And get into debt all the time. Is the untouchable's debt ever cleared?

BELLI *(In tears)*

You are right, master. What the boys did is in the past. I tried to reason with Appa. He will not listen. It is possible to clear the debt at the plantation, is it not?

SANKA

The bullocks...I can still buy them from him, in spite of all his arrogance earlier. Even with their wounded legs. Let him bring them here when he thinks he can show his face to me.

BELLI

I will make sure of that, master. You are very kind.

SANKA

I will give him a good price—more than what he will get in the market. I will do that for him.

BELLI

He will be ever grateful for that, Master, I can assure you.

SANKA

I will not simply give money, keep that in mind. I will not give a loan. But if it a sale of the bullocks I will give him a good price for it.

BELLI

I am sure he will agree, master.

SANKA

I am not so sure.

BELLI

I will make him agree, master.

(Cross fade to hut. Choma is where he was earlier. Belli enters and approaches him.)

CHOMA

I do not agree!

BELLI

Appa, it is your last chance, your only chance.

CHOMA

I will not sell the bullocks – not to the landlord, not to anybody else.

BELLI

We are doomed.

CHOMA

You said there were two ways.

BELLI

We can repay the plantation in labour.

CHOMA

We will repay in full.

BELLI

But who will do that?

CHOMA

We will decide soon.

BELLI

Whoever goes, it will not be you. I can go myself. One of the boys will stay back and look after you. That will be Kala. I will take Neela with me.

CHOMA

All that can be decided later. There is a party of guests arriving. We must prepare to receive them.

(Cross fade to drum)

DRUM

Guests! As if the burden of death and despair was not enough, Belli had now to take care of the guests.

As with guests everywhere, in all parts of this land, in big cities, small towns and even tiny villages not even on a map, guests are known to arrive without invitation, arrive in large numbers, and arrive with large appetites. Choma's family might be untouchables, but they had obligations as hosts to entertain other members of the community if they happened to come for a visit. They had to be fed, and they had to be plied with toddy before, during and after the feed. Sometimes they stayed long. Sometimes they did not know when they were leaving.

(The cyclorama shows a community campfire)

The end of the rainy season, before harvesting begins, is a lean period for wage earners on farms. There is no work, and there is no pay. It is the best time to move out of one's own village and visit others. This can go on as long as two months. If your own kitchen is bare you can always rely on the hospitality of your kinsmen. Feeding the guests was clearly something that Choma could not be concerned with. It was Belli's responsibility. Belli had meticulously left ample quantities of rice and paddy with the landlord's wife for safe custody. It was for the lean season. But now it was nearly used up. There was not even a pinch of salt in the kitchen and, as everybody knows, borrowing salt from another house is shamelessness of the lowest order.

The guests pitched in with weaving baskets that paid for the toddy. Choma led them to the sweet potato patch, and with everybody digging them up there was enough for two days. They danced a lot around the fire, Choma drumming happily for them and joining them in dance. It made Choma feel better. It was good that his mood was lifting. It also made the group more hungry, more thirsty. One evening Choma announced in a great burst that they would go on a rabbit hunt. Haam!

Armed with sticks and nets they were off in a flash. Belli now had to get the fat and spices to cook rabbit meat. The group was lucky in snaring eight rabbits. Reaching Biruma's toddy shop well after he had shut down they negotiated a round of drinks in exchange for two rabbits. That took care of one night and one day. How long more? Belli was seriously worried. She confided in Choma. The kitchen was now quite empty. There was no stock of grain either in there or at the landlord's house. Choma was too drunk to understand. He admonished her for having lost her senses and assured her that fate was on their side after all.

And fate came knocking in the form of a dead she buffalo.

(A peasant enters, covering his face and head with a sheet)

PEASANT

Choma! Choma, are you there? Choma!

CHOMA *(Leaving the group and entering, unsteady)*

Who are you?

PEASANT *(Hesitantly)*

Ramappa.

CHOMA

From the other side of the pond? What brings you to my humble hut at this time of night?

PEASANT

I had to wait till it was dark, so nobody saw me coming here.

CHOMA

So you are here now. What is it?

PEASANT

A she buffalo of ours...died this afternoon.

CHOMA

A she buffalo is dead.

PEASANT

Yes...Will you come and take it away.

CHOMA *(Understanding, feigning disinterest)*

I have guests...I cannot leave home now.

PEASANT

If you have guests, you can all feast on buffalo meat.

CHOMA

It is all right for you to say that. What do we do with the meat? We need a heap of other things to cook buffalo meat? Where can we get all that?

PEASANT

You can wake up the grocer and get them.

CHOMA

But it costs money. We are poor people.

PEASANT

We can't leave the dead buffalo there.

CHOMA

Come tomorrow, and we will see.

PEASANT *(Taking out some coins)*

Here, four annas. Will that do?

CHOMA

We will see. Let me ask the guests.

(The peasant exits. Choma joins the guests. There is a cry of joy from the cyclorama.)

DRUM

The carcass was shifted immediately. The Muslim grocer was awakened and the necessary supplies lined up. He was promised the skin and the horns, for which the group was lent eight annas for another round of toddy. It was a grand feast. Everybody joined the celebration. Belli too. They danced through the night. Even Badu was seen raising his snout to the moon in celebration.

The guests left at last. The next day was Friday. Manuel arrived, as punctual as the messenger of Yama.

(Fade out. A long wail from a dog. Choma's hut. Belli and Choma are arguing. Manuel is seated and watching.)

MANUEL

So...You had a diversion in the story. Guests and merrymaking and feasting, I am told. Well, the time has come to get back to work. What have you decided?

CHOMA

I will come.

MANUEL

You? What work will you do on the plantation? You will keep drinking, and the debt will keep growing. We need young hands.

CHOMA

But Kala and Neela—they are children.

MANUEL

Belli, you can come. You can bring one of the boys.

CHOMA

Belli leave home? How can she?

MANUEL

The boys are not children anymore. You don't need Belli here. She can work on the plantation.

BELLI

Appa, you must decide. Either you sell the oxen and pay off the plantation, or you let me go and pay it off in labour.

(Choma is greatly agitated. He moves about trying to say something, he stammers, he tries again, but does not succeed in saying anything. Belli calms him down and gets him to sit.)

BELLI *(To Manuel)*

It is decided. I will come. Neela will join me. He is a big boy now. He will look after me. Kala will stay back and look after Appa. *(A moment of silence and Choma rises to bid them good bye. He hugs Belli. They are both weeping.)*

MANUEL

It is a good decision. This way your earnings will be put to good use, and not washed away in drink.

CHOMA

Whatever happens, you must be back before the next festival in Panja. Promise me that.

BELLI

I promise.

CHOMA

Kala and I will walk with you till the next village. Let's go.

(The group leaves. Fade out.

Fade in cyclorama. A group of men undertaking a journey, led by Manuel.)

SCENE 8

The labour lines. On the cyclorama we see a long row of small rooms. Manuel leads a group onstage. They are carrying bundles and small trunks. Among them is Belli. Manuel speaks to the imagined group.

MANUEL

This is where you will all stay! You can see that there are people in some rooms already. You can choose your rooms from those that are empty. The untouchables are all on this side. On that side is the path going up to the plantation—all the levels of the plantation right up to the top. We start work at six in the morning. Make sure you are on time. There will be cuts in your pay if you are late. Any questions?

BELLI

Where do we get water? *(Manuel glares at her)*

For drinking...for washing. *(One in the group points to a spot.)*

MANUEL

There is a stream there. He will show you. If you keep your eyes open you will see for yourself.

Your wage has been fixed at five rupees per month. *(There are protests)*

I know it was more last season! But we have had a bad season. The price of coffee beans in the market had a big fall. So...you can only be given five rupees. It will go up to six rupees after six months if things improve.

(Addressing Belli) You...You will be paid twelve *annas*[2] at the end of every week. The rest will be adjusted against your debt.

BELLI

What is the work we have to do, sir?

MANUEL

Whatever you are told. You will do what you are told.

(Manuel leaves)

BELLI *(Calling)*

Neela! You can get water from the stream down there. Two pots will do. We can look at storing water tomorrow. Don't play in the water. You have not been well through the journey. It should not get worse. I will be in the third room in this line. Bring the water there.

(Crossfade to a small desk with a chair. A man is seated with his back to us, busy with some papers. Manuel is standing next to him.)

MANUEL *(Pleased)*

They will never clear the debt. They have already found their way to the toddy shop. We can expect them to remain with us for a long time. All except two of them. Old Choma has sent his daughter and younger son. They will work hard and save. They may return in four months. No more than six months.

(Crossfade to Belli. She is talking to Neela inside.)

---

2 Anna is the pre-independence coin fraction of a rupee; 16 annas made a rupee.

BELLI

No, you can't go to work yet. Not till your fever is completely gone. And no playing with the boys. There is a shrine at the foot of the hill. I will make sure we get the right charms for you there and the herbs to be added to your gruel. I will spend whatever time is needed to get you well.

(Crossfade to the desk. The man is seated with his back to us. Manuel is standing next to him with Belli.)

MANUEL

This is her, sir, Choma's daughter. Her younger brother is also with us, but is not at work today. The two of them are here as replacements for his two sons. *(The man turns his chair and faces Manuel and Belli. It is Michael, the proprietor and director of the estate.)*

MICHAEL

So...The old man has sent his daughter. Do you think you can clear his debt? Drinking all the time, increasing his debt all the time. *(Belli is speechless. Manuel nudges her to speak.)*

BELLI

Yes, sir.

MICHAEL

Yes, sir, what? You will clear the debt? Or will you also be raising the debt all the time?

BELLI

I will work hard, sir. I will do whatever...

MICHAEL

Let's see...Choma's account here...it says you still owe us fifteen rupees.

BELLI *(Between Manuel and Michael)*

Fifteen rupees, sir? I thought...

MICHAEL

Whatever you might think, it is fifteen rupees that must be cleared.

MANUEL *(Quickly)*

Exactly what I told them, sir. The debt must be cleared.

MICHAEL

She looks like a good worker. Make sure she clears the debt within this season.

MANUEL

Can be done, sir, can be done.

(He leads Belli off. Belli at the labour lines.)

BELLI

Fifteen rupees, not twenty-five. Only fifteen rupees now. It must have been a mistake. Or we must have heard it wrong – what with all the sorrow surrounding us. He must have meant fifteen rupees. He is a good man. He took Neela and me in the bus from Belthangady. The others took three days and two nights, walking all the way. He brought us by bus. He is a good man. They talk rough, that is their way, but they are different at heart.

Neela! How you loved that bus ride! It was the first time in your life! You were seeing a bus for the first time. You finally got inside a bus and rode in it for so many hours! It was the first time for me too. We will get into a bus once again very soon, Neela! You will get well soon, then we will go back to work, and in no time we will clear the debt once and for all. We will have some money to take home with us. Appa and Kala will be so happy to see us. We will pick up a new shirt for Kala at the bus stop shop in Beltahngady. One for you too. Badu will be barking and dancing all around you. I hope Kala is looking after Appa. He is so young. Anyway, just a few months more. I will be there to take care of Appa. But first I have to take care of you. You must get well soon. *(Manuel enters, looking for Belli.)*

MANUEL

There you are! I saw in the register that your attendance has been irregular. Taking off every now and then.

BELLI

It's like this, sir...

MANUEL

I have heard enough excuses in my life, enough stories. And your brother, Neela. Absent for so many days.

BELLI

He is in there, sir. He is ill. He has had a fever the last six days. You can go in and see for yourself. I have been attending to him.

MANUEL

I see. I will give you till the end of this week. You must be back full time from Monday, your son and yourself. *(He starts to leave, returns)*

You know that every day's absence makes your stay here longer.

BELLI

I know, sir. I am trying hard to give you what you want from us.

MANUEL

Let me see what I can do to help you. I will shift you from plantation work to work in my house. That way you can also attend to Neela easily.

BELLI *(Overwhelmed)*

Sir...You are too kind.

MANUEL

Yes, we will shift you straight away. You can report for work at the bungalow from this evening.

(To cyclorama. We see a series of vignettes as passage of time and Belli's fall:

- *Belli serving Manuel coffee*
- *Belli holding his jacket while he puts it on*

- *Manuel presenting her a sari*
- *Manuel teasing Belli*
- *Manuel holding Belli's face in his hands...*
- *Finally, Manuel leading Belli off, his arm around her.*

This may be done by any other dramatic device as decided by the performing group.)

(The labour lines again. Manuel is seated. Belli is standing, looking upset.)

MANUEL

You have to tell me. You have been like this for three whole days.

BELLI

How can I?

MANUEL

All right, keep it to yourself. I cannot do anything if you don't tell me.

BELLI

Give me some time.

MANUEL

We don't have too much time. The missus will be back from her home town one of these days. We will not be able to...

BELLI

That is the trouble.

MANUEL

What trouble?

BELLI

People are talking, saying nasty things. The other day Neela's friend taunted him with an abuse. Thank god, he didn't understand what it meant. How can I face him if he finds out? What will I do in the village if it reaches there?

MANUEL

It will all be forgotten soon. You have enough money now.

BELLI

Your generosity.

MANUEL

Your debt will be cleared. You will go away. Everything closed and everything forgotten.

BELLI

Closed? I thought...

MANUEL

To be forgotten. You understand, I am sure.

BELLI

Who am I to have an opinion on this matter?

MANUEL

Anyway, Michael sir wishes to see you.

BELLI

Michael sir? See me?

MANUEL

He has sent me to fetch you.

BELLI

See me for what?

MANUEL

Who knows? Maybe he wants to settle the accounts. Maybe he wants to give you a bonus. Who knows, he may be thinking of a new job for you.

BELLI

I see...

MANUEL

I knew you would see.

BELLI

When does he want to see me?

MANUEL

Now.

BELLI

Just now?

MANUEL
Just now.

BELLI
Why? I don't even know him.

MANUEL
Don't know him?

BELLI
I don't know him. He doesn't know me.

MANUEL
Who did he meet last week on the forest trail when he was taking his dogs for a walk? Who did he take to the hunting cabin the other side of the stream?

BELLI
Oh...

MANUEL
People will be talking soon, saying nasty things. Neela's friends will be taunting him with new abuses.

BELLI
I didn't know what was happening!

MANUEL
You knew how to count money.

BELLI
It was not like that! You have to believe me, it was not like that!

MANUEL
Not like what? What was it not like?

BELLI
Not like you...

MANUEL
So, you want to tell me what he was like? You want to show me?

BELLI
No! That is not... He is the master of the plantation. He is the master over all of us. We have to do what we are told.

MANUEL

You are right. We have to do what we are told. Right now, he is telling you to report to him. He has told me to take you to him.

BELLI

What should I do?

MANUEL

Go to him.

BELLI *(Distraught)*

I don't know what to do!

MANUEL

Follow me!

(Crossfade to desk. Michael is seated as before. Manuel and Belli enter, stay a few paces away. Michael turns to face them. There is a long pause. Michael signals to Manuel to leave. He does. Michael beckons to Belli. She approaches hesitantly. Michael, still seated, caresses her lightly. She does not respond. He draws her and holds her closer, seats her on his lap.)

MICHAEL

I know. It is difficult here. You are shy. You are beautiful when you are shy. Come to the bungalow. I will wait for you there.

(Michael rises, fondles her in parting and leaves. Belli remains frozen. Crossfade to the labour lines. Belli rushes in, agitated.)

BELLI

Neela! Neela, where are you? Get here at once. Here, take this shawl. Put all your things in it and bundle them up. We have to leave. Don't ask questions! Get ready fast. Don't leave anything behind. Take every little thing you have and put it in the bundle. Where are we going? We are going home! We are free! Good, good! Go down to the stream and wait. I will be with you in a minute.

(Belli picks up her own bundle and rushes out.
Crossfade to desk. Manuel is with Michael.)

MICHAEL

She can't be found, you say? My estate supervisor is telling me that a coolie working on this estate is missing, and she cannot be found!

MANUEL

Sir, we have searched every corner of the estate – all the labour lines, the warehouses, the tool-sheds, the abandoned huts, every place.

MICHAEL

You don't think...

MANUEL

It is possible, sir. She has been talking about home for some time now. After all, she and her brother have cleared the debt.

MICHAEL

Is the debt cleared? Completely?

MANUEL

She seemed sure when she mentioned it, sir. She said you told her that. I would have made sure sister and brother were held here longer.

MICHAEL

Still, she cannot leave without reporting to the office. She cannot leave without informing you!

MANUEL

What should we do now, sir?

MICHAEL

Put up a search party. She must be found and brought back.

MANUEL

Sir, I have already done that. Two men who are strong and fast on the road have gone after her. I sent them as soon as it was known that she was missing.

MICHAEL

At least you had the sense to do that. Good! It is over twelve hours already. When do you think your men will be back with the two of them?

MANUEL *(Looking off)*

One of them is coming up this way right now, sir. He is alone. I don't see the two of them. *(Calling off)* This way! Come up here!

(A coolie enters. He is carrying a length of cloth that looks like a ragged half sari.)

MICHAEL

Have they been found?

COOLIE

Not exactly, sir. We reached the river crossing near the Haiguli shrine, knowing they would take that route. It is shorter than taking the crossing at the next village. This is what we found.

MANUEL

You mean she has drowned?

COOLIE

There was a priest on the bank of the river, sir. He said he found this half sari. It was floating downstream and got caught in a fallen tree branch. The current has been strong the last two weeks, sir. The priest says the woman must have been sucked in and drowned.

MICHAEL

Belli's half sari...Are you sure it is hers?

MANUEL

It looks like her sari, sir.

COOLIE

Even the priest thinks so, sir. She used to be seen at the shrine now and then, along with the boy.

(Fade out.)

SCENE 9

Choma's hut. It is dark. This scene, like the earlier one when Chaniya returns, is played in near darkness, with the outline of the hut and the outlines of characters barely visible. Belli enters quietly.

Crossfade to drum.

DRUM

Belli found her way back to the village. Clever girl! It was late at night, and people were dropping off after a hard day's toil on near empty bellies lined with toddy. Not wanting to wake up Kala or Choma she got Neela to lie down next to the oxen. He fell asleep immediately. Just as she prepared to lay herself down quietly before the hut Badu ran up to her, barking excitedly.

BELLI

Badu, Badu! Shhh! Quiet! All right, all right, I will play with you, but stop barking now! You will wake up everybody. Here, lie down here. Quiet, now. We will play in the morning.

CHOMA *(From inside)*

Who? Badu! Who is it? *(He steps out)* Who is this?

BELLI

Appa...

CHOMA

Belli?

BELLI

Yes, appa, your Belli!

CHOMA

Belli! You are back!

(Cyclorama. There is celebration around a campfire. Choma's drumming is lively. So is the dancing and singing.

Crossfade to drum.)

DRUM

Belli's return was among the greatest joys in Choma's life. It helped erase the bitter memories of the tragedy of losing his two older sons in one stroke. Over the next few days he spent a lot of time with Belli, dreaming of happy days ahead. He gave me a new skin, from the hide of a fully grown monitor lizard.

(Cross fade to Choma and Belli outside the hut)

CHOMA *(Proud of Belli)*

Not a single *anna* owed anymore! Are you sure? *(Belli nods, smiling)*

I am so proud of you. You have done what none of us grown men could do. You saved all that you earned, didn't squander it away.

BELLI

I was thinking of you and Kala all the time. I had to get back as quickly as I could.

CHOMA

You had Neela to look after too. And yet you managed everything so well. You worked hard, I am sure. It was such a large sum of money to clear. All because of this sinful old man...

BELLI

We all have our weaknesses, appa...Yes, it was a large amount. It does not matter how you came to be in that debt. It is all over now. It does not matter what I had to do. The important thing is that it has all been cleared now.

CHOMA

Yes, yes. All clear. I will go to the landlord and tell him. I will start working hard myself now. I will hold my head erect. And you know what? I will start looking for a husband for you! *(Belli reacts with uncertainty)*

Yes, I will! I had my eye on that slim young man who was playing the flute last night.

BELLI

Appa...

CHOMA

They told me later that he was already promised to a girl from another village. No matter! I will spread the word and look out myself at the festival in Panja next week.

BELLI

Appa, I don't know if I am ready for marriage now. Who will look after you? Who will take care of Kala and Neela?

CHOMA

Silly girl! Of course you are ready for marriage! I am surprised there were no men after you in the plantation. There must have been, right?!

BELLI *(Changing subject)*

I am here, no? Now let me attend to the work here.

CHOMA

You can begin by giving the boys a good bath. Look at their hair. All caked with mud.

BELLI *(Hesitant)*

We will see.

CHOMA

You have bathed them ever since they lost their mother. You have done everything a mother can do for them.

BELLI

They are big boys now, not children anymore. They may not like being bathed by me.

CHOMA

Nonsense! Take them to the river bank and give them a good scrub. You take them there and I will go and speak to the landlord.

(Choma exits. Belli remains still. She picks up the drum, holds it close to herself for a few beats. She speaks to the drum.)

BELLI

He must never know. Nobody will ever know. I am not the Belli who left this village nine months ago. But it is all over. It is all left behind. You...He tells you all his stories, his toils, his woes. You have them all stored inside you. Only you can tell Choma's tale. Will you ever listen to a tale of Belli? Will you understand?

(She keeps the drum down, rises and moves to the cyclorama, where she enacts the tragedy of Kala's drowning as the drum narrates it.)

DRUM

What can I say? The sweetness of jaggery and the bitterness of neem always go together. No sooner had Choma discovered a new joy in his life, there was a fresh tragedy waiting to overtake him. Belli took Neela and Kala to the river bank to bathe them, awkward for the first time, but not revealing it. She will have me tell this story.

BELLI

Stay here. I will go and get a dry gourd to give you a good scrubbing. Sit at the bank here. Don't try to wade in the water. *(She moves away)*

DRUM

They didn't listen. They decided to step into the stream. The feel of the cool water surrounding their bodies and flowing past their thighs was more joy than the bath by a picky older sister.

BELLI *(From off)*

Kala! Neela! Don't go in any further. It is slippery.

DRUM

And treacherous.

BELLI

It gets deep suddenly.

DRUM

And you can't swim.

BELLI *(Rushing in, using the entire width of the cyclorama base for the following)*

Kala! What have you done?! Neela!! Don't step in. You will also get sucked in. *(Shouting across)* Anybody there! Please! Can you pull this boy out of the water?! Neela! Go and fetch Appa! Anybody you can find!

DRUM

A boy on the other bank leapt forward to help.

BELLI

Yes! This way! You can see his head there!

DRUM

But no, the boy was stopped by his family. They held on to him and dragged him back.

BELLI

What are you doing? Why are you holding him back? My little brother is drowning!

DRUM

She knew very well why the boy was being held back.

BELLI

No!! No!!!

DRUM

It was over in less than a minute. He went down a third time, gasping, swallowing even more water, his face contorted, his gaze fixed on Belli.

BELLI

Noooooo!!! *(She collapses into a heap)*

(Choma rushes in, looks at Belli, rushes to the river bank, realises what has happened, goes over to Belli and stands above her, frozen.)

DRUM

The family on the other bank collected their things and hurried away. Choma, his daughter and the lone surviving son remained on their side of the stream, speechless, crushed by the twin tragedies of an avoidable death and their unshakable lowly caste. They remained there with no thought of time or what they should do or where they should go. Belli and Choma sat still, staring at the river. Neela, god bless his innocent soul, lay down and fell asleep. Seeing him curled up, his head resting on her lap, Belli decided that she should return to the hut and cook a pot of gruel for all three of them. She led Neela away. Choma stayed back longer. The loneliness was worse without her there. He picked himself up and walked home.

(Choma's hut. He and Belli are seated in front of the hut. They are still. They speak after several moments of silence.)

BELLI

Did you pay your respects to the landlord?

CHOMA

I did.

BELLI

Good.

CHOMA

I paid my respects.

BELLI

It is good that you did.

CHOMA

I went to his house to pay my respects after my first son died. I went and paid my respects after my fourth son died.

BELLI

What did he have to say?

CHOMA

He said life must go on.

BELLI

It must.

CHOMA

What do they mean when they say that life must go on?

BELLI

It means...

CHOMA

Yes?

BELLI

I don't know. It must mean something.

CHOMA
It must. Life must mean something for it to go on.

BELLI
Did you talk to him about starting work?

CHOMA
Yes.

BELLI
You were going to make one last try about...

CHOMA
I did. I said it was the only thing left to live for.

BELLI
And he said...?

CHOMA
He said he understood.

BELLI
He understood.

CHOMA
He understood, he said. He had nothing against me or our caste, he said. He would like to help. But...

BELLI
But he cannot help.

CHOMA
Not as long as his mother is alive. We could take up the idea after she died, he said.

BELLI
What do you think?

CHOMA
What can I think? How can I wish for his mother's death so that I become a farmer?

BELLI
Shall I tell you what I think?

CHOMA
What is that?

BELLI

You should think about Guruva. You do think about him now and then, don't you?

CHOMA

How can I not think about him?

BELLI

All right, he hurt you by getting married without your knowledge.

CHOMA

Selling his soul to another religion for her sake.

BELLI

All right, he married a Christian girl. But they are the same people as us. Don't you agree that they are the same people?

CHOMA

If you say so.

BELLI

So what is Guruva now? He is a farmer. He tills his own land. What is more important to you? Being a farmer on your own land? Embracing their religion? Or remaining faithful to our gods, but remaining wretched untouchables. *(A long pause. Choma stares ahead.)*

You should speak to the priest.

(Crossfade to drum)

DRUM

Choma was willing to listen. There was merit in the argument. And coming from Belli it sounded even more reasonable. What had their gods done for them? Heaped them with misery, one tragic blow after another. What had they to feel grateful about? Yes, Choma's mind was made up. They would embrace Christ. It was not for nothing that they called him the Saviour. One question remained: how could he go back to the Christian priest after having rejected the Church earlier? The answer to the question was brought by Manuel, who was visiting the village for the next round of recruitment.

(Manuel enters and walks over to Choma. Belli, startled, looks down.)

MANUEL

I got the news about your last son in the village...I am very sorry. *(Choma does not respond)* I am glad to see Belli again. She is well, I hope. In the plantation she was reported as missing...That can mean many things.

CHOMA

She has cleared all the debts. That is why she is here.

MANUEL

Of course, of course. I am not here to demand anything from you. Or from her. I have come to offer my sympathy after your recent loss.

CHOMA

We are not accustomed to such sympathy.

MANUEL

The landlord was telling me that you are going to start working again. That will be soon, I hope. It is good for you. The monsoon preparations have to begin immediately.

CHOMA

Hang the landlord!

MANUEL

You have to think of your livelihood, your children's future.

BELLI

We have decided to move out of this village.

MANUEL

Move out? Where will you go? What will you do?

BELLI

The church is very kind to people like us. We will find a new place to make a home. Who knows, we may start working on our own farm.

MANUEL

Like Guruva. He is happy as a farmer now.

CHOMA

Have you met him?

MANUEL

Just the other day, in Kokkada, on my way here.

CHOMA

How is he? How is my Guruva?

MANUEL

He is happy. He is keeping well too. In fact he has been longing to see you. He did not know about Chaniya's...He was wondering how he may visit you here.

BELLI

And we have been wondering how we may visit his village. That way we can meet the priest too.

MANUEL

I can tell him that on my way back. He will be happy to hear that you have forgiven him. He may like to bring his wife to visit you too.

BELLI *(Hesitantly)*

Appa, you should go to meet Guruva yourself. Tell him he is welcome to visit us.

MANUEL

Yes, you should go to Kokkada and meet him yourself.

BELLI

Let him know that you have decided to become a Christian. He will mention it to the priest and arrange a meeting for you.

CHOMA

You are right. It was my foolish pride that made me cut him off. I will go to Guruva straight away. When the priest sees what a fine pair of bullocks I have he will be too happy to give me some land. I will bring my Guruva back with me for a visit. We will have a proper celebration. *(Choma drapes a shawl on himself, picks up a stick and starts on his trek to Kokkada. Belli steps away, head bent. Manuel steps up to her and places his hand on her shoulder. She turns. He takes her face in his hands. She cannot resist him. She leads him into the hut.*

Choma's trek. He sits for a rest break.)

CHOMA

Badu! You know we are going to see Guruva, don't you? Clever dog! And you want to spot him before I do! Always twenty steps ahead. Clever dog! Here, sit down with me for a while. I have some sweet potato in this bundle. I know you would much rather have sweet pig meat. But sit down for a while and rest. We have a long trek ahead.

Look at him go! He is in a hurry. Badu! No need for such excitement. We will get there in good time. *(He is on the move again)*

Stop barking, Badu. What is it? Why do you want me to turn that way?

Aah, the Panjurli shrine...Of course, you remembered. All right, all right, I will follow you. Yes, yes, we always stop here on our journeys. Look at that dog! How he stretches himself flat before Panjurli in total submission. Clever dog! He does not know that in another few days we will not be stopping at this shrine anymore.

(Choma prostrates himself. Optional: a gigantic projection of Panjurli on the cyclorama. Choma is shaken.)

Panjurli!!! A thousand apologies! Mercy! Mercy on this foolish servant of yours! How could I have ever entertained the thought of abandoning you?! You have been our true god, our only god! Mercy! Mercy!!

(Choma rises and beats himself with the stick he is carrying. He drops to the ground again, weeping convulsively. Crossfade to the drum.)

DRUM

You will know that Choma's tale is drawing to a close now. It is almost time for me to leave you. I will be called to duty soon. I have to go where I am needed most.

(Crossfade to Choma's hut. Choma enters and rushes to the hut.)

CHOMA

Belli! Belli, I have sinned! You have to forgive me! God, Panjurli forgive me! I have sinned! Belli, forgive me!

(Choma enters the hut. There is a long shriek from Belli, followed by a thunderous roar from Choma.

A moment later Manuel comes tumbling out of the hut. He leaves hurriedly, buttoning up. Finally, Belli steps out, stands still for a moment and collapses on the ground before the hut.

Fade out. When the lights come on again, Belli is seated where we last saw her, the drum in her hand.)

BELLI

He beat everybody and everything in his way. He beat Badu and drove him out of the village. He beat Neela. He took the bullocks to the spot deep in the forest where he had found them as calves and let them loose. He offered them as a feast for any passing panther. He chopped up the plough and set them ablaze. He sat before the fire and laughed like a madman.

He spared me. He did not touch me. He did not come near me. I longed for him to beat me too. I longed to cling to him and beg him to beat me to death. All I did was to sit here, pouring out my heart to you. You should be by his side. He is dying. He needs you. He cannot live without you. He cannot die without you.

(Choma steps out and walks up to Belli. She places the drum at his feet. He picks it up and enters the hut. A moment later the drumming begins. A very slow fade out begins as the drumming builds up. It continues in the dark for a while and stops abruptly.

Optional: Crossfade to cyclorama. Choma is silhouetted, sitting cross-legged, drum raised high in one hand.

Fade in spot on Belli.)

BELLI

Choma's tale has been told. His spirit has joined his maker. It is over.

Fadeout.

Close of Play.

BANGALORE LITTLE THEATRE

Six Decades of Wholesome Community Theatre

In 1960, a small group of committed persons in Bangalore sought a theatre experience that could be a genuine alternative to the order of the day that was called BBC Theatre – British Bedroom Comedy. The group included the talented couple, Scott and Margaret Tod, and at least four other expats, along with a handful of Bangaloreans. They had a vision of a Community Theatre best described by the slogan invented 25 years later: *Think Globally, Act Locally.* Bangalore Little Theatre came into existence with a play reading in the last week of September that year. The first production on boards in December 1960 was Moliere's *The Prodigious Snob*, more commonly known as *The Would-be Gentleman*

In 1962, within a year of inception, BLT arrived at a character and identity for itself: to maintain pride in its strictly amateur status, but to conduct its affairs in a thoroughly professional manner. The group gave itself a constitution and, through that, a participatory style of functioning. The group was seen as belonging to a membership, and therefore to be managed transparently by a elected management committee. The founding members were the first to give way to younger members to take the group forward.

Way back in 1963, BLT produced its first Indian play in English, an original adaptation of *Mrichhakatika* (The Toy Cart of Clay) by a founder-member, Prof B Chandrasekhara. Since then, the group has maintained the conscious policy of producing Indian plays periodically – translations, adaptations, original scripts, by its own members and others. Not surprisingly, two of the six awards for contemporary playscripts instituted for the first time by *The Hindu* in 1993 landed in BLT. The first prize was for the play by Vijay Padaki, *Credit Titles,* a political satire on intellectual property rights for patenting life forms. A Special Prize was awarded to another member, Ambika (Poile) Sengupta

Old-timers of BLT have often been asked the secret of the group's long life when, in contrast, we see hundreds of cases of groups starting with a bang and dropping by the wayside in a couple of years. The difference, it seems, is in the simple fact that BLT is a community-based organisation and, therefore, a membership driven group. From this fact has followed a number of guiding principles that appear to have served BLT well over the years. For instance:

- The participatory and transparency principles in management (with all financial transactions completely open and made available to the entire membership)
- The highly open leadership structure around an elected Managing Committee (rather than being founder-centric or personality-driven)
- The constant development of new talent, including new directors (rather than being dependent on the same old hands or breeding star complexes)
- The pursuit of the higher purpose, the constitutionally-enshrined objective of promoting the theatre and related arts in Bangalore (rather than the attitude of 'let's do another play')

All of this actually makes it far more difficult to 'manage' the organisation. It is so much easier to let a charismatic leader take charge and 'run' the group as he (or she) wishes.

The significance of these principles is understood better when we see that a sizeable majority of the theatre talent in Bangalore, including the more recognised names, has been in BLT productions, workshops and training programmes earlier. They continue their affiliation with BLT even if they perform under other banners.

Related to this point is one other indisputably important feature of BLT. It is the only English- language theatre group in Bangalore (perhaps anywhere in India) with strong links to the local-regional theatre, building bridges across language divides.

Many of the stalwarts on the Kannada stage and screen have been either life members of BLT or have been prominently involved in some capacity or the other. After all, among the founders were personalities like Prof B Chandrasekhara, Nani, Shivaram, Seetharam, V Ramamurthy and S Ramaswamy. Then there were CR Simha, Vimala Rangachar, SG Ramachandra, KC Sekhar, Suresh Heblikar, Paddu, Shankar and Arundhati Nag, Ashok Rao.... And many many more – including some who went on to become Presidents of Karnataka Nataka Academy! Indeed, BLT has been a substantial support to Kannada theatre groups in their start up stages.

BLT has invested heavily in training and outreach activity. In the late 1970s, BLT introduced for the first time in Bangalore a comprehensive introductory programme for newcomers to the theatre, based on the Stella Adler system. Since the mid '80, the group has made its Summer Project on Theatre (SPOT) a regular training event. It has come to be recognised as the most prestigious training event in the city, because of the quality of inputs provided. And it continues to be a part of BLT's social commitment. Other groups and productions snap up the talent from these training projects.

In 1993, the group initiated an annual Festival of Short Plays (SHORTS), aimed at promoting theatre activity among the college and youth population. With the audience response as enthusiastic as seen, the scale of the Festival may well be enhanced considerably in the coming years.

As a socially-responsible theatre society, BLT has readily taken on many a fundraising production for worthy causes. In 1970-71, BLT's production of the new play by Badal Sircar, *Evem Indrajit*, was the first fundraising event to contribute to the Prime Minister's Fund for the Bangladeshi (then East Bengal) refugee crisis. An original script, *Head Start*, by Vijay Padaki, was produced for CRY in January 1996. Since then BLT has made a constitutional commitment to dedicate one production for a charity every year. The group also provides various kinds of help to theatre projects in colleges, schools, clubs and other institutions.

With the high repute in training and outreach activity, it was only logical for BLT to set up an Academy of Theatre Arts in 2008. The stated mission of the Academy is to enrich the theatre institutional system through the thrust programme of *Theatre Education,* thus building the societal base for the true appreciation of the theatre and, indeed, all of the performing arts.

THE SERIES EDITOR

Vijay Padaki is a Theatre Educator based in Bangalore. He has worn two caps for most of his life with equal facility. He has been active in the theatre for sixty years. He has been a management professional for over forty-five years.

Vijay is a psychologist and behavioural scientist by training, and founder-director of The P&P Group, a management resource centre that has programmes of research, consulting and training in the areas of Organisation and Institutional Development. A good part of the work of The P&P Group is devoted to the effectiveness of large development programmes. Among his earlier assignments he headed the Human Resources Division of India's oldest cooperative R&D institution, Ahmedabad Textile Industry's Research Association (ATIRA), which also helped set up the first Indian Institute of Management in Ahmedabad. Later, he was a member of the founding faculty at Indian Institute of Management, Bangalore, the founder of a Centre for Management for the textile industry in Ahmedabad, and a Visiting Professor at Indian Institute of Science, Bangalore to initiate a programme in R&D Management. He was a Senior Associate at the National Institute of Advanced Studies in its early years.

Vijay joined Bangalore Little Theatre in 1960, the year of its inception, and later served the company in many capacities–as actor, director, trainer, writer, designer and administrator, including two stints each as Secretary and President. In 2008, the institutional set up was restructured. Bangalore Little Theatre Foundation was created as a Public Charitable Trust. It was done with the purpose of reinforcing the organisation's strengths in outreach activity, and thus *rededicating the commitment to social development goals beyond performance.* The Trust requested Vijay to provide the leadership to a newly-created Academy of Theatre Arts in its formative years. The Academy is developing a long term programme thrusts to strengthen the institution of theatre education and practice in India.

Vijay has been responsible for institutionalising several activities of BLT, such as the annual summer workshop for newcomers to the theatre (SPOT), from which has emerged a large number of the theatre personalities in Bangalore, the History of Ideas programme of biographical plays, the Courtyard Theatre programme, and the Children's Theatre programme, which includes the annual flagship children's play as a partnership production to support a charity. Vijay conceived and initiated the highly successful Trainer-Training programme and the Directors Training programme in Bangalore.

He has forged several international partnerships with BLT over the years. The John F Kennedy Centre for Performing Arts in Washington invited him to serve as an advisor to the India Festival in 2011. The same year, he gave the Harold Clurman lecture at the Stella Adler Studio in New York. More recently, the Ministry of Culture invited Vijay to initiate a programme of Arts and Heritage Management in India.

Vijay has written over 50 original plays. He has also adapted or translated several play scripts. Seagull Books has published a volume of two Gujarati plays translated by him. In 1993, Vijay won the award for the best contemporary play script instituted by *The Hindu* for the play *Credit Titles.*

vijay@bangalorelittletheatre.org

PUBLICATIONS IN THE SERIES

This edition commemorates the 60th year of Bangalore Little Theatre.

Volume 2: THE HISTORY OF IDEAS
Programme of new plays

From BLT's highly acclaimed History of Ideas programme, plays include ***The Prophet and the Poet,*** based on the Gandhi-Tagore exchanges; ***Finding Ananda***, rediscovering the life and work of Swami Vivekananda, with the Bengal Renaissance as the backdrop; ***Tiger! Tiger!*** revealing the humanistic side of Tipu Sultan; ***Monsters in the Dark,*** an original adaptation of the Pulitzer award book *The Emperor of All Maladies* by Siddharyha Mukherjee, sub-titled A Biography of Cancer; ***Einstein's Dreams,*** an original dance theatre adaptation of the novel by the same title by Alan Lightman.

Volume 3: CHILDREN'S THEATRE
Programme of new plays

Contains plays from BLT's hugely successful Children's Theatre programme, this volume includes ***The Ungrateful Man,*** a tale from the Panchatantra; ***The Magic Drum,*** a collection of stories from the book by the same title by Sudha Murty; ***Ali Oh Baba,*** a retelling of the tale from the 1001 Arabian Nights; ***The Court Jester,*** the tales of Tenali Rama.